Pro Microservices in .NET 10

A Holistic Approach to Building Microservices in C#

Second Edition

Sean Whitesell
Rob Richardson

apress®

***Pro Microservices in .NET 10: A Holistic Approach to Building Microservices in C#,
Second Edition***

Sean Whitesell
KIEFER, OK, USA

Rob Richardson
Provo, UT, USA

ISBN-13 (pbk): 979-8-8688-2048-9
https://doi.org/10.1007/979-8-8688-2049-6

ISBN-13 (electronic): 979-8-8688-2049-6

Copyright © 2025 by Sean Whitesell and Rob Richardson

This work is subject to copyright. All rights are reserved by the Publisher, whether the whole or part of the material is concerned, specifically the rights of translation, reprinting, reuse of illustrations, recitation, broadcasting, reproduction on microfilms or in any other physical way, and transmission or information storage and retrieval, electronic adaptation, computer software, or by similar or dissimilar methodology now known or hereafter developed.

Trademarked names, logos, and images may appear in this book. Rather than use a trademark symbol with every occurrence of a trademarked name, logo, or image we use the names, logos, and images only in an editorial fashion and to the benefit of the trademark owner, with no intention of infringement of the trademark.

The use in this publication of trade names, trademarks, service marks, and similar terms, even if they are not identified as such, is not to be taken as an expression of opinion as to whether or not they are subject to proprietary rights.

While the advice and information in this book are believed to be true and accurate at the date of publication, neither the authors nor the editors nor the publisher can accept any legal responsibility for any errors or omissions that may be made. The publisher makes no warranty, express or implied, with respect to the material contained herein.

Managing Director, Apress Media LLC: Welmoed Spahr
Acquisitions Editor: Ryan Byrnes
Editorial Assistant: Gryffin Winkler

Cover designed by eStudioCalamar

Cover image by Pixabay.com

Distributed to the book trade worldwide by Springer Science+Business Media New York, 1 New York Plaza, New York, NY 10004. Phone 1-800-SPRINGER, fax (201) 348-4505, e-mail orders-ny@springer-sbm.com, or visit www.springeronline.com. Apress Media, LLC is a Delaware LLC and the sole member (owner) is Springer Science + Business Media Finance Inc (SSBM Finance Inc). SSBM Finance Inc is a **Delaware** corporation.

For information on translations, please e-mail booktranslations@springernature.com; for reprint, paperback, or audio rights, please e-mail bookpermissions@springernature.com.

Apress titles may be purchased in bulk for academic, corporate, or promotional use. eBook versions and licenses are also available for most titles. For more information, reference our Print and eBook Bulk Sales web page at http://www.apress.com/bulk-sales.

Any source code or other supplementary material referenced by the author in this book is available to readers on GitHub. For more detailed information, please visit https://www.apress.com/gp/services/source-code.

If disposing of this product, please recycle the paper

*This book is dedicated to you, the reader.
Writing good software is hard enough. Learning and conquering the development of microservices is an even greater challenge. I hope this book serves you well in your journey to developing great solutions for your users.*

Table of Contents

About the Authors xiii

About the Technical Reviewer xv

Acknowledgments xvii

Foreword xix

Introduction xxi

Chapter 1: Introducing Microservices 1

   Benefits 2

      Team Autonomy 3

      Service Autonomy 3

      Scalability 4

      Fault Isolation 5

      Data Autonomy 7

   Challenges to Consider 7

   Microservice Beginning 9

   Architecture Comparison 10

   Microservice Patterns 12

      API Gateway/BFF 12

      External Configuration Store 14

   Messaging 14

      Business Process Communication 15

      Message Format 17

      Transport 17

   Testing 18

      Test Pyramid 18

TABLE OF CONTENTS

E to E	19
Service	20
Unit Tests	20
Automation	21
Deploying Microservices	**21**
Versioning	21
Containers	22
Pipelines	22
Cross-Cutting Concerns	**23**
Monitoring	23
Logging	24
Alerting	25
Testing the Architecture	26
Summary	**27**
Chapter 2: Other Software Patterns	**29**
Monolith	30
What Is It	31
Pros and Cons	31
Best Use-Case	32
Modular Monolith	32
What Is It	33
Pros and Cons	33
Best Use-Case	33
Layered Architecture	34
What Is It	34
Pros and Cons	34
Best Use-Case	35
Event-Driven Architecture	36
What Is It	36
Pros and Cons	36
Best Use-Case	37

Pipeline Architecture 37
What Is It 37
Pros and Cons 38
Best Use-Case 38
Micro-Kernel 38
What Is It 39
Pros and Cons 39
Best Use-Case 39
Service-Oriented Architecture 40
What Is It 40
Pros and Cons 40
Best Use-Case 41
Microservices 41
What Is It 42
Pros and Cons 42
Best Use-Case 42
Summary 43
Choose the Right Tool for the Job 43

Chapter 3: Searching for Microservices 45
The Business 45
Domain-Driven Design 46
Domain 47
Subdomains 47
Ubiquitous Language 48
Bounded Contexts 48
Aggregates and Aggregate Roots 49
Event Storming 51
Setup 52
Color Coding 52
The Meeting 54
Seeing the Domains 58

TABLE OF CONTENTS

Domain Models 59

    Focus on Behavior 60

    Domain Modelling 60

Decomposition 60

Becoming a Microservice 61

Summary 62

Chapter 4: ASP.NET Is a Great Place for Microservices 63

A Brief History of .NET 63

    .NET Framework 63

    .NET Core 65

    Modern .NET 67

Ways to Build Microservices in ASP.NET 68

    ASP.NET MVC 69

    ASP.NET Razor Pages 73

    ASP.NET Web API 74

    ASP.NET Minimal APIs 76

    Azure Functions 79

    KEDA Functions 82

Aspire 84

    Summary 86

Chapter 5: First Microservice 87

Interprocess Communication 87

API First Design 88

Transport Mechanisms 89

    REST 89

    gRPC 90

File ➤ New ➤ Project 91

Contacting Google's Routes API 95

    App Settings 95

    Testing What We Have 95

Swagger	97
Leveraging gRPC	98
Incorporating gRPC	99
Testing gRPC Endpoint	103
Modify the Monolith	104
Service Discovery	104
Summary	105

Chapter 6: Microservice Messaging 107

Issues with Synchronous Communication	107
Limits of RPC	108
Messaging	108
Architecture	109
Reasons to Use Messaging	109
Message Types	110
Message Routing	112
Broker-less	112
Brokered	112
Consumption Models	113
Competing Consumers	113
Independent Consumers	114
Delivery Guarantees	115
At Most Once	115
At Least Once	116
Once and Only Once	116
Message Ordering	117
Building the Examples	118
Building the Messaging Microservices	118
Running RabbitMQ	119
First Project	119
Building the Invoice Microservice	120

ix

TABLE OF CONTENTS

Building the Payment Microservice 122

Testing the Competing Consumers 123

Building a PubSub Demo 124

Drawbacks of Messaging 125

Summary 126

Chapter 7: Decentralizing Data 129

Current State 129

The Rule 130

Database Choices 131

Availability 131

Sharing Data 133

    Duplicate Data 134

Transactional Consistency 137

    CAP Theorem 137

    Transactions Across Microservices 138

    Sagas 139

CQRS 145

Event Sourcing 147

    Scenarios 151

Eventual Consistency 152

Data Warehouse 154

Materialized View 155

Splitting the Monolith 156

    Moving Code 157

    Strangler Pattern 159

    Feature Flags 159

Splitting the Database 159

Summary 162

TABLE OF CONTENTS

Chapter 8: Testing Microservices 165
Cost of Errors 165
What Not to Test 166
What to Test 166
    Code 167
    Performance 167
    System Failure Handling 168
    Security 169
Testing Levels 169
    Unit Testing 170
    Integration Testing 171
    Component Testing 172
    Contract Testing 173
    Service Testing 174
    End-to-End Testing 175
    End-to-End Testing Microservices 175
Consumer-Driven Contract Testing Deep Dive 178
    Consumer Project 179
    Consumer Test Project 182
    Provider Test Project 186
Summary 188

Chapter 9: Deploying Microservices 189
Containerize a .NET Microservice 189
    Containerize .NET with a Dockerfile 190
    Containerize .NET with the .NET SDK 194
Deploy a Containerized .NET Microservice 196
    Deploy to Azure Kubernetes Service (AKS) 197
    Deploy to Azure Container Apps 202
    Deploy to Azure App Service 203
    Other Deployment Options 205
Reverse Proxy 206

xi

Kubernetes Ingress	207
Application Gateway	209
API Management	212
YARP	213
Reverse Proxy Roundup	217
Summary	217

Chapter 10: Healthy Microservices 219

Is It Healthy?	219
Where Do We Look?	220
OpenTelemetry	221
Aspire	224
Adding more Instrumenters to .NET Aspire	225
Custom Logs, Traces, and Metrics	226
Azure Application Insights	232
Effective Monitoring	233
Debugging with Logs	236
Summary	238

Index 239

About the Authors

Sean Whitesell is the president of SkyForge Consulting, a Microsoft MVP, and an Azure Cloud Architect with several years of experience designing and implementing enterprise cloud solutions. He has led the Tulsa .NET User Group since 2009 and has been programming and working with electronics for over 20 years. Sean is dedicated to helping developers and IT professionals adopt modern cloud technologies and best practices.

Rob Richardson is a software craftsman, building web properties in ASP.NET, Node, React, and Vue. He is a Microsoft MVP, a published author, a frequent speaker, and a diligent teacher of high-quality software development. You can find his recent work at robrich.org/presentations.

About the Technical Reviewer

Mike Benkovich is a developer, business owner, Microsoft Azure MVP, and an online instructor. Mike worked at Microsoft from 2004 to 2012 where he helped build developer communities across the United States. In 2009, he started a Toastmaster club for geeks called TechMasters in Minneapolis where they still grow speakers for conferences. Today, he is a LinkedIn Learning Instructor for Azure and has developed many online courses. Mike actively works in Azure Cloud Governance and Software Delivery consulting. Learn more on www.BenkoTIPS.com.

Acknowledgments

There are challenges, and there are life goals. Writing this book has certainly been an accomplishment of a life goal. I could not have done this alone. There are people in my life that have given phenomenal support, and I'm eternally grateful.

To the Lord for helping me through challenging times, especially the ones I get myself into.

To my wife and biggest cheerleader, Barb, thank you for your unceasing support. It is so much more than I deserve. You have been so understanding of my goals and the challenges that come along with them. To my daughter, McKayla, you are my gem and are the reason I fight hard to be a good dad. Remember, the best goals are worth fighting for.

To Michael Perry, I can't thank you enough. Your willingness to help me is amazing. I appreciate our discussions, where I get to learn so much from you. I'm thankful I got to learn from your book *The Art of Immutable Architecture*. Details in your book really helped this book and me as an architect.

To Floyd May, thank you so much for your friendship and our time on the whiteboard discussing microservices. I really appreciate your guidance.

To Phil Japikse, thank you so much for helping me get started with this book project. I appreciate your guidance throughout this book.

To Josh Brown, thank you so much brother for helping to spur ideas and the great discussions about databases.

To Rob Richardson, thank you for helping me get this book done. I appreciate being able to lean on your expertise.

—Sean Whitesell

I would like to thank the Lord whose inspiration I rely on daily. His help has been instrumental in accomplishing this work.

—Rob Richardson

Foreword

Software development is undergoing a significant transformation. The industry is shifting away from traditional monolithic application development, where large teams deliver substantial projects on an infrequent basis, toward microservice-based development. In this modern approach, applications are decomposed into smaller, independently versioned components developed by focused teams, enabling faster release cycles.

This updated book serves as a comprehensive guide for utilizing the latest versions of .NET to build microservices. Readers will gain practical knowledge on implementing containers, Kubernetes, Docker, and messaging systems within microservice architectures. Additionally, the book covers new features in .NET including Aspire, gRPC, Minimal APIs, and best practices for deploying and monitoring microservices in Azure production environments. Sean and Rob, both recognized experts with extensive experience in .NET and ASP.NET application development, bring valuable insights throughout this book. I am confident you will find their expertise beneficial as you advance your skills and develop innovative solutions.

—Scott Hunter
VP Director, Azure Developer Experience (formerly drove .NET and ASP.NET)
Microsoft

Introduction

The microservice architecture breaks software into smaller pieces that can be independently deployed, scaled, and replaced. There are many benefits to this modern architecture, but there are more moving pieces.

In the olden days, we compiled the entire software product into one piece and deployed it infrequently. Deployment was hard, so we opted not to do it very often. With the advent of containers, deployment has become much easier. We can now break our application into lots of little pieces – microservices. When one microservice needs more horsepower, we can scale up only this portion of the web property. If a feature needs to work differently, we can deploy only this microservice, avoiding the churn with the entire system.

With this power come some additional layers of complexity. In the legacy monolithic software applications, we merely made a function call if we wanted to call into another part of the system. Our internal methods now have IP addresses, multiple instances, maybe load balancers distributing the load, and many more moving pieces.

How do we discover the address of the microservice? How do we scale to just the right level of availability without wasted cost? This is the magic of microservices, and this is the purpose of this book. You'll learn how to design, architect, build, test, containerize, deploy, and monitor applications to build robust and scalable microservices.

Who Should Read This Book

In some respect, anyone involved with software projects related to distributed architecture should read this book. Even if a software project is not a distributed architecture but may become one, this book will shed some light on understanding existing business processes that may need to be handled by microservices.

From development managers to product owners to developers will find this book useful in understanding many complexities of a microservices architecture. Application architects and developers will gain quick insight with the hands-on code samples. The step-by-step coding approach covers examples with direct microservice calls as well as by messaging communication.

INTRODUCTION

Book Organization

The microservices architecture is multifaceted and complex. Chapter 1 covers many of the subjects involved in this architecture style. Chapter 2 introduces other software patterns besides microservices. After all, microservices isn't the right solution for every software problem. In Chapter 3, we use a fictional story to help convey the purpose of breaking apart a monolithic application to a microservices architecture. We cover using Event Storming and Domain-Driven Design tenants to help understand existing business processes to determine where and why to create a microservice. In Chapter 4, we look at existing ASP.NET hosting options and new features in .NET 10.

In Chapter 5, we cover direct communication with microservices using HTTP and gRPC. This chapter is also where you begin creating microservices using Visual Studio 2025 with C# and .NET 10. Chapter 6 covers asynchronous messaging communication through an enterprise service bus.

Chapter 7 covers breaking apart data from a centralized data store to distributed data stores. We also cover Saga patterns for handling transactions across multiple systems.

In Chapter 8, we cover testing the microservices including both unit testing and integration testing using ASP.NET. We also cover testing the microservices that communicate using messaging. You will create the test projects for both communication styles.

Chapter 9 covers containerizing microservices in Docker containers using both a Dockerfile and via new .NET 10 SDK commands. Then we'll deploy the microservices to various Azure services including Kubernetes. We then discuss reverse proxy options including YARP to avoid complex multidomain setup.

In Chapter 10, we cover health concerns for microservices using OpenTelemetry, the industry standard mechanism for harvesting logs, traces, and metrics from microservices and other cloud infrastructure. We cover creating custom logs, traces, and metrics in ASP.NET microservices. You'll learn how to use Aspire for local development and how to use Azure Application Insights in production to ensure microservices are performant and functioning correctly.

CHAPTER 1

Introducing Microservices

Twitter, PayPal, and Netflix had serious problems. Problems like scaling, quality, and downtime became common and increasing issues. Each had a large, single-code base application known as a "monolith." And each hit different frustration points where a fundamental architecture change had to occur. Development and deployment cycles were long and tedious, causing delays in feature delivery. Each deployment meant downtime or expensive infrastructure to switch from one set of servers to another. As the code base grew, so did the coupling between modules. With coupled modules, code changes are more problematic, harder to test, and lower overall application quality.

For Twitter, scaling servers was a huge factor that caused downtime and upset users. All too often, users would see an error page stating Twitter is overcapacity. Many users would see the "Fail Whale" while the system administrators would reboot servers and deal with the demand. As the number of users increased, so did the need for architecture changes. From the data stores, code, and server topology, the monolithic architecture hit its limit.

For PayPal, their user base increased the need for guaranteed transactions. They scaled up servers and network infrastructure. But, with the growing number of services, the performance hit a tipping point, and latency was the result. They continuously increased the number of virtual machines to process the growing number of users and transactions. This added tremendous pressure on the network, thereby causing latency issues.

Netflix encountered problems with scaling, availability, and speed of development. Their business required 24×7 access to their video streams. They were in a position where they could not build data centers fast enough to accommodate the demand. Their user base was increasing, and so were the networking speeds at homes and on devices. The monolithic application was so complex and fragile that a single semicolon took down the website for several hours.

In and of itself, there is nothing wrong with a monolith. Monoliths serve their purpose, and when they need more server resources, it is usually cheap enough to add more servers. With good coding practices, a monolith can sustain itself very well. However, as they grow and complexity increases, they can reach a point that feature requests take longer and longer to implement. They turn into "monolith hell." It takes longer to get features to production, the number of bugs increases, and frustration grows with the users. Monolith hell is a condition the monolith has when it suffers from decreased stability, difficulty scaling, and nearly impossible to leverage new technologies.

Applications can grow into a burden over time. With changes in developers, skillsets, business priorities, etc., those applications can easily turn into a "spaghetti code" mess. As the demands of those applications change, so do the expectations with speed of development, testing, and deployment. By pulling functionality away from monolithic applications, development teams can narrow their focus on functionality and respective deployment schedule. This allows a faster pace of development and deployment of business functionality.

In this chapter, you will learn about the benefits of using a microservices architecture and the challenges of architecture changes. You will then learn about the differences between a monolithic architecture and a microservices architecture. Next, we will begin looking at microservices patterns, messaging, and testing. Finally, we will cover deploying microservices and examine the architected infrastructure with cross-cutting concerns.

Benefits

For large applications suffering from "monolith hell," there are several reasons they may benefit by converting to a microservice architecture. Development teams can be more focused on business processes, code quality, and deployment schedules. Microservices scale separately, allowing efficient usage of resources on infrastructure. As communication issues and other faults occur, isolation helps keep a system highly available. Lastly, with architectural boundaries defined and maintained, the system can adapt to changes with greater ease. The details of each benefit are defined in the following.

Team Autonomy

One of the biggest benefits of using a microservice architecture is team autonomy. Companies constantly need to deliver more features in production in the fastest way possible. By separating areas of concern in the architecture, development teams can have autonomy from other teams. This autonomy allows teams to develop and deploy at a pace different than others. Time to market is essential for most companies. The sooner features are in production, the sooner they may have a competitive edge over competitors.

It also allows for but does not require different teams to leverage different programming languages. Monoliths typically require the whole code base to be in the same language. Because microservices are distinctly different applications, they open the door to using different languages, allowing flexibility in fitting the tool to the task at hand.

With data analytics, for example, Python is the most common programming language used and works well in microservice architectures. Mobile and front-end web developers can leverage languages best suited for those requirements, while C# is used with back-end business transaction logic.

With teams dedicated to one or more microservices, they only hold the responsibility for their services. They only focus on their code without needing to know details of code in other areas. Communication will need to be done regarding the API endpoints of the microservices. Clients need to know how to call these services with details such as HTTP verb and payload model, as well as the return data model. There is an API specification available to help guide the structure of your API. Consider the OpenAPI Initiative (https://www.openapis.org/) for more information.

Service Autonomy

As team autonomy focuses on the development teams and their responsibilities, service autonomy is about separating concerns at the service layer. The "Single Responsibility Principle" applies here as well. No microservice should have more than one reason to change. For example, an Order Management microservice should not also consist of business logic for Account Management. By having a microservice dedicated to specific business processes, the services can evolve independently.

Microservices often interact with one another to process complex business logic. Despite this interaction, the system retains its flexibility through loose coupling, ensuring that code can evolve independently without compromising the architecture.

With loose coupling between microservices, you receive the same benefits as when applied at the code level. Upgrading microservices is easier and has less impact on other services. This also allows for features and business processes to evolve at different paces.

The autonomy between microservices allows for individual resiliency and availability needs. For example, the microservice handling credit card payment has a higher availability requirement than handling account management. Clients can use retry logic and error handling policies with different parameters based on the services they are using.

Deployment of microservices is also a benefit of service autonomy. As the services evolve, they release separately using "Continuous Integration/Continuous Deployment" (CI/CD) tools like Azure DevOps, Jenkins, and CircleCI. Individual deployment allows frequent releases with minimal, if any, impact on other services. It also allows separate deployment frequency and complexity than with monolithic applications. This supports the requirement of zero downtime. You can configure a deployment strategy to bring up an updated version before taking down existing services.

Scalability

The benefit of scalability allows for the number of instances of services to differentiate between other services and a monolithic application. Generally, monolithic applications require larger servers than those needed for microservices. Having microservices lets multiple instances reside on the same server or across multiple servers, which aids in fault isolation. Figure 1-1 shows a relationship between the number of code instances and the size of the code.

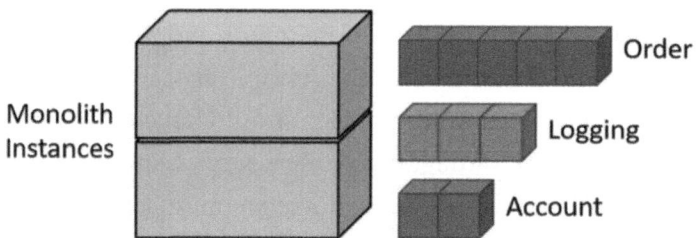

Figure 1-1. *Example of instance and size of code*

By utilizing a microservice architecture, the applications can leverage servers of diverse sizes. One microservice may need more CPU than RAM, while others require more in-memory processing capabilities. Other microservices may only need enough CPU and RAM to handle heavy I/O needs.

Another benefit of having microservices on different servers than the monolith is the diversity of programming languages. For example, assuming the monolith runs .NET Framework, you can write microservices in other programming languages. If these languages can run on Linux, then you have the potential of saving money due to the operating system license cost.

Fault Isolation

Fault isolation is about handling failures without them taking down an entire system. When a monolith instance goes down, all services in that instance also go down. There is no isolation of services when failures occur. Several things can cause failure:

- Coding or data issues
- Extreme CPU and RAM utilization
- Network
- Server hardware
- Downstream systems

With a microservice architecture, services with any of the preceding conditions will not take down other parts of the system. Think of this as a logical grouping. In one group are services and dependent systems that pertain to a business function. The functionality is separate from those in another group. If a failure occurs in one group, the effects do not spread to another group. Figure 1-2 is an oversimplification of services dependent on other services and a dependency on a data store.

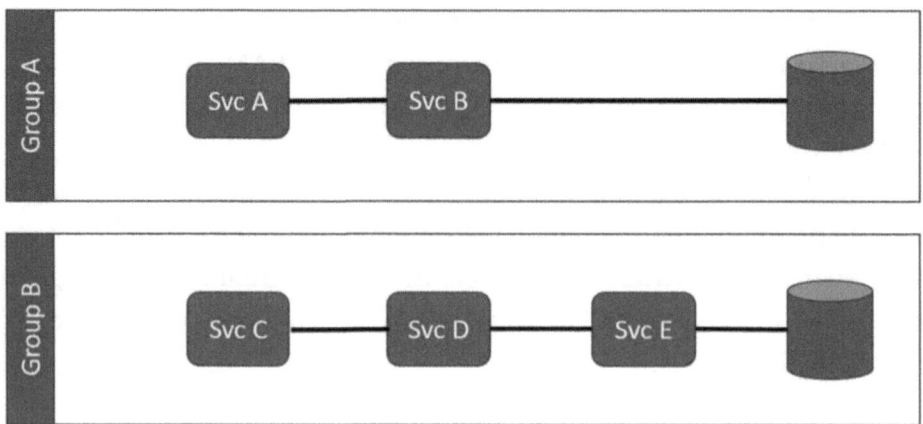

Figure 1-2. *Depiction of fault isolation*

As with any application that relies on remote processing, opportunities for failures are always present. When microservices either restart or are upgraded, any existing connections will be cut. Always consider microservices ephemeral. They will die and need to be restarted at some point. This may be from prolonged CPU or RAM usage exceeding a threshold. Orchestrators like Kubernetes will "evict" a pod that contains an instance of the microservice in those conditions. This is a self-preservation mechanism, so a runaway condition does not take down the server/node.

An unreasonable goal is to have a microservice with an uptime of 100% or 99.999% of the time. If a monolithic application or another microservice is calling a microservice, then retry policies must be in place to handle the absence or disappearance of the microservice. This is no different than having a monolithic application connecting with a SQL Server. It is the responsibility of the calling code to handle the various associated exceptions and react accordingly.

Retry policies in a circuit breaker pattern help tremendously in handling issues when calling microservices. Libraries such as Polly (http://www.thepollyproject.org) provide the ability to use a circuit breaker, retry policy, and others. This allows calling code to react to connection issues by retrying with progressive wait periods, then using an alternative code path if calls to the microservice fail X number of times.

Data Autonomy

So far, there have been many reasons presented for using a microservice architecture. But they focus on the business processes. The data is just as important, if not more so. Monolithic applications with the symptoms described earlier most certainly rely on a data store. Data integrity is crucial to the business. Without data integrity, no company will stay in business for long. Can you imagine a bank that "guesses" your account balance?

Microservices incorporate loose coupling, so changes deploy independently. Most often, these changes also contain schema changes to the data. New features may require new columns or a change to an existing column, as well as for tables. The real issue occurs when the schema change from one team impacts others. This, in turn, requires the changes to be backward compatible. Additionally, the other team affected may not be ready to deploy at the same time.

Having data isolated per microservice allows independent changes to occur with minimal impact on others. This isolation is another factor that encourages quicker time to production for the business. Starting a new feature with a new microservice with new data is great.

With separate databases, you also get the benefit of using differing data store technologies. Having separate databases provides an opportunity for some data to be in a relational database like SQL Server, while others are in nonrelational databases like MongoDB, Azure Cosmos DB, and Azure Table Storage. Having a choice of different databases is another example of using the right tool for the job.

Challenges to Consider

Migrating to a microservice architecture is not pain-free and is more complex than monoliths. You will need to give yourself room to fail. Even with a small microservice, it may take several iterations to get to exactly what you need. And you may need to complete many rounds of refactoring on the monolith before you can support relocating functionality to a microservice. Developing microservices requires a new way of thinking about the existing architecture, such as the cost of development time and infrastructure changes to networks and servers.

If coming from a monolith, you will need to make code changes to communicate with the new microservice instead of just a simple method call. Communicating with microservices requires calls over a network and, most often, using a messaging broker. You will learn more about messaging later in this chapter.

The size of the monolithic applications and team sizes are also factors. Small applications, or large applications with small teams, may not see the benefits. The benefits of a microservice architecture appear when the overwhelming problems of "monolith hell" are conquered by separating areas.

Many companies are not ready to take on the challenges and simply host monolithic applications on additional servers and govern what business logic they process. Servers are relatively cheap, so spreading the processing load is usually the easiest "quick" solution. That is until they end up with the same issues as PayPal, Twitter, and others.

Developers may push back on the idea of microservice development. There is a large learning curve for the intricate details that need to be understood. And many developers will remain responsible for various parts of the monolithic applications, so it may feel like working on two projects simultaneously. There will be the ongoing question of quality versus just getting something to production. Cutting corners will only add code fragility and technical debt and may prolong a successful completion.

A challenge every team will face is code competency. Developers must take the initiative to be strong with the programming language chosen and embrace distributed system design. Design patterns and best practices are great as they relate to the code in monoliths and inside the microservices. But new patterns must also be learned with how microservices communicate, handling failures, dependencies, and data consistency.

Another challenge for teams developing microservices is that there is more than code to consider. In the later section "Cross-Cutting Concerns," items are described that affect every microservice, therefore every developer. Everyone should be involved in understanding (if not also creating) the items that help you understand the health of the architectural system. User stories or whatever task-based system you use will need additional time and tasks. This includes helping with testing the system and not just the microservices.

Microservice Beginning

With a primary system needing to work with other systems, there arose an issue of the primary system being required to know all the communication details of each connected system. The primary system, in this case, is your main application. Since each connected system had its own way of storing information, services it provided, and communication method, the primary system had to know all these details. This is a "tightly coupled" architecture. Suppose one of the connected systems changes to another system, a tremendous amount of change was required. Service-Oriented Architecture (SOA) aimed to eliminate the hassle and confusion. By using a standard communication method, each system could interact with less coupling.

The Enterprise Service Bus (ESB), introduced in 2002, was used to communicate messages to the various systems. An ESB provides a way for a "Publish/Subscribe" model in which each system could work with or ignore the message as they were broadcasted. Security, routing, and guaranteed message delivery are other aspects of an ESB.

When needing to scale a service, the whole infrastructure had to scale as well. With microservices, each service can scale independently. By shifting from ESB to protocols like HTTP, the endpoints become more intelligent about what and how to communicate. The messaging platform is no longer required to know the message payload, only the endpoint to give it to. "Smart Endpoints, Dumb Pipes" is how Martin Fowler succinctly stated.

So why have microservices gained so much attention? With the cost of supportive infrastructure, it is cheaper to build code and test to see if one or more microservices are the right way to go. Network and CPU have tremendously increased in power and are far more cost-effective today than yesteryear. Today, we're able to rapidly process large volumes of data with mathematical models and analytics, allowing us to acquire insights quicker than ever before. For about $35 USD, a Raspberry Pi can be bought and utilized to host microservices!

Cost is a huge factor, but so are the programming languages and platforms. Today, more than a handful of languages like C#, Python, and Node are great for microservices. Platforms like Kubernetes, Service Fabric, and others are vastly capable of maintaining microservices running in Docker containers. There are also far more programmers in the industry that can quickly take advantage of architectural patterns like SOA and microservices.

CHAPTER 1 INTRODUCING MICROSERVICES

With the ever-increasing demand for software programmers, there also exists the demand for quality. It is way too easy for programmers to solve simple problems and believe they are "done." In reality, quality software is highly demanding of our time, talents, and patience. Just because microservices are cheaper and, in some cases, easier to create, they are by no means easy.

Architecture Comparison

Since most microservices stem from a monolithic application, we will compare the two architectures. Monoliths are the easiest to create, so it is no surprise this architecture is the de facto standard when creating applications. Companies need new features quickly for a competitive edge over others. The better and quicker the feature is in production, the sooner anticipated profits are obtained. So, as nearly all applications do, they grow. The code base grows in size, complexity, and fragility. In Figure 1-3, a monolith is depicted that contains a user interface layer, a business logic layer with multiple services, and a persistence layer.

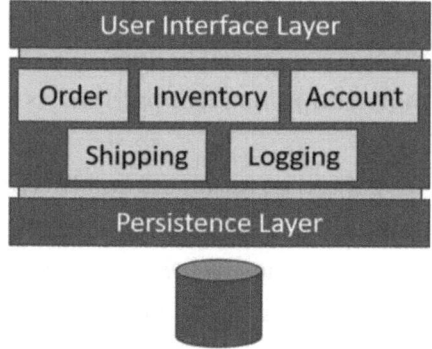

Figure 1-3. *Depiction of three-tier architecture*

A monolith, in the simplest term, is a single executable containing business logic. This includes all the supportive DLLs. When a monolith deploys, functionality stops and is replaced. Each service (or component) in a monolith runs "in process." This means that each instance of the monolith has the entire code base ready for instantiation.

With the microservice architecture, shown in Figure 1-4, business logic is separated out into out-of-process executables. This allows them to have many instances of each running on different servers. As mentioned earlier, fault isolation is gained with this separation. For example, if shipping is unavailable, orders would still be able to be taken.

CHAPTER 1 INTRODUCING MICROSERVICES

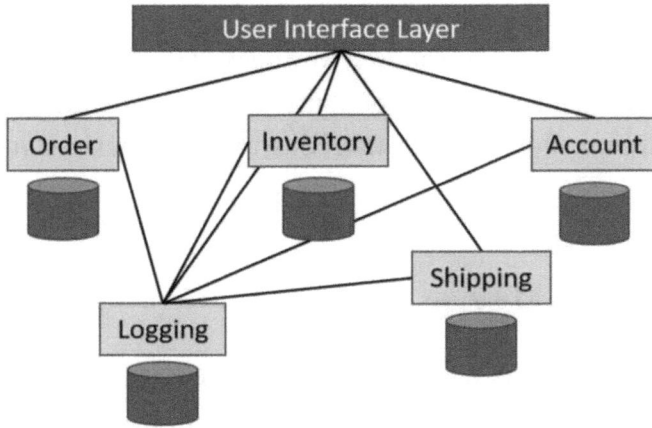

Figure 1-4. *Example of microservice architecture*

What is most realistic is the hybrid architecture, shown in Figure 1-5. Few companies fully transition to a microservice architecture completely. Many companies will take a sliver of functionality and partially migrate to a microservice solution.

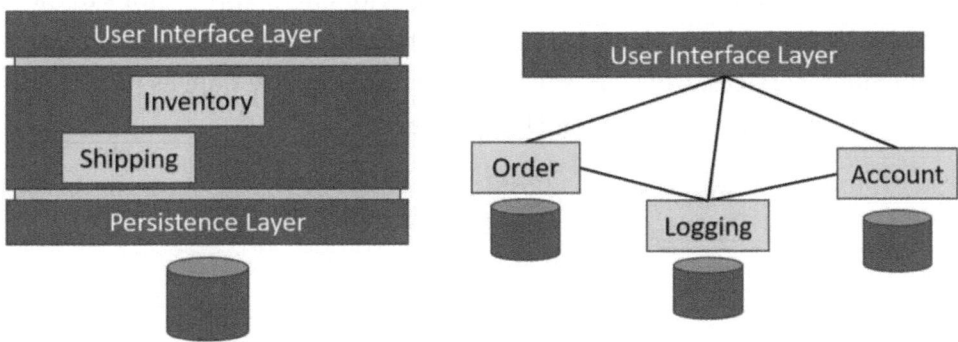

Figure 1-5. *Depiction of hybrid architecture*

When migrating from a monolithic to a microservice architecture, there is a huge danger when too much business functionality is in one microservice. For example, if the order microservice has tight coupling in the code with inventory management, and all of that logic was brought over, then you end up with a distributed monolith. You have gained some separation benefits while retaining many of the burdens the monolith has.

CHAPTER 1 INTRODUCING MICROSERVICES

When you decide to venture down the path of creating microservices, start small. By starting with a small code base, you allow a way back. If the microservice is beyond time, cost, or patience, you will need to undo or abort changes to the monolith. While making these changes, continuously execute tests on the monolith looking for breaking code you did not expect.

Microservice Patterns

Every microservice architecture has challenges such as accessibility, obtaining configuration information, messaging, and service discovery. There are common solutions to these challenges called patterns. Various patterns exist to help solve these challenges and make the architecture solid.

API Gateway/BFF

The API Gateway pattern provides a single endpoint for client applications to the microservices assigned to it. Figure 1-6 shows a single API Gateway as an access point for multiple microservices. API Gateways provide functionality such as routing to microservices, authentication, and load balancing.

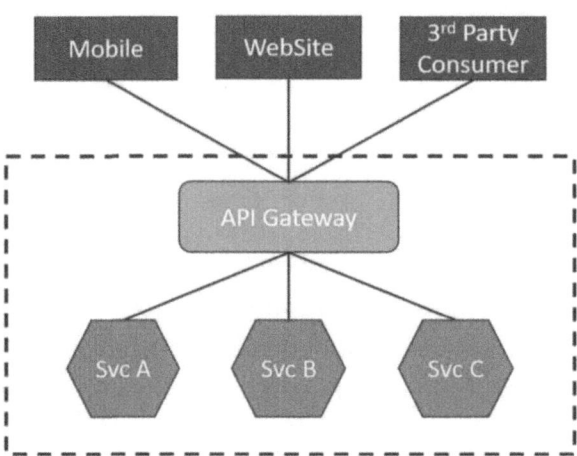

Figure 1-6. *Single API Gateway access point*

12

CHAPTER 1   INTRODUCING MICROSERVICES

Depending on the scale of the architecture and business needs, a single API Gateway may cause another problem. The number of client applications may increase. The demands from those client applications may grow. At some point, separation should be done to split client applications apart by using multiple API Gateways. Design pattern Backends for Frontends (BFF) helps with this segregation. There are multiple endpoints, but they are designated based on the types of clients being served.

In this example, depicted in Figure 1-7, one application calling the microservices could be an MVC web application, whereas another client could be a mobile application. Also depicted is for connections from third-party consumers.

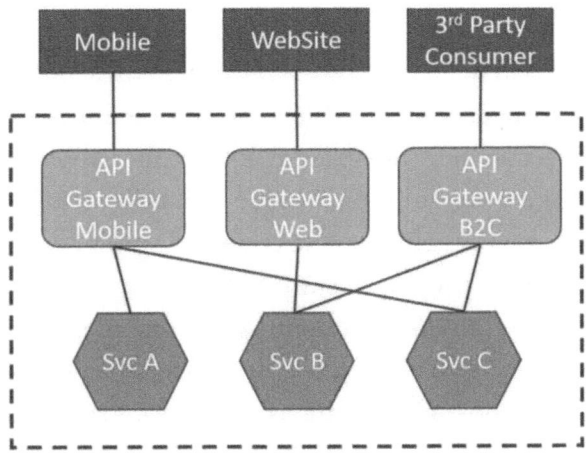

Figure 1-7. *Designated API Gateway endpoints*

Mobile clients usually do not get/need all the content compared to a full website. Using the BFF pattern with API Gateways allows for that separation of handling the differences.

Consider the end user may be responsible for data usage charges. If the mobile application does not need that much information "ready" compared to the full website version, then the separation of end-user view management calls for the BFF pattern.

There are precautions when using an API Gateway pattern. There is a coupling of microservices to the API Gateway. As microservices evolve, so does the infrastructure. API Gateways must be maintained so there is not too much coupling. An API Gateway should not be more responsible than necessary. There may be a point at which multiple API Gateways are created, and microservices split between them. This would help with another precaution where the API Gateway can be a bottleneck and may add to any latency issues.

External Configuration Store

Nearly all microservices will need configuration information, just like monoliths. With the ability to have many microservices instances, it would be impractical for each instance to have its own configuration files. Updating information across all running instances would be overwhelming. Instead, using the External Configuration Store pattern provides a common area to store configuration information. This means there is one source of the configuration values.

The configuration information could be stored in a data store such as SQL Server or Azure Cosmos DB. Environment-specific settings could be stored in different Configuration Stores allowing the same code to work in Dev vs. Staging or Production. Of course, each instance will need to know how to get to the Configuration Store. This information is in the local configuration files. This means there is just enough information in these files on where and how to get all other application settings.

The information in the Configuration Store may change at any time. A challenge here is knowing when to get the settings. The code can either get all the settings at startup or as needed. If only retrieving at startup, then the behavior of the microservice will not change until restarted. With some settings, this is fine, such as retrieving the environment it is running in. This may be useful with logging. If the microservice is running in Dev, then the verbosity of logging is much higher. If not Dev, then only log the additional information in certain conditions like error handling. That setting is not likely to change. Some settings do change and should be checked often. Settings like an HTTP timeout value or a maximum number of retries in a business function may change and affect the behavior.

Messaging

As microservices are designed to fit various business needs, their communication methods must also be considered. With monolithic applications, methods simply call other methods without the need to worry about where that method resides. With distributed computing, those methods are on other servers. Interprocess communication (IPC) mechanisms are used to communicate with microservices since they are over a network.

With microservice communication, we need to consider "why," "what," and "how" data is sent. Business processes and use cases help determine the layout of messaging needs. These determine the "why" there is communication with microservices. The "what" is the data format as not all contents in the messages are the same and they will vary based on purpose. Lastly, transport mechanisms are used to transfer message content between processes. This covers the "how" messages are sent to endpoints.

Business Process Communication

There are multiple ways of communicating between business processes in a microservices architecture. The simplest but least versatile method is using synchronous calls. The three other ways are asynchronous and provide various message delivery methods.

RPC

The synchronous way is for when a request needs an immediate response. For example, a microservice has a financial algorithm and responds with data based on the values passed into the request. The client (monolith client or another microservice) supplies the parameter values, sends the request, and waits for the response. The business process does not continue until it has received an answer or an error. This type of call is a Remote Procedure Call (RPC) as it is direct and synchronous from the client to the service. Using RPC should be limited in use. These have a high potential of adding unnecessary latency for the client and should only be used when the processing inside the microservice is small.

Fire-and-Forget

The first type of asynchronous call is a fire-and-forget style. The client does not care if the microservice can complete the request. An example of this style is sending a notification email. A business process may need to inform a user about an event, such as a successful transaction or a subscription renewal, and calls a microservice dedicated to sending emails. The business process continues without waiting to confirm whether the email was sent successfully.

Callback

Another style of asynchronous call is when the microservice calls back to the client, notifying when it is done processing. The business process continues after sending the request. The request contains information for how the microservice is to send the response. This requires the client to open ports to receive the calls and passing the address and port number in the request. With many calls occurring, there is a need to match the response to the request. When passing a correlation ID in the request message and the microservice persisting that information to the response, the client can use the response for further processing.

Consider the example of a barista. You place your order for a latte. The barista takes down the type of drink and your name. Then two parallel processes occur. One is the process of creating the drink. The other is processing payment. Only after the drink is ready and payment succeeds are you called. "Sean, your latte is ready." Notice there are two pieces of information used as a correlation ID. The customer's name and the drink name were taken at the time of the order and used to tell the customer the order has completed.

This example also shows a synchronous business process. I did not start waiting for the drink until after the order was taken. Then two asynchronous processes occurred: one to create the drink and the other to take payment. After those two processes were completed, another asynchronous process was initiated. I was notified the drink is ready and where to pick it up. During the time the latte is being made, I could read a newspaper or even cancel the order. This notification type is called a "domain event."

Pub/Sub

This leads to another asynchronous call style, Publish/Subscribe (Pub/Sub). This is a way of listening on a message bus for messages about work to process. The sender publishes a message for all the listeners to react on their own based on the message. A comparison of the Pub/Sub model is a newspaper company. It publishes a single issue daily to multiple subscribers. Each subscriber can read and react independently to the same content as all other subscribers.

A persistent-based Pub/Sub model is where only one instance of a listener works on the message. Building on the fire-and-forget model is a logging example. As an event that requires logging occurs, a message is created containing content to be written. Without persistence, each subscriber would log the message and cause duplicate records. Using the persistence model, one subscriber locks the message for processing. Other listeners may pick up the next message, but only one message is processed. Now, only one log entry is created for each event. If the subscriber fails to complete their task, then the message is aborted, and another subscriber can pick it up for processing.

Message Format

The format of the data in the messages allows your communication to be cross language and technology independent. There are simply two main formats for messages: text and binary. The human-readable text-based messages are the simplest to create but have their burdens. These formats allow for the transportation to include metadata. With small- to medium-size messages, JSON and XML are the most used formats. But, as the message size increases, the extra information can increase latency.

Utilizing a format such as Google's Protocol Buffers (`https://developers.google.com/protocol-buffers/`) or Avro by Apache (`https://avro.apache.org/`), the messages are sent as a binary stream. These are efficient with medium to large messages because there is a CPU cost to convert content to binary. Smaller messages may see some latency.

Out of the box, ASP.NET Core can use JSON or XML as the payload format. For all the references with ASP.NET Core and microservices, JSON is the chosen format. In the call to and from the services, the data is serialized and deserialized using JSON. Most of the time, using JSON is fine given the size of the payloads.

Transport

Transportation mechanisms are responsible for the delivery of messages to/from the client and microservices. There are multiple protocols available such as HTTP, TCP, gRPC, and Advanced Message Queuing Protocol (AMQP). As you read earlier, there are direct and indirect ways of sending messages. These are direct calls to a microservice with sockets opened waiting for a caller. Port 80 is the standard port HTTP traffic, and port 443 for Transport Layer Security (TLS) encrypted HTTP traffic.

Generally, HTTP is used but TCP web sockets is an alternative. The drawback with synchronous messaging is there is a tighter coupling between the client and services. The client may know about details it should not need to care about, such as how many services are listening and their address. Or the client must do a DNS lookup to get an address for a service.

Representational State Transfer (REST) is an architectural style that is quite common today when creating Web APIs and microservices. For example, to retrieve data, the call uses the HTTP verb GET. To insert, modify, or delete data, the HTTP verbs POST, PUT, UPDATE, and DELETE are used. The specific verb is declared in the code of the service endpoints.

As a microservice architecture develops, there may be microservices calling other microservices. There is an inherent risk of latency as data is serialized and deserialized at each hop. An RPC technology called "gRPC Remote Procedure Call" (gRPC) is better suited for the interprocess communication. gRPC is a format created by Google using, by default, protocol buffers. Where JSON is a string of serialized information, gRPC is a binary stream and is smaller in size and, therefore, helps cut down latency. This is also useful when the payload is large, and there is a noticeable latency with JSON.

For asynchronous calls, messages are sent using a message broker such as RabbitMQ, Redis, Azure Service Bus, Azure Event Hubs, Kafka, and others. AMQP is the primary protocol used with these message brokers as it defines publishers and consumers. Message brokers ensure the delivery of the messages from the producers to the consumers. With a message broker, applications send messages to the broker for it to forward to the receiving applications. This provides a store-and-forward mechanism and allows for the messages to be received at a later time, such as when an application comes online.

Testing

Testing is just as crucial to product development as coding. A huge problem is when code performs incorrectly. We can make the most elaborate software that performs at amazing speed and return invalid answers. It does not matter how fast your code runs to a wrong answer.

Just like code, tests are multifaceted. From simple code handling a small amount of business logic to classes with many dependencies, targeted tests are needed to ensure the accuracy and reliability of our products.

Test Pyramid

The test pyramid is a visual representation of testing levels. Figure 1-8 is based on Mike Cohn's concept in his book *Succeeding with Agile*. It represents the number of tests compared to each level, speed, and reliability. The unit tests should be small and cover basic units of business logic. Service tests are for individual microservices. And end-to-end tests are the slowest and most unreliable as they generally depend on manual effort and the least amount of automation.

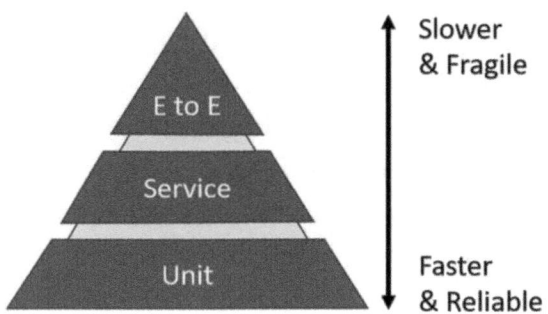

Figure 1-8. *Testing pyramid*

E to E

End-to-end tests, sometimes referred to as system tests, are about testing the system's interactions that use microservices and their interaction with other services. These tests may include UI level tests using manual effort or automated tests using products like Microsoft's Playwright. System tests verify subsequent calls retrieve and update data.

Figure 1-9 shows a block of tests executing against a System Under Test (SUT), which calls multiple microservices. Testing at this level is very slow and fragile compared to unit tests.

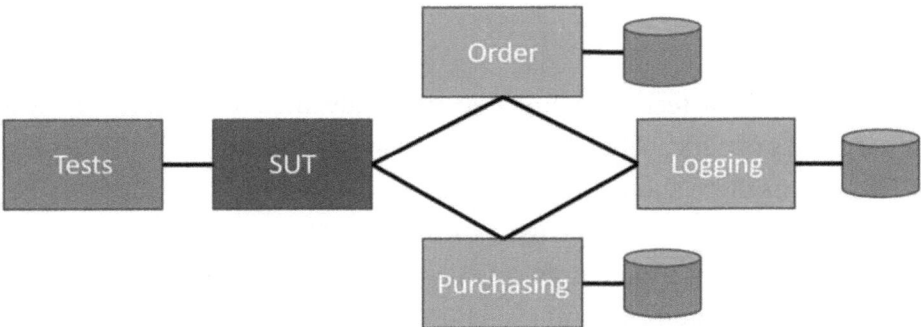

Figure 1-9. *Depiction of end-to-end testing*

Service

Component tests are for testing a microservice apart from other services like other microservices or data stores. You use a mock or a stub to test microservices that depend on a data store or other microservices. Mocks and stubs are configured to return predetermined responses to the System Under Test (SUT).

A stub returns responses based on how they are set up. For example, in Figure 1-10, a stub could stand in for a data store or other long-running method. When called for saving a new order, it returns the order and other information as if it was just saved. This helps the speed of testing since it skips time-consuming, out-of-process logic and only returns premade data.

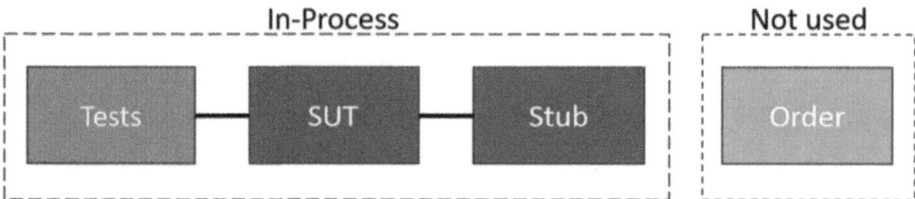

Figure 1-10. *Using stub for testing*

Mocks help verify dependencies are invoked. Mocks also require a setup of predetermined responses. They are used to help test behavior, whereas a stub helps with testing of state. For example, when calling a `createOrder` method, verify that the method to create a log message was also called.

Unit Tests

Good unit tests are the fastest to execute and, generally, the most reliable. They are at the most basic level of code. Unit tests should not invoke calls outside of the executing process. This means there should be no calls to data stores, files, or other services. These tests are for testing the details of business logic. The scope of these tests varies in opinion. Some say the test should only cover code within a single method. Others say the test can go across many methods and even into other classes. To keep them fast, reliable, and maintainable, keep the scope of the tests small.

Automation

Using a Continuous Integration/Continuous Deployment (CI/CD) pipeline should be considered a must-have. They help with the automation of testing and deployment. It is highly recommended to use a build step in your CI/CD pipeline that is performing the unit tests. Integration tests are generally much longer in execution time, so many companies do not add them to the CI/CD pipeline. A better recommendation is to have them executed nightly, at least, or on some other schedule.

Deploying Microservices

Microservices are independent applications. Although their code and business functionality may have come from a monolith, they now have a life of their own. Part of that independence is deployment. As discussed earlier, one of the benefits is deployment apart from a monolith and other microservices. This section discusses factors on versioning tactics, wrapping in containers, hosting in orchestrators, and deployment pipelines.

Versioning

As newer releases of microservices are deployed, versioning takes consideration. Leveraging a versioning semantic from SemVer (`https://www.semver.org`), there are three number segments that are used:

- Major – Version when you make incompatible or breaking API-level changes
- Minor – Version when you add functionality in a backward-compatible manner
- Patch – Version when you make backward-compatible bug fixes

Using Semantic Versioning applies to your APIs as well as any NuGet packages you create. With your API, if using REST, you can add a version in the URL, for example, "api/v1/account."

As you build multiple microservices, there will be common functionality that each service will use. You will quickly build a framework that may include logging, monitoring, and alerting. In this framework, you can use NuGet packaging for each piece. With these packages, you can use Semantic Versioning if using NuGet 4.3.0 or above and Visual Studio 2017 version 15.3 or above.

Containers

Containers allow for executables, their dependencies, and configuration files to be packaged together. Although there are a few container brands available, Docker is the most well-known.

Deploying microservices can be done straight to servers or more likely virtual machines. However, you will see more benefits from running containers. By using containers, you can constrain resources like CPU and RAM, so processes that consume too much CPU or have memory leaks do not kill the server on which they reside. They are easier to manage. Controlling the number of container instances, running on certain servers, and handling upgrade/rollback and failures can all be handled by using an orchestrator. Orchestrators like Docker Swarm, Service Fabric, Kubernetes, Azure Container Apps, and others manage containers with all the features just mentioned but also include features like network and security.

Pipelines

With development processes like Continuous Integration and Continuous Deployment (CI/CD), you can leverage tools that help automate testing and staged releases. Tools like CircleCI, Jenkins, Travis, Azure DevOps, and GitHub Actions, to name a few, can be set up to perform various tasks. You can set them up to be either manually executed or triggered when code is checked into a repository.

Using Azure DevOps, for example, you can set up Builds that are triggered when code is checked in. Executing tasks pull code from the assigned repository, run unit tests and/or integration tests, build a container image, push the image to a container registry, like Azure Container Registry (ACR), and notify an orchestrator of the new image. In this example, you can have code checked in, trigger a build, and within a short time your code is running in a development or staging cluster. You can also set up Builds and Releases on a time-based schedule so, for example, hourly or nightly environments are updated.

Also, "Azure DevOps" have automatic or manually triggered Releases. An automated Release is triggered with a completed Build. Manually triggering a Release provides the option to specify a current or previous build version. With Release tasks, you can have more thorough tests performed, and if passing, the container images can feed a production cluster.

Microservices should be treated as independent applications with their own deployment pipelines. This autonomy allows them to evolve separately from monolithic systems and other microservices. To support this independence, each microservice should also have its own repository, which further facilitates its ability to develop separately.

Cross-Cutting Concerns

There are aspects that are not specific to microservices but do apply to the infrastructure. These are just as important as microservices. If a microservice became unavailable at 2 am, how would you know? When would you know? Who should know? These cross-cutting concerns help you understand the system's whole health. Understanding the health of a system helps with capacity planning and troubleshooting. If the system is showing signs of resource starvation, you may need more containers or servers. Troubleshooting is also important to help identify bugs, code fixes, and infrastructure-related items like network bandwidth.

Monitoring

To say that your microservice is running well means nothing if you cannot prove it and help with capacity planning, fault diagnosing, and cost justification.

Evaluate good monitoring solutions. Prometheus (`https://prometheus.io`) is a great option, but it is not the only good one available. And, although Prometheus is great, it has a steep learning curve. Whatever you find, make sure you build in time to learn how to use it well. After data is captured, you will need something to display that information. Tools like Grafana (`https://grafana.com`) are for displaying captured metrics via Prometheus and other sources.

Using Prometheus and Grafana helps you know if a server or Node (if using Kubernetes) is starving for resources like CPU and RAM. You can also use monitored information like call volumes and response times to know if you need to add servers to the cluster. This tremendously helps with capacity planning.

Implementing a form of health check provides you access to information in various ways. One of which is knowing the microservice is not dead and responds to requests. This is a "liveness probe." The other is in what information goes back to the client. Consider adding an entry point that uses HTTP GET, for example, `HTTP://{service endpoint}/health`. Have the liveness probe return details about the microservice and list the health of various service-specific details:

- Can connect to data store
- Can connect to next microservice hop
- Necessary data for troubleshooting and incident reporting
- Version that can be used to verify latest version has been deployed

The liveness probe may return an HTTP code of 200, signifying the microservices are alive. The response contents contain the health status. Each microservice will have different data to respond with that you define to fit your architectural needs. The returned data can then feed monitoring resources. You may need to add custom adapters to feed systems like Grafana. There are .NET libraries for Prometheus that capture data and are customizable.

Logging

Logging information from microservices is as vital as monitoring, if not more so. Monitoring metrics are great, but when diagnosing fault events, exceptions, and even messages of properly working calls, logging information is an absolute must. First, decide what information you need to keep. Then decide how to keep and retrieve that information.

A centralized logging system provides a great way to accept information that may come from multiple systems. This is known as "Log Aggregation." Services like Splunk are third-party tools for log management. Microservices log information to stdout or stderr. This information is captured and sent to Splunk, where it can be correlated and viewed.

Consider the information you need to keep, for example, messages that include the application name, machine name, timestamp in Coordinated Universal Time (UTC), and brief description. Another option may include a serialized Exception type and stack trace. If you do capture the Exception, I recommend looping through Inner Exceptions to capture all bubbled events. The main piece of information may be wrapped in Exception layers, and you do not want to miss the details. The stack trace will certainly help with identifying code lines, class, and additional information needed for further research.

As with any logging mechanism, there will be costs associated. You will need some way of capturing the log information as well as storing it. Loggly (https://www.loggly.com) is a logging system with many connectors for a variety of systems. The monolith and all microservices can use the libraries and have all logs stored in a central storage location.

Alerting

With data monitored and captured, development teams need to know when their microservices have issues. Alerting is the process of reacting to various performance metrics. It is common for CPU utilization to hit 100% momentarily. The issue is when the process exceeds a CPU threshold too long and risks resource starvation or impacting other processes. Setting alerts based on situations like high CPU utilization or RAM starvation is simple. The following is a list of example metrics you should create alerts for:

- High network bandwidth usage
- CPU usage over a threshold for a certain amount of time
- RAM utilization
- Number of inbound and outbound simultaneous calls
- Errors (exceptions, HTTP errors, etc.)
- Number of messages in a service broker's Dead Letter Queue (DLQ)

Tools like Grafana, Azure Log Analytics, and RabbitMQ have their alerting features. Grafana can alert on most of the items in the preceding list. You will need to set up alerts in multiple systems. If your choice of service broker does not contain alerts, you may need to consider writing a custom metrics handler or see if an open source option is available.

CHAPTER 1   INTRODUCING MICROSERVICES

An additional option is using webhooks to send information to a Slack channel. This way, there is a message that multiple people can see. With alerts that are severe enough to warrant paging someone in the middle of the night, there are tools like ZenDuty. This is configurable with an escalation policy to page one or more people depending on the types of alerts.

Testing the Architecture

A previous section covered code and service testing. This section is about testing the cross-cutting concerns of the infrastructure. With monitoring, logging, and alerting in place, are they set up correctly? As your microservice architecture evolves, so should these items. The tools for these items also need upgrades and modifications as the architecture changes.

In a non-production environment, intentionally cause a failure. Consider the following questions as a starting list of items to evaluate. As you go through the list, add to it. Find the details that are specific to your case and add them to your checklist. Quickly, you will gain a trust level in the tooling, your settings, the microservices, and the team's ability to respond.

- Was the failure logged?
- Do the log entries reflect enough detail to identify the server, microservice, etc.?
- Is the failure due to code, network, third-party call, or data store? Something else?
- Does the failure appear on the monitoring tool?
- Was an alert generated?
- Did the alert go to the development team responsible?
- Did the alert contain enough information to start troubleshooting properly?
- Are there multiple failures noticed? Should there be one or multiple?
- Did the code retry using a "retry policy"? Should it? Was the retry adequate?

- After resolving the failure, did the alert stop? Does logging show correct activity?
- Are you able to produce a report of the failure that includes information from the monitoring tool, correlated log entries, alerts, and from those who responded?

Now consider systematically causing more failures. With each one, go through your checklist. Refine the checklist and, more importantly, fix the items discovered during this testing.

Summary

We just went over a lot of information with a large, broad stroke. The topics mentioned are just the tip of the knowledge iceberg compared to the depth of knowledge encompassing microservice architecture. Adopting a microservice architecture is not easy nor cheap. With all the challenges, it does take allowance to fail, teamwork, and time to do it right. For many companies, the benefits easily outweighed the challenges. They saw the benefits of autonomy with teams, services, and data. They can scale their services and make the best use of their servers.

There are many patterns available for microservices. It would take another book to cover them all. But the API Gateway, BFF, and External Configuration Store will quickly serve you well. They apply to even the smallest microservice architecture.

The communication with microservices may change in your architecture. The easiest is to use synchronous RPC. But you may find yourself changing to use the asynchronous methods with a message broker since it is more extendable.

Always consider testing throughout the development cycles. Unit testing will provide confidence in the accuracy of the understanding of the business logic for the minute code. With microservices, there is an added layer of testing complexity. Testing the service layer is possible and made easier to automate with mocks and stubs. Then, when nearly ready for production, the system tests to verify that the system is operational and functional.

When developing microservices, consider automating builds using CI/CD automation tools like Jenkins and Azure DevOps. The pipelines handle so many of the mundane processes and free up developers for more coding. Also, include in the build pipelines test execution for more stable releases to various environments.

The cross-cutting concerns are for the environments hosting microservices. You should be able to monitor the health of each service and hosting server. Set up alerts to notify the right people to jump to action if/when issues occur. When they happen, logging will be crucial for troubleshooting and debugging.

Lastly, manually test the architecture. Cause issues to occur so that you know your monitoring shows enough information, logging has recorded vital clues, and alerts are notifying correct response team members. The microservice architecture will evolve just like the microservices. The infrastructure will need the same attention as the code receives.

CHAPTER 2

Other Software Patterns

This chapter teaches the reader about other software patterns. This book is focused on microservices, a great software pattern. But it isn't the only software pattern. Lest we fall into a scenario where we seek for the golden hammer, let's educate the reader that other tools exist in an architect's toolchest. Just because microservices are awesome doesn't mean it's the correct tool for every job.

Why are we discussing other software patterns in a microservices book? Microservices isn't the only software pattern. We'll definitely focus most intensely on building microservices in .NET. But there are other great tools for building high-quality software. In this chapter, we'll show the other architecture tools you can choose from. Definitely choose the correct tool for your task.

A software pattern is a description of a particular way of architecting a system, the various components of the system, and how they interact. We use software patterns as metaphors to allow teams and developers to clearly identify common techniques and to choose appropriate designs for a system.

Let's imagine an auto mechanic's toolchest. In the chest there's a hammer, a set of screwdrivers with various heads, maybe Allen wrenches of various thicknesses, saws with blades to cut various materials, and a socket set with sockets of various sizes. Each socket in the socket set is carefully labeled with the size of the bolt head that it can turn. Because each tool has a specific name, a mechanic can ask a helper, "Can you hand me the 8mm socket?" and the helper can choose the correct tool. If we had no names for these, the helper could just as easily hand over the hammer. Or perhaps if the mechanic only said "screwdriver," they'd get handed a Phillips head when they needed a hex head screwdriver.

Like tools in an auto mechanic's toolchest, software developers have various names for software architecture patterns. When an architect identifies the system is best as a monolith, developers can now avoid building an event-driven architecture. Because we have these names, we can communicate easily and clearly about our intentions and implementations.

CHAPTER 2   OTHER SOFTWARE PATTERNS

Like any good tool, there is a proper way to use it and an improper way to use it. Software architecture patterns are no different. There are proper applications for a software pattern, and places where a software pattern doesn't fit. There is no golden hammer, and there is no "best" software pattern. Rather every pattern has an appropriate use-case, and each is correct for a specific problem.

This book is focused on the microservices pattern. Microservices are great for creating loosely coupled systems of easily deployable, easily replaceable components. This can be perfect for some systems, but is definitely not the right fit for all systems. In this chapter, we'll briefly explore other architecture patterns. If the needs of your system better fit another architecture pattern, you can pivot away from this book to a book specific to that pattern.

Monolith

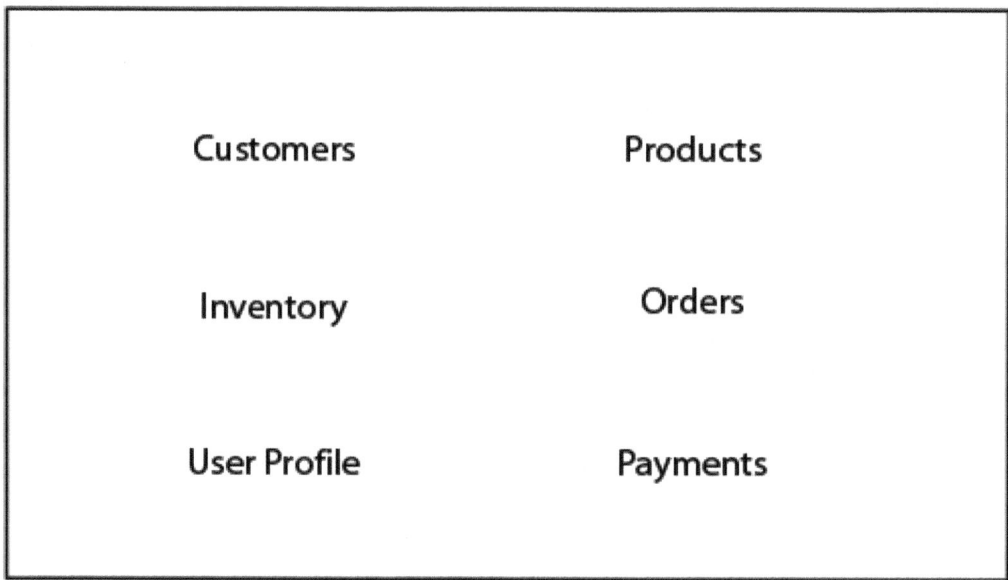

Figure 2-1. *A monolithic application has all system features in one deployed package*

What Is It

The monolithic software pattern is characterized by a single codebase compiled and/or deployed into a single running application. The monolith is likely the first software pattern an architect will learn. As seen in Figure 2-1, all development is done in a single repository and deployed as a single binary or single collection of binaries. Any change in the system requires redeploying the entire system.

Pros and Cons

When using the monolith pattern, any change requires redeploying everything. This can be great because everything has a single version. Often this is bad because deploying anything requires changing everything. And if everything changes, we now need to revalidate everything. Will QA run all the integration test cases across the entire system with every small code change? Can we afford the time or cost necessary to do that?

A monolithic application is perfect when it's deployed to a client's environment where we have less control over hosting and configuration. A monolith is deployed as a single unit, so customers need not configure lots of pieces.

When first beginning a new project, a monolith is a great starting point. When you first begin building the system, the seams between components may not be obvious yet. During development, you may abandon or completely change pieces of the application. As you first start, consider keeping the entire application in one fast-moving repository and deployed as one deployment package. As the application matures, discover the seams between components, and refactor into smaller pieces deployed separately.

A monolithic application often has a consistent interface because it was all designed together. Consumers of a monolith therefore can expect consistency in API calls.

It can be difficult to evolve and change a monolithic application. Often intertwined behaviors and system functions lead to convoluted code and awkward work-arounds to compensate. This leads to highly coupled code, causing unexpected bugs when the system evolves. Where a smaller or more distributed system might make multiple copies with slight variations or configuration changes, a monolith may have a single, super-configurable, super confusing implementation. This technical debt can be difficult to solve.

Developers are quick to align with the DRY principle. Short for "Do not Repeat Yourself," it's a technique for combining similar functions into one configurable function so any change to the business rule will instantly propagate to every use-case that runs

CHAPTER 2 OTHER SOFTWARE PATTERNS

the rule. In general, this is a great technique to contain maintenance issues. However, in a large monolithic system, this can be a hindrance. As we chase code changes in the name of DRY, we create infinitely complex modules that require extreme configuration and experience to use. In a monolith, DRY code can be more costly to maintain and harder to reason about.

Best Use-Case

The best use-case for a monolith is when deploying to machines you don't own. A single product can be deployed and configured in one go. Another good use-case for monolithic systems is when beginning a new project where you haven't yet discovered system components. Until the seams between the components present themselves, a monolith is easier to construct and quickly iterate.

Modular Monolith

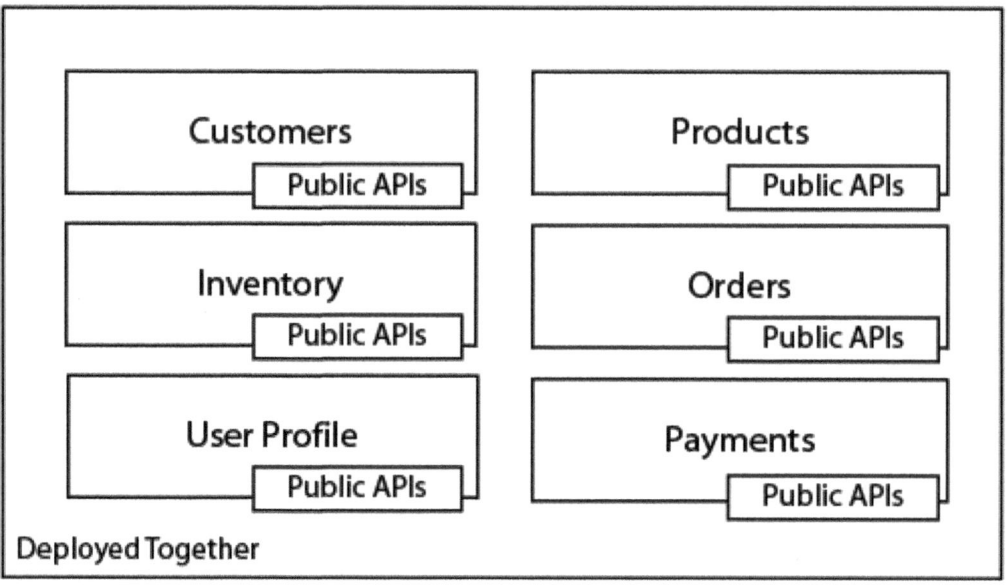

Figure 2-2. *A Modular Monolith has lots of pieces with public endpoints but all are deployed at once*

What Is It

A modular monolith is a step from monolith toward microservices, but also a worst-case scenario of both monolith and microservices. In a modular monolith, application pieces are split into small components, offering loose coupling and easy component upgrades and replacement (Figure 2-2). However, the entire application is still deployed at once.

Pros and Cons

A modular monolith includes the worst cons of both monolithic systems and microservice systems. Like a monolith, any change in any component requires redeploying everything. With everything changing, everything needs to be revalidated. Like microservices, we can't just test each component in isolation, but we must test the interaction between components. These integration tests are more complex and don't easily lend themselves to mocking. Without mocked dependencies, tests may test more than necessary, and that leads to slower test runs to accomplish the same validation.

Modular monoliths are a great temporary solution as you're beginning to break apart a monolithic application. Perhaps you're first focusing on separating the codebase into components, and you'll next refactor the deployment process to allow individual components to be deployed in isolation.

Best Use-Case

Modular monolith is a great transition state when moving from a monolith to microservices. But don't spend too long here. It includes all the cons of both microservices and monoliths.

Layered Architecture

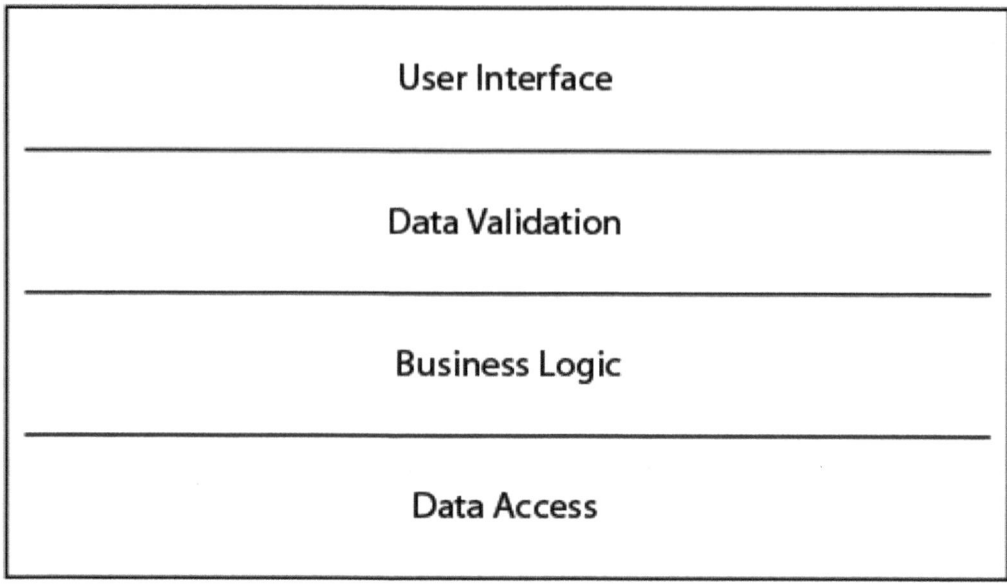

Figure 2-3. *Layered architecture has distinct layers for technical features*

What Is It

Layered architecture, as seen in Figure 2-3, is like lasagna. You have various horizontal tiers representing technologies or system functions. Typically, one will have a data tier, a business layer, perhaps a validation layer, and finally a user interface layer. If you get fancy, you might have a business rules engine layer or a database entities layer or data-transformation layer.

Pros and Cons

What's great about a layered architecture is you can clearly delineate responsibilities – it's obvious where new code should go and what it should look like. It's easy to clone a similar class, change the name, and update the properties or methods to fit the new item.

What's unfortunate about a layered architecture is the separations are not on user feature groups, but often on technology boundaries. This leads to scaling concerns. When deploying, we have two options:

1. Compile all the layers into a monolith: In this approach, the application is still deployed as a single piece, so any change in any part of the system requires redeploying the entire system.

2. Compile each layer into a separate microservice: Though this sounds like a move toward a microservices architecture, it's actually a step backward. A request from a user must now make three or five or more network request through the horizontal microservice layers to get to the data store. Each network request adds latency and potential integration problems.

In either deployment scenario, we still can't scale different system functions separately. For example, if the user login feature is getting hit particularly hard, but user profile features aren't used often, we still have to scale the entire system to meet the need.

Layered architecture was historically used when we started noticing cracks in the monolith. We searched for a way to break the monolith apart, and as technologists, easily found seams in the technologies. This does produce more loosely coupled code, but doesn't allow easy feature replacement or individual module scale like a microservices platform.

Best Use-Case

As you build any other architecture, you may introduce layers in each component to better separate concerns into testable pieces. For example, in a microservice, separating business logic from data storage allows us to easily mock data storage when testing business logic functions.

Event-Driven Architecture

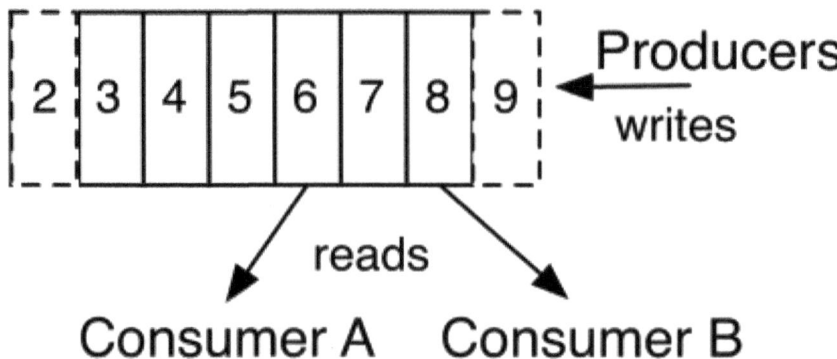

Figure 2-4. Producers save events, and asynchronously consumers read them

What Is It

Event-driven architecture is an extension of microservices. In both microservices and event-driven architectures, each piece is built and deployed separately. In a microservices architecture, components often call each other via REST, GraphQL, or gRPC calls. In event-driven architecture (Figure 2-4), each piece publishes events to an enterprise service bus. Other components can subscribe to the event feed, and take necessary down-stream actions if the event is relevant. In an event-driven architecture, the current state of the system may not be known. Instead, the system is eventually consistent.

Pros and Cons

Event-driven architecture is great for systems that focus on asynchronous communication and very loose coupling. Each component can spit out various events describing actions taken or processes completed. Down-stream systems can choose to subscribe to the event stream, and take action if the event is relevant to them.

In an event-driven architecture, an enterprise service bus (such as Kafka, EventGrid, or MassTransit) allows a separation between the publishing and the consuming systems. This removes a major source of system down-time. No longer does the other system need to be online to get the job done. A publisher can publish as fast as they can, and a consumer can slowly chew through the queue. In fact, a publisher can publish to the service bus even if the consumer is offline. By comparison, if the publisher made a REST call to the consumer, both systems would need to be operational for the call to succeed.

Event-driven systems often lend themselves to event streams where only the changes are noted. For example, the payment microservice may publish events related to successfully or unsuccessfully charging the user's credit card, but the message likely doesn't include the full order. Since messages only contain the changes, it can be difficult to infer the current state of entities in the system. A consumer may need to replay a large portion of the event history to reconstruct the current state. A consumer might choose to cache the current state, mitigating this concern.

Best Use-Case

Event-driven architecture is great for asynchronous systems where components need not process at the same speed. When dependencies can be asynchronous, event-driven architecture allows a separation between publish and subscribe, compensating for system instability or downtime.

Pipeline Architecture

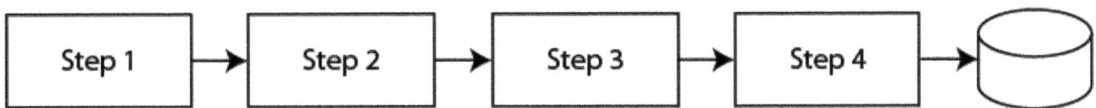

Figure 2-5. *A pipeline of sequential steps to complete a complex workflow*

What Is It

A pipeline architecture (Figure 2-5) is a linear process represented by a series of components. Each component modifies the data in a specific way. Perhaps the pipeline ingests data from one source, cleans and transforms it, and exports it into a data warehouse.

Pros and Cons

Pipeline architecture is great for systems that look like assembly lines, constructing complex results through a series of steps. In each station, the component can take specific actions to contribute to the overall process.

The pipeline architecture is similar to an event-driven architecture in that data may flow downstream to other processes. Unlike an event-driven architecture that focuses on asynchrony, a pipeline architecture instead focuses on a linear process. Much like a call stack, each component in the linear process waits for the previous step to complete.

In a pipeline architecture, the stream of data can be bigger than monolithic data processes, but separating into distinct steps makes data processing slower.

Best Use-Case

A pipeline architecture is great for a complex series of steps where discrete actions can be separated and scaled individually.

Micro-Kernel

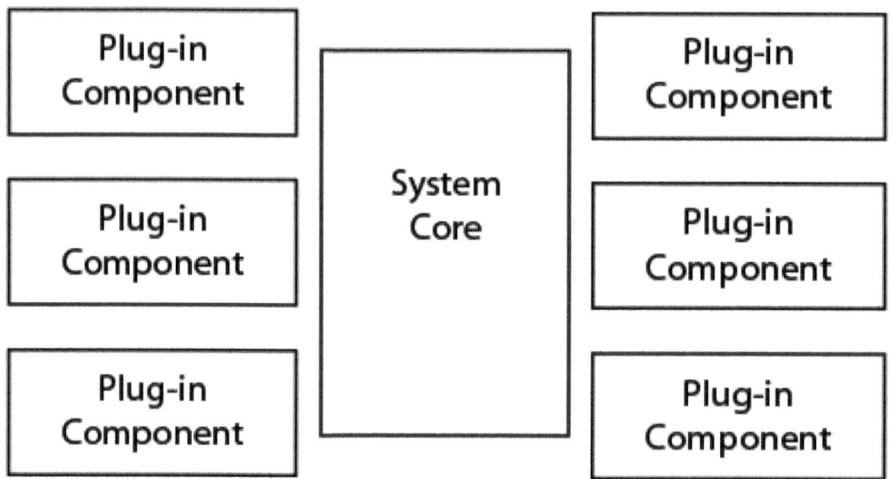

Figure 2-6. Micro-kernel architecture has a small core and many plug-in components

What Is It

In a micro-kernel architecture (Figure 2-6), the core of the solution is kept very minimal. Plugins augment the core features to accomplish individual tasks.

Pros and Cons

Consider a tax calculation system that accounts for local, regional, and national tax rates. Perhaps the tax rates change frequently or are complex to calculate. In this case, the core system is tasked with the overly simplistic requirement of "calculating the taxes," and a relatively stable publicly consumable interface is necessary. However, the individual laws and statutes dictate a constantly evolving mechanism for calculation. It may even be a challenge to identify if a tax rate applies to a particular purchase. In this case, we can build a stable "calculate the tax" service with a generic interface that takes in details such as location, date, and products purchased. Within this service, we can load each plugin, identify if it applies, then call the plugin's function(s) to do the calculation.

In a microkernel architecture, we can choose to deploy only a single plugin if that's all that has changed. This can lead to efficiencies in development and deployment as only a small portion of the system needs to be revalidated.

In a microkernel architecture, it's often a difficult matter to infer whether a new feature should be in the system core or in a plugin. What if two plugins need similar features, but this adjustment doesn't apply to other plugins? Should the core expand to avoid code duplication? It takes careful skill to construct and preserve an ideal micro-kernel.

A great example of a micro-kernel architecture is the Node.js ecosystem. In the core of Node.js, there's really only a few features. The most prominent are 1. listen to sockets, and 2. access the file system. Most major features we think of as "Node.js features" live in node_module libraries loaded dynamically into application code. Express.js, Angular, Three.js, and others build upon the core Node.js to produce very different results for dependent applications.

Best Use-Case

When a system requires a very diverse set of functions that evolve quickly, a microkernel architecture can keep the core system very stable while allowing plugins to grow organically.

Service-Oriented Architecture

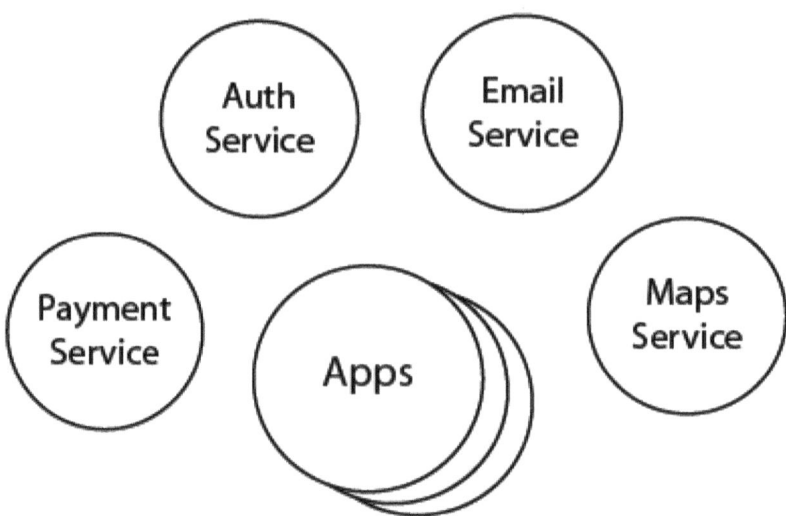

Figure 2-7. *Service-oriented architecture has common enterprise services so teams don't need to reinvent the wheel*

What Is It

Service-oriented architecture (Figure 2-7) is an organizational pattern of communicating between systems and teams using reusable services. Perhaps one team builds an email distribution service, and any team needing to send emails invokes this service. This removes duplication and streamlines use of best practices and/or regulatory compliance across the enterprise.

Pros and Cons

Service-oriented architecture breaks an organization's needs into enterprise services consumed by other teams. By comparison, microservices concerns itself with a single product, arranging features into smaller pieces.

Enterprise services are a great way to create reusable nuggets of feature, avoiding the need for each enterprise team to reinvent it themselves. This can lead to operational efficiencies, but can also lead to complexity and competition. What if the enterprise email service doesn't include attachments or both an HTML and plain text body? What if the enterprise email service doesn't support adding bcc recipients with no "to" address? In this case, the team requiring this feature would need to petition the other team for support. Does this need align with both teams' priorities and urgency? Or do we need to compete with other priorities to get the need met?

A service-oriented architecture where common services emerge can lead to technological stagnation. Now that the problem is solved by "them," we don't need to worry about it ... but we also must get "them" to fix and evolve it to match changing business trends or technology improvements. We are no longer in control of the speed and quality of the software.

If we can't talk the other team into evolving the service, the team could choose to "go rogue," to create a clone of the functionality with necessary adjustments. Though this gets the team unblocked, it defeats the entire purpose of organizational efficiency.

Best Use-Case

In large organizations with great inter-team communication and servant-leadership mindset, service-oriented architectures can lead to great organizational efficiencies.

Microservices

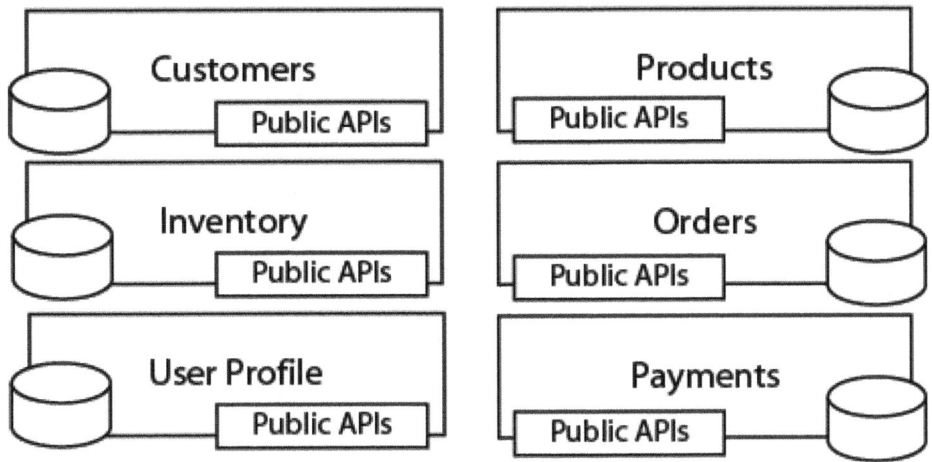

Figure 2-8. *Microservices are built and deployed separately*

What Is It

Microservices is a pattern of separating system features into small components. In Figure 2-8, we split the system vertically by function. For example, the user login microservice is separate from the order entry microservice. Each microservice includes data validation, data storage, and business functions. Each microservice is built and deployed independently, making a single system into a mesh of interrelated services and agents, each with a specific task.

Pros and Cons

The microservices approach is great for larger systems where the total features are difficult to manage in a single system. Each microservice accomplishes a single task, and is built and deployed individually.

In a microservices system, each component is only a small portion of the system's functionality. This means that while one can thoroughly unit- and integration-test a microservice, one still doesn't know if it works as expected. It isn't until we test the interaction between components that we discover if the entire product works together. Sadly, these tests between components can't be mocked – we really do need the full components to validate their cohesion. So we may not be able to fully test the system until all the components are deployed. Nonproduction environments may help with this, but ultimately, we need to run some tests in production to fully validate the software.

In a microservices system, different components can be in different programming languages. We can pick the best development environment for the task at hand, mixing and matching technologies across the microservice suite. In general, we tend to lean into what we know, so single-language microservices architectures are completely fine.

Best Use-Case

Microservices are a great choice for larger systems or when the system architecture calls for very distinct features. Each microservice is deployed and scaled individually, allowing for easy adjustment or replacement.

Summary
Choose the Right Tool for the Job

In Table 2-1, we see a summary of all the software patterns. There's great diversity in approaches here. It might be easy to dismiss some patterns as completely ineffective. Alas, each tool has a proper use. Much like a mechanic's toolchest, these software patterns allow developers to craft the perfect system to accomplish stakeholder needs. With unique names, developers can communicate their intent to other engineers. A screwdriver is different from a hammer, and a monolith is different from a microservices architecture. With a familiarity of software patterns, you can easily choose the right tool for the job.

Table 2-1. *Software Pattern Summary*

Software pattern	Quick summary	Best use-case
Monolith	All pieces deployed and scaled at once	– Getting started – Deploying to environments outside your control
Modular Monolith	Small components all deployed at once.	– Temporary spot when transitioning from monolith to microservices
Layered Architecture	Data tier, business tier, ux tier, and others	– Separate technologies into easily cloneable pieces – Clearly know where new code goes
Event-driven Architecture	Each service publishes events. Those that want to listen can subscribe.	– Asynchronous processes where eventual consistency is sufficient
Pipeline Architecture	A series of steps in a linear process	– Complex processes that can be broken into discrete steps
Micro-kernel	A small, stable core feature-set augmented by plugins	– Very diverse system functions around a stable core set of principles
Service-based Architecture	Organizational needs are solved by generic services from other teams.	– Large organizations with great inter-team communication
Microservices	Small components deployed and scaled individually	– Easily scale or replace system features without affecting other features

CHAPTER 3

Searching for Microservices

This chapter uses a mock scenario to understand a client's problems with an application critical for their business. You will see how a workshop-style meeting, called Event Storming, helps software developers understand the customer's business and their application in need of help. You will also learn about Domain-Driven Design (DDD) and how developers can use it to prepare for decomposing a monolithic application into microservices. To head in the right direction, we will start with a brief introduction to the customer's business. This introduction will help you understand a little about the customer's struggles, which will aid with an example of analyzing the need for microservices.

The Business

Our hypothetical client company Hyp-Log is a shipping logistics middleman coordinator for hotshot deliveries. Hotshot deliveries are point-to-point transfers of goods or materials that require a level of expedience that may not be attainable by larger carrier firms.

Hyp-Log's value to its customers derives from its ability to source the best possible price given the type, size, and weight of a given shipment. In essence, Hyp-Log took all their rate spreadsheets and the analysis that staff were performing manually and built a "rate engine" to perform those same calculations with greater speed, higher accuracy, and better overall customer experience.

CHAPTER 3   SEARCHING FOR MICROSERVICES

A previous employee of Hyp-Log created a custom application for them. Although the application has helped in many ways, a few business processes remain as manual effort. With growing demands, Hyp-Log decides to have a company make the programming changes necessary. Code Whiz is the hypothetical software development firm hired to make the code modifications.

There are several challenges when it comes to managing shipments without automation. Let's consider an owner/operator in a carrier company. This person is not only the owner of the company, responsible for all the back-office administrative tasks, but this person is also responsible for quoting shipments and delivering said shipments. That is an awful lot of tasks for one individual. Here is where the monolithic carrier portal shines, and the application removes the burden of quoting each shipment. The rating engine uses carrier-provided rate sheets, fleet availability, and capabilities to generate quotes for customer shipments automatically, thus removing the burden of a quotation from the carrier.

After a few years of using spreadsheets and calling carriers for quote information, they decided to have an application made to handle their processes. An employee created an application to facilitate as much of the work as possible. That application became affectionately known as "Shipment Parcel Logistics Administration – Thing," aka "SPLAT." *Naming things is hard.*

SPLAT has three main user types: customers, carriers, and administrators. It provides a way for customers to submit load requests, pick a carrier based on a list of quotes, and provide payment. Carriers can manage their fleet and base costs per mile plus extra costs based on particular needs. Some loads require a trailer, are hazardous material, or even refrigerated.

Domain-Driven Design

Before we can leverage Domain-Driven Design (DDD), we need to define a few things. We will go over a few tenants of DDD: Domain, Ubiquitous Language, Bounded Contexts, and Aggregates with Aggregate Roots.

Domain

DDD is a way of developing applications with an intended focus on a domain. The domain is the realm for which you created the application. For instance, if the application is primarily designed to manage accounting-related functionality, its domain would be accounting rather than anything else.

In the case of Hyp-Log, their domain is hotshot load management. Other domains may exist in the company, like Human Resources and Insurance, but they are not relative to why Hyp-Log exists as a company. They are ancillary domains for a company to function, but they do not help Hyp-Log stand out among competitors.

Eric Evans is the founder of DDD and author of *Domain-Driven Design: Tackling Complexity in the Heart of Software*. This chapter will leverage pieces of DDD to help understand the hotshot domain and determine when/where to create microservices. DDD was not created for the use of microservices but can be leveraged for the development of microservices. That said, this book does not explain every piece of DDD.

Subdomains

A subdomain is a grouping of related business processes. For example, you may have a group of processes for Accounts Payable, Accounts Receivable, and Payroll in an accounting domain. The business processes related to each other for generating and processing invoices belong to the Accounts Receivable subdomain. In comparison, the business processes for managing time sheets, wages, and federal forms belong to the Payroll subdomain. At this level, we are only referring to the business processes. This grouping of focus is known as the Problem Space.

The code that provides the functionality in a subdomain should also exist in groups separate from others. The groups of code that provide functionality for their subdomain are called a bounded context. The bounded context exists in what is known as the Solution Space. We will discuss more on bounded contexts in another section. When we decide what code should become a microservice, you will see how the subdomain type weighs in.

There are three subdomain types: Core, Supportive, and Generic.

- Core – Each core subdomain in an application contains one or more bounded contexts that are critical to the company.

- Supportive – The supportive subdomains are not deemed critical but contain code that is supportive of the business.

- Generic – Lastly, generic subdomains are those that are replaceable with off-the-shelf solutions.

Ubiquitous Language

One of the most important artifacts of DDD is the Ubiquitous Language (UL). The UL is a collection of phrases and terms that helps everyone involved to have a clear and concise understanding of business processes.

Some phrases like "user submits a request" are not clear to the full meaning and context to which it belongs. Rephrasing helps to build a UL that is quickly understood. For example, "the customer provides a coupon code" and "the customer issues dispute request" have entirely different contexts though both have a "user" and are "submitting a request." The clarification is crucial so that everyone involved in the project's development understands the specifics of business processes.

There are times when terms have overloaded meanings. Depending on the context, terms like "ticket" can mean various things. To say "a user submits a ticket" needs clarification to the specific context. Is this referring to a customer submitting a support ticket? Or is this referring to a driver submitting a ticket to a machine in a parking garage to pay for parking? Having a well-formed UL helps alleviate confusion between teams and can make for more concise use cases.

UL should also extend to the code. Developers tend to shy away from long class and method names. But having concise names for namespaces, classes, and methods helps the code stay in line with the UL. As time goes on and developers change roles or jobs, having code in line with the UL helps other developers come up to speed in a shorter amount of time.

Bounded Contexts

A bounded context is a collection of codes that implements business processes in a subdomain distinctly different from other processes. For example, consider an application at a manufacturing plant. The code for inventory management of purchased parts is different than inventory management of manufactured parts. Because the business processes differed between purchased parts and manufactured parts, the code providing business functionality is also different. By using ubiquitous language here, the term "part" is distinguished to the various purposes to become "purchased part" vs. "manufactured part." Thus, there is a bounded context, determined by the language around the term "part."

Identifying bounded contexts can be done by a couple of different tactics. As mentioned, language is an indicator of a boundary, making a bounded context. Functionality that uses specific language in the namespaces, class names, and method help identify a bounded context and its purpose. Consider, too, the terms used in the functionality. For example, the term invoice is an obvious clue. But CustomerAccount may not be enough of a clue. In cases like these, look for verbs. What is acting on or with the CustomerAccount? Two possibilities of action are the creation of a customer account, while another is notification.

Aggregates and Aggregate Roots

Not surprisingly, there can be multiple classes in a bounded context. There is a relationship between the classes based on dependency. This dependency may be due to inheritance or composition. Each group of these classes is an Aggregate and the top-level class in an Aggregate Root.

There is a rule, provided by Eric Evans, that states that classes in an aggregate may call on each other or an aggregate root of another aggregate even if it is in another bounded context. The idea is that no class in a bounded context may leverage a class directly in another bounded context without going through the root of an aggregate. This rule is an architectural form of encapsulation. It prevents building dependencies that quickly become fragile.

Let's consider the following example. There is an aggregate for handling health care benefits in the Benefits bounded context shown in Figure 3-1. There is an aggregate root with dependent classes handling benefits such as retirement, health insurance, and short-term disability. In the Payroll bounded context, there is also an aggregate. It has dependent classes for handling details like time sheets, federal forms, and direct deposit. Each aggregate, in the separate bounded contexts, has its own Employee class. This duplication of the Employee class allows employee functionality to be separate and not become a God class. God classes contain functionality for multiple bounded contexts, thus blurring the lines and making them harder to evolve.

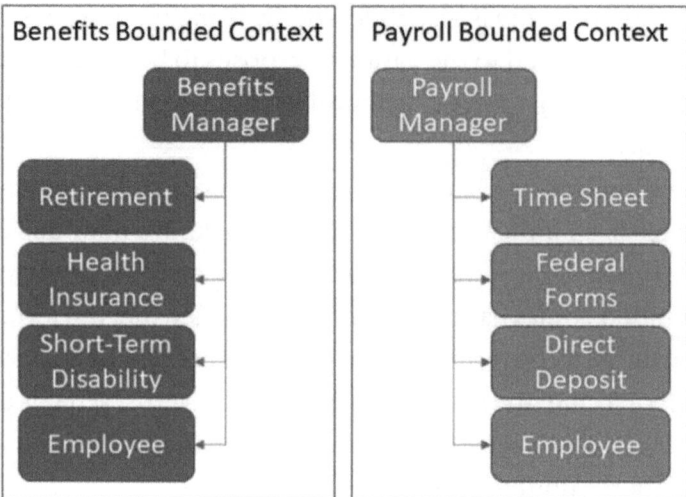

Figure 3-1. Example of aggregates

Should any class in the benefits aggregate be allowed to call the employee object in the payroll aggregate and change its state? No. Allowing any class to call any other class in a different aggregate could affect the integrity of the data in that employee's state. When changes to an employee's benefits affect their paycheck, then the code in the benefits aggregate should only make calls to the payroll aggregate root. Adhering to this rule allows for business rules to be in place to protect the integrity of the employee data and other related classes. Another example is that changes to an employee's benefits should not change their direct deposit information.

Going back to our larger example of the hotshot shipping company, the Load Request class is related to Load and Customer classes handling new load requests in the SPLAT application. In Figure 3-2, you see the Load Request class is the aggregate root. To access load information in the request, you should not go directly to the Load class but rather through the Load Request class. Going directly to the Load Request class allows it to either provide the functionality to alter the state of a Load or Customer. In the absence of functionality, the root can protect the integrity of the state of the information.

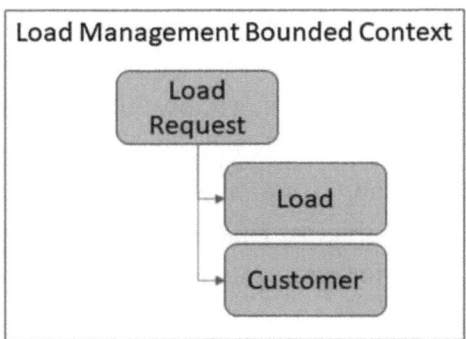

Figure 3-2. Shows Load Request class as the aggregate root

Domain-Driven Design is a large topic and takes a while to fully grasp all the details and integrate them into daily software development. The aspects I covered will help in the discussions about how the developers at Code Whiz analyze and create code that fulfills the needs for Hyp-Log. In the next section, we will cover a way of analyzing an existing code base.

Event Storming

The team at Code Whiz decided to use a workshop-style meeting called "Event Storming" with the members at Hyp-Log. Though not the only way to help understand business processes, it is great for identifying various domains that the development team will later be modeling. Alberto Brandolini originally invented Event Storming to help identify aggregates in DDD. It is also extremely useful for companies to understand existing systems better and develop the requirements needed for a software project. Alberto has a website on Event Storming at `https://eventstorming.com`.

In Event Storming, software developers learn from subject matter experts, known as domain experts, how the industry operates and how that company operates. The meeting is to help everyone involved gain a common understanding of how things currently work and to show processes that need to change. Event Storming meetings help new development team members come up to speed and with domain experts new to their position. A domain expert may retire, and someone without years of knowledge must take over that role. In such cases, domain experts can also gain a complete understanding of the various pieces of a system.

Several of these meetings will take place throughout the development effort. Although it would be nice to have everything discussed and all requirements gathered before development starts, doing so will inevitably allow for misunderstandings or incorrect assumptions. It may also be more effective to have many small meetings than a few long and daunting. The relative domain experts approve the solutions created by the developers for the various problems. This approval process helps prevent a deviation between what the domain experts and development team understand about the business processes.

Setup

Event Storming is best done on large walls using paper rolls, sticky notes, and pens. Since many people can work together, provide enough space for the sticky notes when working with multiple subdomains. It is common to use hallways to allow for enough room for people to work around each other.

Digital options are available but somewhat discouraged. Although using a site like Miro (https://miro.com) is a good option, it is difficult for multiple people to collaborate effectively. One advantage an online resource like Miro has over using real sticky notes is the ability to grab a group of sticky notes and move around the board quickly.

Color Coding

To distinguish types of activities, use sticky notes of various colors. There are many suggestions on color schemes to use. Whatever color scheme you choose, make a legend like the one noted in Figure 3-3. Considering the size of the wall used during the Event Storming sessions, you may want to make copies of the legend for various areas.

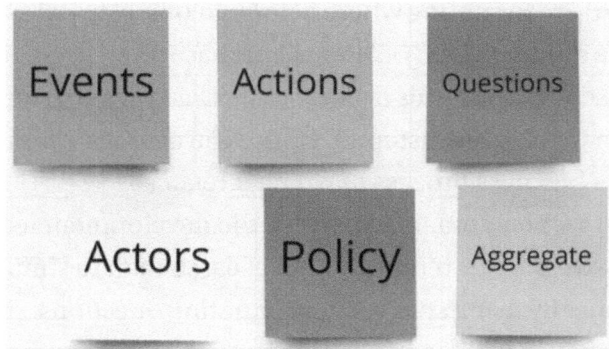

Figure 3-3. Event Storming legend

- Orange – Domain Events
- Blue – Actions/Commands
- Yellow – Actors
- Purple – Policy
- Green – Aggregate
- Red – Questions

Domain events (orange) are business processes that are noted in the past tense. They are in the past tense as they have occurred, and other items are affected by these events. Actors (yellow) either cause a domain event or are responsible for initiating an action/command. For example, the Customer actor initiated the "Order Submitted" domain event by completing an online order.

Actions/commands (blue) are artifacts that either trigger a domain event or are a process triggered by a domain event. For example, if an "Invoice Created" domain event occurred, an action could be to "Notify Customer."

Policies (purple) are for noting where special business rules come into play. For example, with a domain event of "Items Purchased," note an action for a warehouse employee to pick the items. A policy may note that an item weighing over 50 pounds requires two people to lift. Another example is if an item weighs over 200 pounds, then a forklift is required. Policies are to note where such attention is needed but not meant to cover every case.

Aggregates (green) are for noting where a domain object exists. Sticking with the previous example of a domain event of "Items Purchased," an aggregate could be a "Warehouse Pick Ticket." In code, this is likely to be class objects. Another example of an aggregate could be an Invoice or Customer. Notice the aggregate is enough for showing the relationship to the business process to which it relates.

Questions (red) are when domain experts or the development team have questions but no immediate answers. They require some research but are simply flagged so the workshop can continue. By using sticky notes for noting questions, you won't forget the necessary details when it comes time for development. However, development cannot be considered complete without answers to those questions. One example could be "Who decides weight thresholds for the warehouse item policy?"

The Meeting

The Event Storming meeting begins with only noting domain events. The domain experts start filling out orange sticky notes and applying them to the wall. They start with any domain event that comes to mind. From there, add other sticky notes as other events are remembered and thought through. Rearrange the sticky notes as discussions occur and as you discover new order of events.

It is not required to note every domain event at this stage. As the meeting progresses and other sticky notes are applied, you will add other domain events to the storyline. And there is no need to note functionality that occurs at the persistence layer (data store interactions) unless there is business-critical functionality. Hopefully, there is no business logic in the persistence layer as that would not be clean code and make for tighter coupling of dependencies.

Domain events that are not relevant to the problem space should not be on the wall. Domain events like "User Logged into System" should only be on the wall if the problem concerns users logging in. Else, the sticky notes only add confusion. Domain events regarding customers and carriers notified, in this case, should be on the wall as they directly apply to business processes in the problem space. Figure 3-4 shows examples of domain events.

CHAPTER 3 SEARCHING FOR MICROSERVICES

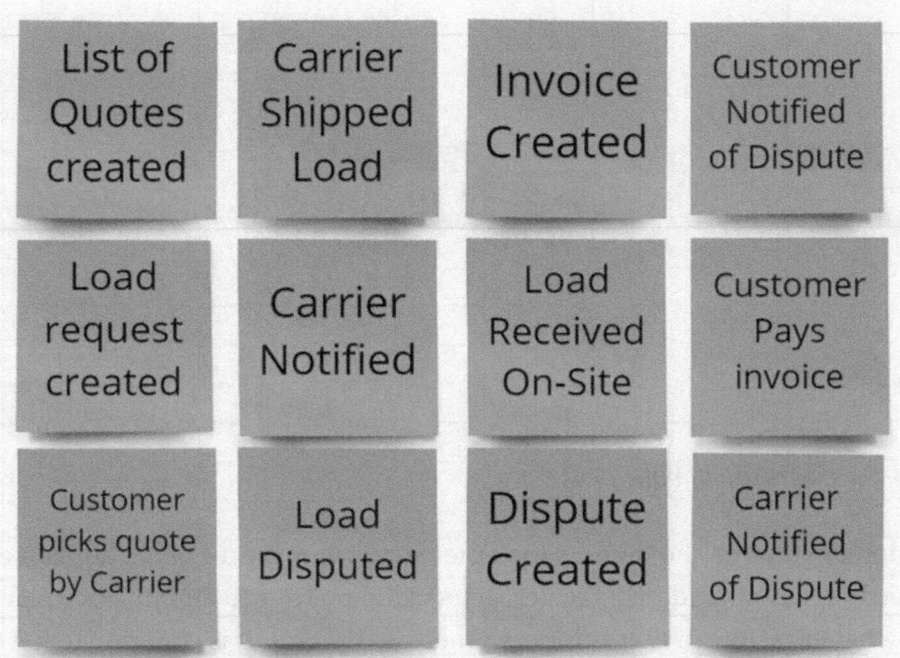

Figure 3-4. Example of domain events

After domain events are applied, ask the group to look for duplicates that do not need to be on the board and apply the order of events. There will be cases where duplicate events should be on the wall. For example, when notifying carriers, there can be more than one time when that event occurs. However, they are context specific. That is, each domain event is relative to the contextual reason it exists.

Figure 3-5 shows a flow of events, also depicting split processes. This split process shows a decision that a load is either accepted or disputed. A parallel process shown is during the dispute handling, where the customer and the carrier are notified. They occur at the same time and are not dependent on each other.

55

CHAPTER 3   SEARCHING FOR MICROSERVICES

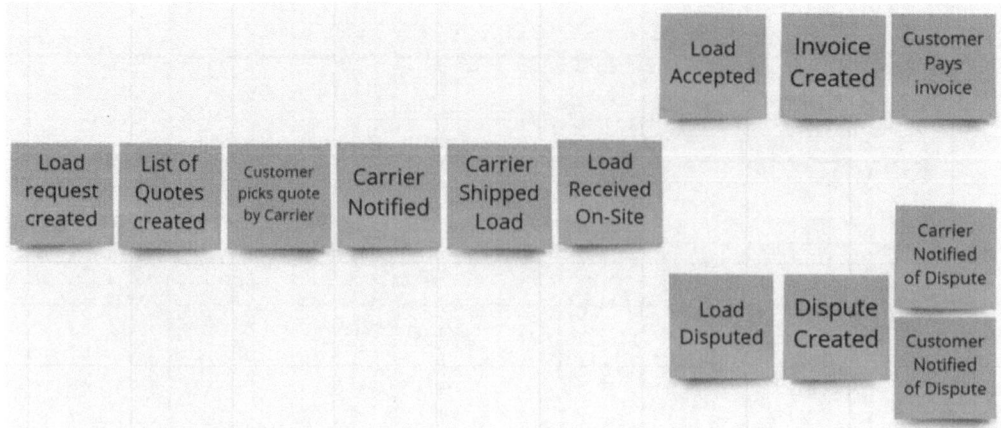

Figure 3-5. *Example of split process*

The domain experts should note the other supporting pieces of the domain events. Add the actions/commands, aggregates, actors, and policies to their relative places showing a better picture of how business processes operate. It is common to have to move many sticky notes to make room for additional supporting notes. Another possibility for duplicate sticky notes is with aggregates. In Figure 3-6, Load, Customer, Carrier, and Invoice can have copies applied to differing contexts. It is cleaner to have copies of sticky notes in cases like this than to move a sticky note.

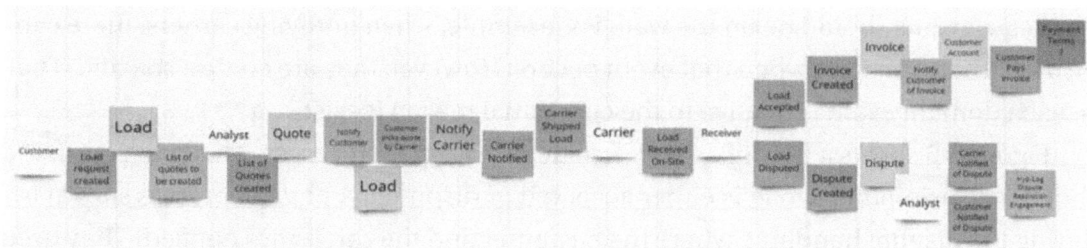

Figure 3-6. *Emerging contexts*

As the teams review the wall of sticky notes and discussions occur, different contexts start to take shape. One such case is for creating a load request, as seen in Figure 3-7. The "Load Request Created" domain event occurs using the Load aggregate and the Customer actor. Another context identified is for creating quotes. That context relies on the actor Annie, our Hyp-Log example administrator who currently must deal with many manual processes and is overworked creating quotes and handling phone calls.

Notice the context for Load Requests and Quoting both rely on the Load aggregate. This reliance could be a case for what DDD calls a "Shared Kernel" relationship because different bounded contexts share code. However, a cursory look reveals that the contexts are not mutually exclusive. They really cannot grow independently, and there is no need for them to do so. So, the line denoting two contexts expands to become one context containing both Load Requests and Quoting.

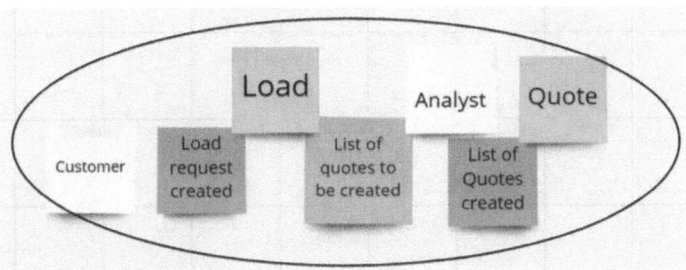

Figure 3-7. *Example of single context*

Other contexts are also identifiable. Depicted in Figure 3-8 are the contexts of Invoicing and Dispute Management. Since the outcome of Event Storming sessions is to reflect the current system, the contexts identified are where code exists and have differing functionality. The code for invoicing should be completely separate from the code for handling disputes. Because of this separation, the code in the various contexts is known as Bounded Contexts. Each bounded context contains business functionality that should be entirely separate from others. This separation allows for the independent evolution of the applicable code.

CHAPTER 3 SEARCHING FOR MICROSERVICES

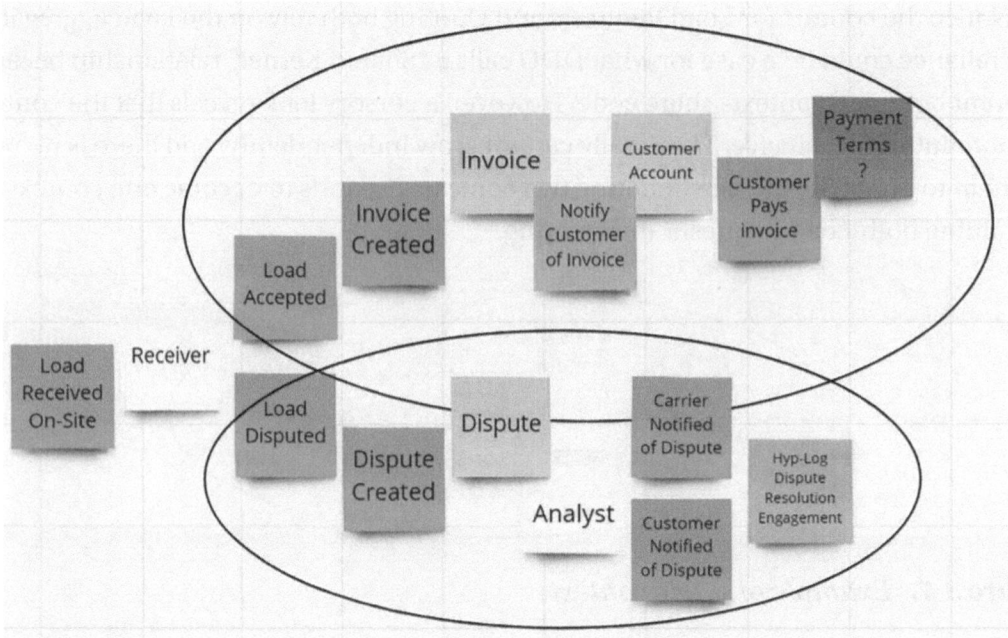

Figure 3-8. *Invoice and Dispute Management contexts*

After each Event Storming meeting, both teams agree on tasks and the related priorities. This way, everyone is engaged and understands the expectations and deadlines. The development team revises and creates work items for the tasks identified. As domain experts evaluate work in progress, some work items may be revised to include rework and sometimes redesign. This rework can happen if the result of development does not meet expectations by the domain experts.

Seeing the Domains

On the wall after Event Storming sessions, the developers can see evidence of bounded contexts. However, how should developers gauge the value of a bounded context compared to another? Another way of asking this question is, how can developers understand the worth a bounded context brings to a company?

The developers group the bounded contexts into subdomains. In Figure 3-9, the subdomains are listed and valued. The Rate Engine subdomain is critical to the business. Without the Rate Engine, Hyp-Log would not provide substantial value to its customers and carriers. Some of the other subdomains are noted as "supportive."

These subdomains are not as critical but are required for the application to process information. For Hyp-Log, the membership, dispute management, and notification subdomains support business processes in other subdomains. Membership is concerned with the logic of registering and maintaining customers and carriers. Notification is only concerned with notifying customers and carriers during different execution of business processes in the Rate Engine subdomain and the Dispute Management subdomain. The Dispute Management subdomain handles issues with loads undelivered, delivered to the wrong place, and incorrect invoice information.

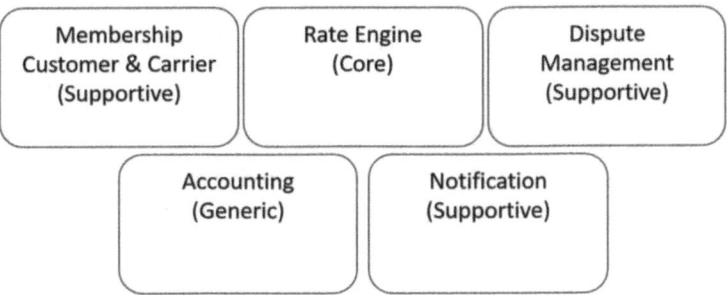

Figure 3-9. Bounded contexts

Understanding the value of a subdomain that a bounded context fulfills helps determine the cost of code change. Code that is in bounded contexts located in core subdomains must have more scrutiny and protection. Because of this, functionality in a core subdomain is less likely to move to a microservice and may very well be better off staying in a monolithic application.

Domain Models

After the first Event Storming meeting with Hyp-Log, the Code Whiz developers started creating code to solve the various issues identified. A domain model is a set of codes created to solve problems in their related subdomains. The Rate Engine subdomain will have a domain model that is separate from the domain model created for handling membership registrations.

As domain models evolve, there will be times when a developer must verify domain experts agree with the new code and when changes occur to existing code. Any code written and previously approved by the domain experts should be tested repeatedly, checking for unintended breaking changes. When using Agile, the Sprint Review is a perfect time for verifying that existing and new changes meet the domain experts' expectations.

Focus on Behavior

Domain models should focus on behavior instead of the state of an object. During the Event Storming sessions, pay close attention to the verbs in the UL. They are clues as to the expected behavior of the domain models. The domain models should also only contain enough code to solve the problems in their subdomain. When a model serves more functionality than needed, it adds the potential for tight coupling, bugs, and failures, making them harder to maintain.

Domain Modelling

Further meetings with the domain experts may show the domain models need to evolve with changes. New requirements may come due to new challenges or when domain experts clarify a business process. Be prepared to throw away a domain model and start over. Although developers dislike having to start over, this is sometimes the best way to come to a more aligned model to what is needed for the business and fellow developers later.

Decomposition

The monolith has been detailed on the wall during the Event Storming sessions. All the important domain events have been identified along with their related actors, commands, and aggregates. Now the development team needs to determine where best to modify the existing code base to fulfill the new requests by their customer.

Of the list of pain points Hyp-Log gave to Code Whiz was the issue with the Rate Engine. Also noted in the Event Storming sessions, the Hyp-Log analyst is responsible for the manual process of retrieving distance information to apply to the quotes. This process is tedious and is impacting the growth of their business. They decided it would be cheaper to apply code changes than hire more people to do this work.

The developers ask for the source code of the existing system. Someone from Hyp-Log gave them a USB flash drive while told it was the only other copy. There is no source code repository keeping the source code safe. Hyp-Log does not realize the danger they are in. With such simple problems arising, Hyp-Log could be in a far worse position.

The developers take a quick cursory look at the code files on the USB drive. They quickly confirm the code is far from clean and is, in fact, a BBoM (Big Ball of Mud) that will take a lot of time to refactor properly. Because of the amount of refactoring it would take to meet the customer's demands, the lead architect decides that retrieving distance information can be done using a microservice that requests data from a third-party API and possibly others.

Using a microservice will allow the existing code to have minimal changes, keep the manual process intact, and have this feature deployed independently of other changes. Another reason for this being a microservice is that it allows other map information providers to be added without changing the monolith.

Another pain point on the list is the lack of a good invoice management system. The analyst does all the invoice handling. She must not only create the invoices but keep track of those not paid and those past due. By having a microservice handle invoices, the current system can be modified as little as possible while providing a more functional solution. But this microservice will be a bit more challenging. There is an existing database with some invoice information. Because any microservice responsible for persistent information must have its own database, the invoice data will have to move. Decentralizing data is covered in Chapter 7.

Becoming a Microservice

Microservices should be considered independent applications free to evolve with little to no dependencies on other parts of a system. They should be maintained or owned by a single team of developers. They also require networking for connectivity for either direct RPC-based calls or messaging-based communication.

The biggest reason for Code Whiz to consider microservices for the SPLAT application is the time-to-market factor. Hyp-Log's business is growing, and the manual processes are holding them back. By making minimal changes to the monolith and adding microservices to solve their main pain points, the application will be able to scale easier over time and handle additional code projects in the future.

Summary

We covered much ground in this chapter. Using our hypothetical company Hyp-Log, you were able to see the business processes of an existing system. You saw how Event Storming was used to understand better what the domain experts know about their system. Event Storming helps everyone be on the same page regarding what business processes exist, how they interact, and what other elements support them.

We also covered DDD at a high level. DDD helps developers by focusing on the domain, subdomains, and related behaviors. You learned about elements of DDD that help the developers leverage to make code cleaner, loosely coupled, and easier to modify for future changes. You also learned that the Ubiquitous Language is a vital piece of DDD that provides contextual support for the development team to better understand the system from domain experts. We also went over aggregates and aggregate roots and how they represent classes with a structure to support a form of encapsulation and how the aggregate roots help protect the integrity of the aggregate.

CHAPTER 4

ASP.NET Is a Great Place for Microservices

This chapter teaches the reader a brief history of .NET and the ways to use .NET for building web properties. We begin with a history of .NET Framework, then look at .NET Core and modern .NET, showing the versatility and "rebirth" of the .NET platform. Then we look at the ways to host websites in .NET: MVC, Razor Pages, Web API, Minimal APIs, and more. This chapter puts in context the value of building in .NET, and encourages developers to move from other languages or at least not move toward other languages.

A Brief History of .NET

.NET Framework

.NET began more than 25 years ago. It has evolved and transformed, and is still going strong. .NET is a great ecosystem to build Microservices – whether serving HTTP traffic through JSON or gRPC APIs or connecting to queues to transform data. With .NET, you can build large monolithic applications and small apps embedded in IoT boards. .NET is a great place to build modern software.

.NET began as an experiment in the late 1990s, and was originally called Next Generation Windows Services (NGWS). In 2001, .NET 1.0 was released. Unlike previous development environments, .NET had managed memory, a JIT (Just-in-Time) compiler, and a common set of runtime libraries – the Common Language Runtime or CLR. .NET ran on a VM-like platform where all memory and processes were managed by the runtime, and applications could allocate memory, then just forget about it, and the memory would get garbage collected when needed. Applications could be written in various languages, compiled into an intermediate language (MSIL), then finally JIT-compiled into a fast native executable to run on Windows on the target hardware.

With the invention of .NET, C# was born. C# combined the best of Visual Basic and the best of C/C++ into a Java-like VM runtime. Like C++, it used object-oriented programming, including inheritance and polymorphism. Like Visual Basic, allocating memory was as easy as declaring it. C# was a great way for C/C++ Windows developers to transition away from COM, COM+, and DCOM to a more modern platform.

On top of .NET, Scott Guthrie prototyped a web server. Unlike Active Server Pages (ASP), this used .NET to make memory management as easy as Visual Basic. It also created a stateful web server to help those familiar with building Windows Forms-based applications to transition to building web applications. There's a familiar designer where users could drag controls from the toolbox, wire up event handlers, and render HTML pages. With this new ASP.NET web server, suddenly any Windows developer could become a web developer.

As .NET and ASP.NET grew from 1.0 to 1.1 to 2.0 to 3.0 to 3.5 to 4, 4.5.2 and finally to 4.7, it added features helpful for modern development. (After .NET Core 2.2, .NET Framework 4.8 was released with security updates.) In 2005, .NET 2.0 brought Generics, Debugger edit and continue, and Click-once deployment. In 2006, v. 3.0 brought Windows Communication Foundation (WCF), Windows Workflow Foundation (WF), Windows Presentation Foundation (WPF), and CardSpace. Most of these haven't stood the test of time. .NET 3.5, released in 2007, brought LINQ, a SQL-like query language for objects, and ASP.NET added AJAX support. Released in 2010, .NET 4.0 added the Managed Extensibility Framework (MEF), Client Profile for deploying to more tightly managed web servers, Portable Class Libraries for deploying to alternate .NET platforms, and the Dynamic Language Runtime (DLR) allowing just-in-time object creation that mirrored PHP-like dynamic programming, and the first version of Tasks for parallel computing. .NET 4.5 was released in 2012, and upgraded Tasks with the *async* and *await* keywords.

ASP.NET also grew with .NET Framework versions. ASP.NET AJAX was released in 2007, offering a convenient abstraction around asynchronous partial page reloads. This allowed ASP.NET developers to not have to worry about creating XMLHttpRequest objects and all the heavy lifting of making async web calls. Instead, they could build as if it was just Web Forms controls with a full post-back, and the magic of ASP.NET would make partial page rendering "just work." Also in 2007, ASP.NET MVC was released, bringing the MVC paradigm popular in Ruby at the time into the .NET ecosystem, and effectively ending the Alt.NET movement. In 2010, ASP.NET released Razor syntax, moving away from the Web Forms syntax coined in ASP.NET 1.0, and adding a much simpler template rendering syntax.

.NET Core

In 2014, .NET Framework was starting to show its age. No longer could it keep up with the rapid release cycle of Ruby and Node.js. .NET's release cycle had always been tied to Windows releases, and .NET only ran on Windows devices. .NET's Compact Framework had made strides into Pocket PC devices, but those too were only Windows. Was .NET to go the way of Cold Fusion and Delphi?

Silverlight made in-roads in moving .NET from Windows to other platforms. Silverlight began in 2007 as a JavaScript-only browser plugin similar to Flash. With Silverlight 2.0, it moved away from solely a video player. It now ran C# and VB.NET, and ran on roughly the same CLR as .NET Framework 3.0. But more impressively, it ran on many browsers and OSs including Mac and Linux.

Sadly, one day Steve Jobs decided that Adobe Flash wasn't good enough for Safari and MacOS, and decided that Safari would stop running browser plugins. Soon other browsers followed, and though the target was Flash, Silverlight got swept up in it too, and expired the same way. Unpatched versions of Internet Explorer 6 still run Flash and Silverlight, but they don't run the modern web. Sadly, Flash and Silverlight are dead.

In the wake of Silverlight, the ASP.NET team started Project K, a reimagination of .NET that was purpose built to run web servers cross-platform. Project K grew into ASP.NET 5 (suggesting an upgrade from .NET Framework 4). As the new platform gained steam, it was renamed .NET Core 1.0, and became not just a web server platform, but a reinvention of all of .NET.

.NET Core 1.0 transplanted the Base Class Libraries (BCL) onto the cross-platform Silverlight runtime. But unlike Silverlight, it ran on servers and clients, not just in the browser. Entity Framework 6 moved to .NET Core 1.0 as Entity Framework Core 1.0. ASP.NET moved onto .NET Core as ASP.NET Core 1.0. Effectively, they replaced the foundation and transplanted the house on top.

.NET Core began as a CLI-first platform. Users could now quickly spin up a .NET Core project from the *dotnet* CLI. Visual Studio and VS Code could also launch .NET projects by running *dotnet* CLI commands. This CLI-first view made it easy to transition in from CLI-heavy platforms like Ruby and Node.js.

As part of the redesign, the authors could build in modern development features. The project file is now a much simpler XML file that doesn't need to list obscure settings or enumerate each file. NuGet packages are a simple reference in the XML file. Modern programming paradigms like Dependency Injection and Inversion of Control (DI and IoC) are baked in, making unit testing far easier. A simple JSON configuration file is automatically combined with environment variables and input parameters into a unified configuration store easily injected into any class. And startup times are much, much quicker as the simpler, modern .NET runtime can drop the legacy weight of a generation of prior decisions.

Unlike previous versions of .NET that were windows-only, .NET Core is now cross-platform, running on Windows, MacOS, and various Linux distributions. Even more impressive, .NET Core is open source, allowing users not only to view the source code, but propose changes. .NET Core is developed in the open through GitHub Issues, and frequently community contributions are included in the final product.

Users looking to upgrade from .NET Framework to .NET Core needed to replace NuGet library references and change namespaces, but not much else needed to change. ASP.NET MVC and Web API worked similarly, and data access with Entity Framework Core (or more commonly "EF Core") was nearly identical to EF 6. In time, WCF and Windows Form would also move to .NET Core, and Blazor experiments could even move Web Forms projects onto .NET Core. The hardest part of the upgrade was if you used Windows-specific features like the Registry or GDI+. Provided your dependencies also had .NET Core (or .NET Standard) editions, the upgrade was pretty painless.

Now that .NET Core was free of the Windows-only ties, it could iterate a lot faster. Releases would come out annually, and include features for Mac, Linux, and Windows. Now that they were free of the legacy weight of .NET Framework, the BCL could move faster, accommodating modern features like gRPC, GraphQL, and web sockets, say nothing of the speed of security fixes.

Like .NET Framework, .NET Core had 1.0, 1.1, 2.0, 2.1, 2.2, 3.0, 3.1, and more. In 2017, .NET Core 2.0 brought more compatibility with .NET Framework classes and HTTP/2. Released in 2019, .NET Core 3.0 brought WCF and Windows Forms from .NET Framework to .NET Core. .NET 3.1 in 2019 brought the first Long-term Support or LTS version of .NET Core. Like Node.js before it, you could now get security updates for significantly longer, catering to enterprise developers who wouldn't necessarily keep up with the fast-paced .NET versions.

Modern .NET

As the team was looking to the next version from .NET Core 3.2, an interesting dilemma emerged. What would this new version be called? There was some ambiguity in the community. "You mean I need to upgrade from .NET 4.8 to .NET 3.1? Isn't 4 bigger than 3?" Should they call the next version 4.0? This would even further complicate the upgrade story. "So I 'upgrade' from 4.8 to 4.0? Are you sure about that?"

Instead of calling it .NET Core 4.0, they chose to skip the 4.0 version, and rebrand it simply as Modern .NET. The next version was to be called .NET 5. Now it was clear that upgrading from .NET Framework 4.8 (or 4.5.2 or 3.5 or anything older) would be to a sensible and obvious larger version number.

Ironically, though .NET dropped the "Core" name, many of the .NET libraries did not. Together with .NET 5 was the release of ASP.NET Core 5 and Entity Framework Core 5. Maybe this was to disambiguate it from the old ASP.NET 5 experiment, renamed from Project K and the old Entity Framework 5 built for .NET Framework that had a big Entity Data Model XML (EDMX) file and designer?

.NET 5 brought the end (or unification) of .NET Framework in 2020. The true upgrade path for .NET Framework apps was now to port to .NET. There was now only one BCL, and the dotnet CLI was the way to run. In 2021, .NET 6 brought hot reload to all projects. In 2022, .NET 7 introduced Ahead-of-time (AOT) compilation which better supported iOS's needs. AOT compilation also can run on a much smaller footprint as it can eagerly trim away unused portions of the .NET BCL and NuGet libraries at the expense of disabling reflection and other dynamic loading. In 2023, .NET 8 introduced MAUI, a unification of the Mono framework and the various XAML platforms including WPF and UWP. Also in .NET 8, we gained Aspire and the semantic kernel, beginning the journey toward observability and AI, respectively. Released in 2024, .NET 9 improved performance and developer experience. Now in 2025, .NET 10 brings the next LTS release with the latest security and performance improvements, developer productivity improvements, cloud-native improvements, and AI improvements including Microsoft.Extensions.AI.

Yes, we've toured through 25 years of .NET extremely quickly. It is nearly impossible to sum up 25 years of history in just a few pages. Alas, we can easily conclude that modern .NET is now a great place to build modern, secure, containerized, cross-platform, open source apps.

With .NET, you can build great

- Desktop apps with MAUI
- Web applications running in Docker containers on Linux
- Phone apps on Android and iOS
- Browser apps with Blazor
- Games with Unity
- IoT projects on Raspberry PIs
- And much more

The same .NET BCL and standard *dotnet* CLI is tailored for each OS and runtime. Though some larger libraries like WCF or Windows Forms may require more OS support, most applications "just work" on Modern .NET. .NET is now a modern development platform for creating any kind of app running on any form factor on most any OS.

Ways to Build Microservices in ASP.NET

That was definitely a whirlwind tour through the history of .NET. We definitely can't do justice to the countless hours of effort and countless minds of engineering that came together to build it. Now we have a modern, secure, cloud-native mechanism for building microservices. .NET is a great place to code.

In .NET, there are now many ways to host microservices, depending on the way users will interact with the service and the complexity of the service you'll build. Do you need a super-light-weight API and don't want to use Node.js? Or do you need a simple website without complex routing? Or do you need an enterprise site with robust Search Engine Optimization (SEO)? Or do you want to focus only on the method, even leaving the process behind? In all of these use-cases, .NET can meet you where you are.

The great news: you can mix-n-match these paradigms in the same application. Modern .NET's focus on middleware added through extension methods means adding some or all of these approaches to the same application is completely possible. It likely doesn't make sense to include them all though – you likely don't have a single app that has all the use-cases bundled into one. Such would definitely qualify for a reference on The Daily WTF[1] site.

---

[1] https://thedailywtf.com/

Let's look at each development paradigm, the pros and cons of each, an example source code from such an app, and identify the ideal use-case for this development approach.

ASP.NET MVC

ASP.NET MVC is the oldest of the platforms, but still great for certain scenarios. ASP.NET MVC focuses on the Model-View-Controller platform where a request comes through the router, chooses a controller based on URL paths that match controller attributes, and runs the matching action (method) on the controller class. As the action method completes, it chooses the Razor view that will marry C# objects with HTML fragments to produce an HTML result.

ASP.NET MVC is perfect for large enterprise applications that produce HTML results. This is great when you need reliable performance and SEO. There is no central controller registration, and with built-in dependency injection (DI), it's easy to build loosely coupled controllers that can be easy to test.

An example ASP.NET MVC controller could look like this:

```
namespace MyMicroservice.Controllers;

public class OrderController(IOrderRepository orderRepository) : Controller
{
  [HttpGet("order")]
  public IActionResult Index()
  {
    var orders = orderRepository.GetAllOrders();
    return View(orders);
  }
  [HttpGet("order/add")]
  public IActionResult Add()
  {
    Order order = new Order();
    return View();
  }
  [HttpPost("order/add")]
  public IActionResult Add(Order order)
```

```csharp
{
    if (!ModelState.IsValid)
    {
        // Fix your errors first
        return View(order);
    }
    var saved = orderRepository.SaveOrder(order);
    return RedirectToAction(nameof(Index));
}
[HttpGet("order/edit/{id}")]
public IActionResult Edit(int id)
{
    var order = orderRepository.GetOrderById(id);
    if (order == null)
    {
        return View("NotFound");
    }
    return View(order);
}
[HttpPost("order/edit/{id}")]
public IActionResult Edit(int id, Order order)
{
    if (!ModelState.IsValid || id != order.Id)
    {
        // Fix your errors first
        return View(order);
    }
    var saved = orderRepository.SaveOrder(order);
    return RedirectToAction(nameof(Index));
}
[HttpGet("order/delete/{id}")]
public IActionResult Delete(int id)
{
    var order = orderRepository.GetOrderById(id);
    if (order == null)
```

```csharp
    {
      return View("NotFound");
    }
    return View(order);
  }
  [HttpPost("order/delete/{id}")]
  public IActionResult Delete(int id, string? confirm)
  {
    orderRepository.DeleteOrder(id);
    return RedirectToAction(nameof(Index));
  }
}
```

As you can see in this example, the Order Repository dependency is an interface that could easily be mocked in a test. The controller logic is simple, also making it easy to test.

A Razor view in this project could look like this:

```cshtml
@model List<Order>

@{
  ViewBag.Title = "Orders List";
}
<div class="row">
  <h1>@ViewBag.Title</h1>
</div>

<div>
  <a class="btn btn-primary" asp-action="Add">Add a new Orders</a>
</div>
@if (Model.Count > 0)
{
  <div class="row">
    <table class="table">
      <thead>
        <tr>
          <th>Id</th>
          <th>CustomerId</th>
```

```
              <th>Order Date</th>
              <th>Order Total</th>
              <th> </th>
            </tr>
          </thead>
          <tbody>
            @foreach (var order in Model)
            {
              <tr>
                <td>@order.Id</td>
                <td>@order.CustomerId</td>
                <td>@order.OrderDate.ToString("g")</td>
                <td>@order.OrderTotal</td>
                <td>
                  <a asp-action="Edit" asp-route-id="@order.Id">Edit</a>
                  <a asp-action="Delete" asp-route-id="@order.Id">Delete</a>
                </td>
              </tr>
            }
          </tbody>
      </div>
}
```

Notice how in this Razor view, we use very simple logic to enumerate items and output HTML. Sadly, the results of a view are a string, so it's difficult to test. However, we're creating the HTML server-side, so we can easily gain a lot by caching pages that don't change often, yielding better performance and easily ranking in search engine results.

ASP.NET MVC apps are great for larger apps that need great SEO and testability. Because the HTML is rendered server-side, it's easy to cache results for performance and speed, perfect for when ranking on search engines is important. There is no central controller registration, and with ASP.NET's built-in DI system, carefully architected controllers are easy to test. If you need SEO and have lots of HTML pages to serve, ASP.NET MVC is great.

ASP.NET Razor Pages

Razor Pages is a relatively new addition to the ASP.NET hosting options. In Razor Pages, a URL's segments exactly map to a folder structure. This can be really handy for simple websites, oftentimes replacing WordPress to give just a touch of interactivity or replacing classic ASP or PHP with a similar development methodology. Like the Web Forms of yesteryear, you can have code-behind C# or VB.NET files if the logic in the page is particularly squirrely.

For example, let's take the URL mysite.com/path/to/page. In Razor Pages, inside the Pages folder, we'd have a *path* folder. And inside the *path* folder, a *to* folder. Inside the *to* folder, we'd have *page.razor* with the page content inside it. Taking a step back, this is probably an awful example. Overly nesting folders is an anti-pattern, and a simpler URL structure like /about-us and /contact-us is probably wiser. One can also use ASP.NET attribute routing in Razor pages websites, removing the need to match urls to folders, though one could easily argue you've now upgraded beyond the ideal use-case for Razor pages, and would be better served by MVC.

Here's the same order list example as a Razor page:

```
@page
@model OrderListModel
@{
  ViewBag.Title = "Orders List";
}
<div class="row">
  <h1>@ViewBag.Title</h1>
</div>
@if (Model.Orders.Count == 0)
{
  <div class="row">
    <p>No orders found in the database.</p>
  </div>
}
<div class="row">
  <table class="table">
    <thead>
      <tr>
```

```html
            <th>Id</th>
            <th>CustomerId</th>
            <th>Order Date</th>
            <th>Order Total</th>
        </tr>
    </thead>
    <tbody>
        @foreach (var order in Model.Orders)
        {
            <tr>
                <td>
                    <a asp-page="./View" asp-route-id="@order.Id">@order.Id</a>
                </td>
                <td>@order.CustomerId</td>
                <td>@order.OrderDate.ToString("g")</td>
                <td>@order.OrderTotal</td>
            </tr>
        }
    </tbody>
</div>
```

Notice in this Razor page we're building simple HTML. If we're replicating a simple WordPress site, maybe we're only rendering posts and other nearly static pages.

Razor Pages websites are great for simple websites where you prefer the simplicity of url-folder routing, where the site's content is mostly HTML. Though you can use code-behind for more complex code, for Razor pages projects, oftentimes you won't need to or a simple *PageModel* is sufficient.

ASP.NET Web API

ASP.NET Web API is great for REST/JSON services. Perhaps these are consumed by other services or consumed by JavaScript apps built in React or Vue.js. In this case we need not render HTML on the server, but need only return data through an API.

CHAPTER 4   ASP.NET IS A GREAT PLACE FOR MICROSERVICES

Like ASP.NET MVC, Web API uses a complex router that can pick a controller and action (method) to match the URL and other parts of the incoming request. Unlike MVC, controller actions often return JSON data directly, and no view is used. Like MVC, a controller is identified by the base class and attributes, and no central registration is necessary.

Here's an example Web API controller:

```
namespace MyProject.Controllers;

[Route("api/[controller]")]
[ApiController]
public class OrderController(IOrderRepository orderRepository) :
ControllerBase
{
  [HttpGet]
  public List<Order> GetList()
  {
    return orderRepository.GetAllOrders();
  }
  [HttpGet("{id}")]
  public ActionResult<Order> GetById(int id)
  {
    var order = orderRepository.GetOrderById(id);
    if (order == null)
    {
      return NotFound();
    }
    return order;
  }
  [HttpPost]
  public ActionResult Add(Order order)
  {
    order.Id = 0;
    orderRepository.SaveOrder(order);
    return CreatedAtAction(nameof(GetById), new { id = order.Id }, order);
  }
```

```
[HttpPut("{id}")]
public ActionResult<Order> Edit(int id, Order order)
{
  if (id < 1)
  {
    return NotFound();
  }
  order.Id = id;
  orderRepository.SaveOrder(order);
  return order;
}
[HttpDelete("{id}")]
public IActionResult Delete(int id)
{
  orderRepository.DeleteOrder(id);
  return Ok();
}
}
```

Notice in this controller we have methods for each of the common HTTP verbs that map nicely to each of the CRUD (Create, Read, Update, Delete) methods. Though we're mostly returning C# objects from these methods, ASP.NET Web API will automatically convert these into JSON responses. If configured to do so, it'll also convert C#'s PascalCase into the typical JavaScript/JSON camelCase and back.

ASP.NET Web API is perfect for enterprise-grade REST APIs. Perhaps it's the backend to a React or Vue.js app running in the browser. Or perhaps it's a GraphQL or gRPC endpoint consumed by other microservices. Because there's no HTML output, this isn't appropriate for user-facing sites.

ASP.NET Minimal APIs

ASP.NET Minimal APIs is great for smaller projects hosting REST APIs. If you've ever gotten overwhelmed with the ceremony of setting up an ASP.NET project, putting attributes on controllers, and all the ceremony and files associated with an app, Minimal APIs may be a great fit. It provides super easy setup, and potentially only a single file in your project. If you outgrow the simple needs, you can always upgrade to Web API's controllers and routing.

Let's imagine a scenario where you need only accept an HTTP post and send an email. Or perhaps you only need to host a JSON file. Or maybe you need to accept a webhook, transform the data, and forward on the intent to a new service or store the data. In each of these scenarios, all the ceremony of controllers, config files, repositories, and other indirection is unnecessary. We just want to get the job done.

With Minimal APIs, you can create a single-file project that does exactly this. You still get the benefits of attribute routing, dependency injection, and new in .NET 10, model validation.

Here's an example Minimal API's *Program.cs* file that hosts a JSON file on an HTTP endpoint:

```
var builder = WebApplication.CreateBuilder(args);

// Learn more about configuring OpenAPI at https://aka.ms/aspnet/openapi
builder.Services.AddOpenApi();
builder.Services.AddHealthChecks();

builder.Services.AddDbContext<MyDbContext>(options =>
  options.UseSqlServer(builder.Configuration.GetConnectionString(
  "MyDbContext")));

builder.Services.AddTransient<IOrderRepository, OrderRepository>();

var app = builder.Build();

// Configure the HTTP request pipeline.
if (app.Environment.IsDevelopment())
{
  app.MapOpenApi("/swagger/v1/swagger.json");
  app.UseSwaggerUI();
}
else
{
  app.UseExceptionHandler("/error");
  app.UseHsts();
}

app.UseHttpsRedirection();
```

```csharp
app.MapGet("/", () => new { message = "Welcome to Pro Microservices in 
.NET 10" });

app.MapGet("/order", (IOrderRepository orderRepository) => orderRepository.
GetAllOrders());
app.MapGet("/order/{id:int}", (IOrderRepository orderRepository, 
int? id) =>
{
  var order = orderRepository.GetOrderById(id ?? 0);
  if (order == null)
  {
    return Results.NotFound();
  }
  return Results.Ok(order);
});
app.MapPost("/order", (IOrderRepository orderRepository, [FromBody] Order 
order) =>
{
  order.Id = 0;
  orderRepository.SaveOrder(order);
  return Results.Created($"/order/{order.Id}", order);
});
app.MapPut("/order/{id}", (IOrderRepository orderRepository, int id, 
[FromBody] Order order) =>
{
  order.Id = id;
  orderRepository.SaveOrder(order);
  return order;
});
app.MapDelete("/order/{id}", (IOrderRepository orderRepository, int id) =>
{
  orderRepository.DeleteOrder(id);
  return Results.Ok();
});

app.MapHealthChecks("/health");
```

```
app.Map("/error", () => Results.Problem());
app.Map("/{*url}", () => Results.NotFound(new {message="Not Found",
status=404}));

app.Run();

// Make it available for testing:
public partial class Program { }
```

In this Program.cs file, we load a JSON config file into a strongly typed object, add it to the IoC container, and make it available on the home page of the application. We also have a swagger page to explore the API surface, a health check page for Kubernetes to validate the container is still running, and error and not found handling should consumers or bad actors start exploring. And it's only 47 lines total! That's a really small program.

If you squint really hard, these *MapGet()* method calls (or *MapPost* or *MapPut*, etc.) look a lot like Node.js's Express. If you've ever had such a small need that C# seemed too much, Minimal APIs can now nicely solve it.

Now let's imagine a new scenario where we have the four CRUD methods (maybe five if we have a GetList method) for three or more entities. Maybe customers, products, and orders. Now that's 15 methods! This "tiny" Program.cs file is now super long. In this example, Minimal APIs no longer makes sense, and it's time to upgrade to Web API's controllers, one controller per entity.

Minimal APIs is definitely not for enterprise-scale applications, but it's perfect for small, single-purpose apps. If we just need a quick web endpoint and don't want all the ceremony of controllers, Minimal APIs is a perfect fit.

Azure Functions

Azure Functions takes it to the next level of simplicity. With Azure Functions, we only specify the method body to handle when a trigger happens. In the web world, this could be an inbound request. But we could also handle other requests like data in an Azure Queue or another data store. Or a timed event could trigger the function. Or any of a host of other triggers could start the function … or many copies of the function in parallel. With Azure Functions, we can easily bind input and output parameters to request details, message queue messages, or IoC dependencies.

CHAPTER 4   ASP.NET IS A GREAT PLACE FOR MICROSERVICES

In all the other hosting strategies we've looked at in this chapter, we're responsible for the process, the web server, and handling all incoming requests – whether they relate to our business logic or not. With Azure Functions, we need only handle the specific request. And because they're so easy to fire up and spin down, it's easy to scale up parallel instances to meet bursting need, and scale back down to save cost.

Azure functions are similar to AWS Lambdas, and are hosted on Azure. The Azure platform takes care of mapping inbound requests to the function instance, and scaling up and down the number of function instances to match the triggered load. The Azure platform also takes care of scaling down to 0 instances when it has received no requests in a while, allowing us to pay nothing while the API is not in use.

Here's an example HTTP trigger Azure function that saves data to SQL Server via EF Core:

```
using System;
using System.IO;
using System.Threading.Tasks;
using Microsoft.Azure.WebJobs;
using Microsoft.Extensions.Logging;
using Microsoft.AspNetCore.Http;
using Newtonsoft.Json;
using Microsoft.EntityFrameworkCore;
using System.Linq;
using System.Net;

public static class SaveUserFunction
{
  [FunctionName("SaveUser")]
  public static async Task<HttpResponseMessage> Run(
    [HttpTrigger(AuthorizationLevel.Function, "post", Route = "users")]
    HttpRequest req,
    ILogger log)
  {
    log.LogInformation("C# HTTP trigger function processed a request.");

    string requestBody = await new StreamReader(req.Body).ReadToEndAsync();
    User user = JsonConvert.Deserialize<User>(requestBody);
```

```csharp
    if (string.IsNullOrEmpty(user.Name) || string.IsNullOrEmpty(user.Email))
    {
      return new HttpResponseMessage(HttpStatusCode.BadRequest)
      {
        Content = new StringContent("Missing name and/or email.")
      };
    }

    try
    {
      using var db = new UserDbContext();
      user.CreatedAt = DateTime.UtcNow;
      db.Users.Add(user);
      await db.SaveChangesAsync();

      return new HttpResponseMessage(HttpStatusCode.OK)
      {
        Content = new StringContent($"User {name} successfully created.")
      };
    }
    catch (Exception ex)
    {
      log.LogError($"An error occurred: {ex.Message}");
      return new HttpResponseMessage(HttpStatusCode.InternalServerError)
      {
        Content = new StringContent("An error occurred while saving
        the user.")
      };
    }
  }
}
public record User(int Id, string Name, string Email, DateTime CreatedAt);
```

```
public class UserDbContext : DbContext
{
  public UserDbContext(DbContextOptions<UserDbContext> options) :
  base(options) { }

  public DbSet<User> Users { get; set; }
}
```

In this Azure Function, we accept an HTTP post, harvest the user details, save to a database, and return a success or failure message to the user. Nothing in this function requires preserving state across sessions, so multiple instances of this function can operate in parallel.

Azure Functions are great when you don't even want to control the running process. A very simple function can easily save to a database, send an email, execute a shard of an expensive computation, or any other small task.

If we needed to build a larger API surface like four CRUD methods to create, read one, update, and delete a user, we'd need four different functions to handle this. Add a Get All method, and we now have five different functions. Clearly, building a CRUD API surface around one or many entities is not a good use-case for Azure Functions. If we needed a larger API surface, we should upgrade to Minimal APIs or Web API.

Azure Functions are purpose-built functions for burstable task execution. The Azure platform takes care of scaling the functions to meet the need, and we only pay while the function instance(s) are running.

KEDA Functions

KEDA is a Kubernetes framework for running and scaling small functions. What's beautiful for a C# function is that any Azure function can easily become a KEDA function when deployed to Kubernetes. In fact, the same HTTP triggered Azure Function need not even be recompiled to host on Kubernetes through KEDA. Though not all Azure triggers are supported, many trigger types transfer naturally into KEDA.

To convert an Azure Function to a KEDA function, we don't need to change the code at all. We need to add a Dockerfile that'll build the function into a container, and we need to add a Kubernetes YAML file that explains how to deploy the function.

Here's an example Dockerfile that publishes an Azure Function as a container:

```
# the build "server" image
FROM mcr.microsoft.com/dotnet/sdk:10.0 AS build

WORKDIR /src

COPY MyFunctionApp.csproj .
RUN dotnet restore

COPY . .
RUN dotnet build -c Release
RUN dotnet publish MyFunctionApp.csproj -c Release -o /dist

# the runtime "server" image
FROM mcr.microsoft.com/azure-functions/dotnet-isolated:4-dotnet-isolated10.0

ENV AzureWebJobsScriptRoot=/home/site/wwwroot \
    AzureFunctionsJobHost__Logging__Console__IsEnabled=true
EXPOSE 80

WORKDIR /home/site/wwwroot
COPY --from=build /dist .
```

This Dockerfile is very different from the Dockerfile we build in Chapter 9. In this Dockerfile, we're using the Azure Functions base image to run our KEDA function. There also is no *ENTRYPOINT* or *CMD* as the base image takes care of that for us.

Next let's look at the Kubernetes YAML file needed to host an Azure Function in KEDA:

```yaml
apiVersion: keda.sh/v1alpha1
kind: ScaledObject
metadata:
  name: my-function
spec:
  scaleTargetRef:
    name: my-function # the deployment name
  triggers:
  - type: azure-queue
```

```
  metadata:
    queueName: my-queue
    connectionFromEnv: ConnectionStrings__AzureStorage
    queueLength: '5'
minReplicaCount: 0
maxReplicaCount: 5
```

In this YAML file, we define the KEDA scaling for this function, referencing the k8s deployment (not shown) and an environment variable in that deployment. This KEDA setup hooks the function to an Azure Queue named *azure-queue*, ensuring that when messages are placed in the queue, function(s) will automatically spin up to process the messages.

To host KEDA functions, you also need to install KEDA. See `https://keda.sh/docs/latest/deploy/` for detailed instructions for installing KEDA into Kubernetes.

To learn more about hosting Azure Functions on Kubernetes with KEDA or to learn about building Dockerfiles for other languages besides C#, visit `https://learn.microsoft.com/en-us/azure/azure-functions/functions-kubernetes-keda`.

KEDA can be a great outlet for making function hosting more vendor agnostic. No longer are we constrained to host in Azure (or AWS or GCP). Instead, we can host the function on any Kubernetes cluster. (Granted, if our KEDA function drains an Azure queue like it does here, we need to run Kubernetes on Azure.)

Aspire

Aspire is not a mechanism for hosting .NET microservices, but it is a great way for orchestrating microservices both during development and when deploying to Azure, Kubernetes, Docker, or other environments. Aspire can start .NET projects, console applications, and containers, orchestrate their dependencies, and collect the logs, traces, and metrics through Open Telemetry.

To create a new Aspire project, open Visual Studio, choose File ➤ New Project, and choose the Aspire starter app. From the options, you can opt to include a Redis container for caching, and you can opt to build an integration test project.

OpenTelemetry has become the industry standard mechanism for collecting logs, traces, and metrics across a fleet of services. It's the perfect mechanism for collecting all the logs in our microservices. When developing and debugging locally, the Aspire dashboard is a perfect way to harvest all these logs, traces, and metrics into a central dashboard, allowing easy startup of the fleet of services, and easy discovery and diagnosis when problems arise.

Aspire is great at connecting services together. Service Discovery can often be a challenge with microservices. "What is the URL for this service in that environment? Do I need the environment suffix like 'dev'?" With Aspire, the URL for all dependent services is automatically injected in as environment variables.

Aspire components make it easy to fall into the pit of success. When you add an Aspire component to the project, you likely don't need to configure it much at all. Rather Aspire will auto-magically inject in the necessary configuration as environment variables as the Aspire AppHost starts the service. Need to connect to a database? Connection strings are a thing of the past. The only downside to Azure components is that searching for docs on a particular technology definitely won't show you the Aspire component way to do it. If you want to learn the technology, maybe taking the old way is a more informed journey. However, if you don't want to learn it, tell the Aspire AppHost to start the container and inject the configuration, then add the Aspire component to your project so it can magically consume the config and initialize the dependency.

Aspire also offers convenient mechanisms for simple deployment. Azure Container Apps is the poster child for Aspire deployment, but new in .NET 10, we can also easily deploy to Kubernetes or Docker. Of course, if we have already solved deployment in our enterprise, we may not need Aspire's deployment mechanism, and may choose to use it exclusively in development.

Aspire can easily be added to existing .NET projects. In Visual Studio, right-click on a web project, choose Add ➤ .NET Aspire Orchestrator Support. When you do this, it'll add two new projects: the AppHost project and a ServiceDefaults project. If you already have these projects in your solution, it'll leverage these projects, adding this new project into place in both.

Aspire is a great way to visualize and launch a fleet of microservices. The elegant dashboard collects logs, traces, and metrics from each subscribed microservice, allowing you to easily visualize HTTP calls as they make their way through the system.

CHAPTER 4   ASP.NET IS A GREAT PLACE FOR MICROSERVICES

Summary

In this chapter, we talked about each of the hosting mechanisms in ASP.NET. We discussed each one's pros and cons and ideal use-cases. ASP.NET MVC and Razor Pages are great for rendering HTML. MVC is better for larger apps while Razor Pages is great for small sites. Web API and Minimal APIs are great for REST APIs. Web API is for larger sites while Minimal APIs is ideal for small things. Azure Functions are great for very small or highly scalable projects while KEDA brings these functions into a container running on Kubernetes. ASP.NET is a great place to build microservices because there's so many options for hosting. See Table 4-1 for a summary of each of the hosting options.

Table 4-1. ASP.NET Hosting Options

Hosting Technology	Ideal Use-case
ASP.NET MVC	Controllers and Views render HTML for enterprise-scale apps that need SEO
Razor Pages	Host a simple website that doesn't need much code-behind
Web API	Controllers render JSON for REST services where the client is other microservices or thick-client browser apps like React and Vue.js
Minimal APIs	Very small web services and single-task applications where the ceremony of controllers isn't necessary
Azure Functions	Focus solely on the method. Scale up to meet demand, and down to 0 when not in use.
KEDA Functions	Host Azure Functions in containers running in Kubernetes

CHAPTER 5

First Microservice

In Chapter 3, we decided that retrieving distance information could be done by calling a third-party Distance Service API. The lead architect decided to make a microservice to provide this functionality. Before we start creating this microservice, we need to understand some crucial architectural details. Microservices are more about software architecture and patterns to solve problems for the business than it is about code. By understanding the business processes that require and use distance information, we can design a better solution.

For each pickup and drop-off location, Annie, the analyst for Hyp-Log, gets distance information from various websites and manually enters it into the SPLAT program.

This is time-consuming and impacts the generation of quotes. When looking at the business process to create quotes, where does a call to a microservice make sense? Before we can answer that question, we need to look at ways microservices communicate.

Interprocess Communication

Every application has processes where logic executes. In the logic, there are calls to functions that reside in memory. However, some functions are not part of the same application processes in distributed systems and may not even be located on the same server. The microservices architecture is an implementation of a distributed system that provides functionality over a network. The various mechanisms for communicating with a microservice are called interprocess communication (IPC). Two such mechanisms for calling a microservice are "direct" and "asynchronous messaging." You can call a microservice directly using Remote Procedure Call (RPC)-style communication. When using this communication style with a third-party resource, you will need to verify that the response time will be adequate for your needs and not add latency that could add other issues.

RPC is a synchronous communication method that has a request and a response. The caller is the client making a request from a function on a server. The caller sends the request and waits for a response. This waiting means that the business logic cannot continue without a specific reply. Because the call to a microservice is over a network, this allows for a separation of concerns. That is, the caller does not need to know about the internals of the microservice.

Understanding how to leverage microservices is very important as each call has a role in the business processes. Since microservices communicate over a network, there is inherent latency to the execution of a business process. If the business process cannot tolerate this additional latency in execution, then that code should not rely on a synchronous microservice.

Using RPC-style communication for microservices has another drawback. The caller must know the network address of the microservices. What happens if the microservice is no longer at that location? How do we handle scaling to several instances of a single microservice? We will start with a hard-coded IP address and then later go over the use of service discovery.

API First Design

Microservices that receive direct requests accept these calls through an Application Programming Interface (API). As fun as it would be to just sling code for our microservice, that would be haphazard and could allow issues to occur. Instead, API first design means focusing on what functionality is exposed and expectations of requests and responses.

An API is one or more functions that are callable by code external to itself. These functions are public entry points that provide encapsulation of business logic. This encapsulation allows for the governance of what logic is available to external callers. These callers may be in different namespaces, classes, or even NuGet packages. When public functions in public classes expose functionality, code in another assembly can call and use that functionality. With Web API, the interfaces are only available via web-based communication protocols, usually Hypertext Transport Protocol (HTTP).

We already touched on understanding a microservice's role in business processes. But how should the microservice be called? This chapter is about RPC-style microservices. Therefore, we need to understand what to expect of this microservice that retrieves information from a third-party distance service. We will build the API first.

That is, we will work out what this microservice will offer functionally. What is the shape/format of the request? Does the request use JSON, XML, or a binary format? Should the request use REST, gRPC, GraphQL, or something else? And what about the response back to the caller?

Transport Mechanisms

When calling any network service like a web server using HTTP, File Transfer Protocol (FTP) server, or Internet of Things (IoT) protocols like MQTT, there is a communication means for data sent to and from the endpoints. The means of communication among the endpoints are using a transport mechanism. There are several transport mechanisms available. In this book, we will only focus on two, REST and gRPC.

REST

Roy Fielding created Representational State Transfer (REST) in 2000 to transfer data using stateless connections. REST provides a form of state over the stateless protocol HTTP. The development of HTTP 1.1 and Uniform Resource Identifiers (URI) standards utilized REST.

REST is best suited for text-based payloads and not binary payloads. Since most data is in memory, it must be transformed, or "serialized," to a textual representation like JSON or XML before being sent to an endpoint. Data is then deserialized back to a binary form stored in memory when received.

REST has operations called HTTP verbs. Here is a list of the most common:

- GET – Used for the retrieval of data
- POST – Used for the creation of data
- PUT – Used for updating data
- DELETE – Used for the deletion of data

The REST standard considers GET, PUT, and DELETE as idempotent. Idempotent actions mean that sending the same message multiple times has the same effect as sending once. For developers, this means we need to pay careful attention to our APIs. When receiving duplicate messages, do not allow the creation of multiple results. For example, if you have duplicate messages that each have instructions to add a charge to a bill for $5.00, the amount should only be affected by one of the messages. POST, on the other hand, is not idempotent. Making multiple calls will likely end up in duplicate records.

gRPC

Another way for microservice communication is with "Google Remote Procedure Calls" (gRPC). Google created gRPC for faster communication with distributed systems by using a binary protocol called Protocol Buffers. Like REST, gRPC is language agnostic, so it can be used where the microservice and caller are using different programming languages.

Unlike REST, gRPC is type specific and uses Protocol Buffers to serialize and deserialize data. You must know the type definitions at design time for both parties to understand how to manage the data. In the section where we use gRPC, you will see how proto definition files define our data structures.

When choosing which transport mechanism to use for microservices, there are some considerations. First, gRPC uses the HTTP/2 protocol, which helps with lower latency. However, you may need to verify various pieces of your network stack are compatible with HTTP/2. Another consideration is knowing when to leverage gRPC. If you know the microservices are public facing, either on the Internet or on a network deemed public, REST is the most likely chosen option. It is the most versatile and easiest to use. If the calls are from internal code such as a monolith or another microservice, you may consider gRPC. Using gRPC will help lower latency and is worth the extra time to set up. Although our microservice is internal facing only, we will start with REST for its simplicity and then show how to integrate gRPC into our project.

So far, we have learned that this microservice will use RPC-style communication with REST for the transport mechanism of data in the request and response. What should the request and response look like, JSON or XML? A brief look at the Google Routes API specification shows they are returning data with JSON. Although we could transform the data to XML for the caller of our microservice, this is just not needed. JSON is a good alternative to XML and is usually a smaller payload in transit and storage.

File ➤ New ➤ Project

For this example, we're going to use the ASP.NET Core Empty project type for the REST frontend and we'll add a Class library project type for the Google Route Service. We're also going to make use of the Minimal API's structure. Our example code is relatively small enough for Minimal API's. It's recommended that if you have a large amount of code that it is either moved to another class or using a controller-based structure like MVC.

This project uses the NuGet packages Microsoft.AspNetCore.OpenApi, Swashbuckle.AspNetCore.SwaggerGen, and Swashbuckle.AspNetCore.SwaggerUI. The project name is DistanceMicroservice. In the Program.cs file, remove any existing lines and replace with the following code.

```csharp
 using GoogleRouteService;

var builder = WebApplication.CreateBuilder(args);

builder.Services.AddOpenApi();
builder.Services.AddSingleton<GoogleRouteServices>();

var app = builder.Build();

IConfiguration config = app.Configuration;

if (app.Environment.IsDevelopment())
{
    app.MapOpenApi();
}

app.UseHttpsRedirection();

app.MapPost("/getdistanceinfo", (Addresses addresses, GoogleRouteServices googleRouteService) =>
{
    var apiUrl = config["googleRoutesApi:apiUrl"]
                ?? throw new InvalidOperationException("URL key, googleRouteApiUrl, not found.");
    var apiKey = config["googleRoutesApi:apiKey"]
        ?? throw new InvalidOperationException("API key, googleRouteApiKey, not found in user secrets.");
```

CHAPTER 5 FIRST MICROSERVICE

```
    var response = googleRouteService.GetRouteInfo(addresses, apiUrl,
    apiKey);
    return response;
})
.WithName("GetDistanceInfo");

app.Run();
```

Create a Class Library project called GoogleRouteService and place in the following code. I recommend renaming the default file from class1.cs to GoogleRouteService. cs. After which, create a project reference from DistanceMicroservice to this GoogleRouteService project.

```
using System.Net.Http.Json;
namespace GoogleRouteService;

public class GoogleRouteService
{
    public async Task<DiscoveredRoutes> GetRouteInfo(Addresses addresses,
    string apiUrl, string apiKey)
    {
      HttpClient httpClient = new();
      httpClient.DefaultRequestHeaders.Add("X-Goog-Api-Key", apiKey);
      httpClient.DefaultRequestHeaders.Add("ContentType",
      "application/json");
      httpClient.DefaultRequestHeaders.Add("X-Goog-FieldMask", "routes.
      duration,routes.distanceMeters");

        var routeRequest = new RouteRequest(
          new Origin(addresses.OriginAddress)
          , new Destination(addresses.DestinationAddress)
          , travelMode: "DRIVE", routingPreference: "TRAFFIC_AWARE",
          computeAlternativeRoutes: true
          , new Routemodifiers(avoidTolls: false, avoidHighways: false,
          avoidFerries: false)
          , languageCode: "en-US", units: "UNITS_UNSPECIFIED");
```

```csharp
    HttpResponseMessage response = await httpClient.
    PostAsJsonAsync(apiUrl, routeRequest);

    var discoveredRoutes = new DiscoveredRoutes(
      addresses.OriginAddress
      , addresses.DestinationAddress
      , string.Empty
      , Array.Empty<Route>());

    if (!response.IsSuccessStatusCode)
  {
      discoveredRoutes.Message =
      $"Error: {response.StatusCode} - {response.ReasonPhrase}";
      return discoveredRoutes;
    }

    var responseBody = await response.Content.ReadAsStringAsync();
    var routes = System.Text.Json.JsonSerializer.Deserialize<Routes>(
    responseBody);
    if (routes is null)
    {
      discoveredRoutes.Message = "Failed to deserialize response to
      Routes.";
    }

    if (routes?.routes is null)
    {
      discoveredRoutes.Message = "Failed to deserialize response to
      Routes or routes array is null.";
    }

    discoveredRoutes.Routes =
      routes?.routes ?? Array.Empty<Route>();
    discoveredRoutes.Message = $"Number of routes found:
      {discoveredRoutes.Routes.Length}";

    return discoveredRoutes;
  }
}
```

CHAPTER 5 FIRST MICROSERVICE

```csharp
public record Addresses(string OriginAddress, string DestinationAddress);

public class DiscoveredRoutes(string OriginAddress, string
DestinationAddress, string Message, Route[] Routes)
{
  public string OriginAddress { get; } = OriginAddress;
  public string DestinationAddress { get; } = DestinationAddress;
  public string Message { get; set; } = Message;
  public Route[] Routes { get; set; } = Routes;
}

public record Routes(Route[] routes);

/// <param name="distanceMeters"> Distance in meters. </param>
/// <param name="duration"> Duration in seconds. </param>
public record Route(int distanceMeters, string duration)
{
  public required int DistanceMeters = distanceMeters;
  public required string Duration = duration;

  // Convert meters to miles
  public double DistanceInMiles =>
    Math.Round(distanceMeters / 1609.34, 2);
}

public record RouteRequest(Origin origin, Destination destination, string travelMode
, string routingPreference, bool computeAlternativeRoutes, Routemodifiers routeModifiers
, string languageCode, string units);

public record Origin(string Address);

public record Destination(string Address);

public record Routemodifiers(bool avoidTolls, bool avoidHighways, bool avoidFerries);
```

Contacting Google's Routes API

Using Google's Routes API allows for up to 10,000 calls per month on their free tier. If you prefer, you can reply with fake data. Using fake data will at least get you up and running until you are able to pay for a service that gives the required information.

Before calling Google's Routes API, you must first sign up and get a few things in order. Start by going to https://developers.google.com/maps/documentation/routes/cloud-setup. Follow the steps on their page to create a project, enable billing, and enabling the API. Enabling the Routes API on your account will provide an API key that you can store in the application's appSettings.json file.

App Settings

Once you have your API key, you need to store that in the appSettings.json file of your main project. In your project, open the file appSettings.json and add this block.

Note It is best not to store any secrets or API keys in configuration files. It is very easy to deploy secrets to production accidentally. Instead, consider using the Secret Manager tool (https://docs.microsoft.com/en-us/aspnet/core/security/app-secrets).

```
"googleRoutesApi": {
  "apiKey": "Enter your API Key here",
  "apiUrl": "https://routes.googleapis.com/directions/v2:computeRoutes"
}
```

Testing What We Have

In Visual Studio 2022, starting with release version 17.6 there is a new window called Endpoints Explorer. This tool can help test our API entry point without additional code. After opening this window, it may contain a reference to the original entry point that you replaced earlier. Refresh the list and you will see the entry point for the new code you have.

CHAPTER 5   FIRST MICROSERVICE

Right-click on the entry for "/getdistanceinfo" and select "Generate Request". This creates a new file based on the project name with "http" file extension. In our example, it is DistanceMicroservice.http. Change the code to match the following.

```
POST {{DistanceMicroservice_HostAddress}}/getdistanceinfo
Content-Type: application/json

{
  "OriginAddress":"101 S. Main St. Chicago, IL",
  "DestinationAddress":"500 S. Main St. Los Angeles, CA"
}
###
```

Before we can send a test request, make sure the application is running. The application can be running in with or without debug mode. The top line of the DistanceMicroservice.http file shows that host address it expects to be running. If needed, modify this accordingly to match what you want to use in the launchSettings.json file.

```
@DistanceMicroservice_HostAddress = https://localhost:7274
```

Just above the line beginning with "POST" is an option to "Send Request". Select this option and it will open a new window to the right showing the results of executing the code for this entry point. You will see the following results.

```
{
  "originAddress": "101 S. Main St. Chicago, IL",
  "destinationAddress": "500 S. Main St. Los Angeles, CA",
  "message": "Number of routes found: 3",
  "routes": [
    {
      "distanceMeters": 3217970,
      "duration": "103788s",
      "distanceInMiles": 1999.56
    },
    {
      "distanceMeters": 3398596,
      "duration": "110417s",
      "distanceInMiles": 2111.79
    },
```

```
    {
      "distanceMeters": 3406657,
      "duration": "110335s",
      "distanceInMiles": 2116.8
    }
  ]
}
```

Swagger

Another way to test the application is using a tool called Swagger. Swagger (https://swagger.io) is a free tool provided by OpenAPI Spec for developing APIs. Adding Swagger is very simple to use, and it will show all the exposed methods that a calling application can call.

Using the Package Manager Console, install packages Swashbuckle.AspNetCore.SwaggerGen and Swashbuckle.AspNetCore.SwaggerUI.

You will need to modify the code to make use of the Swashbuckle packages. In the first block, add the service reference.

```
var builder = WebApplication.CreateBuilder(args);

builder.Services.AddOpenApi();
builder.Services.AddSwaggerGen();
builder.Services.AddSingleton<GoogleRouteServices>();

var app = builder.Build();

IConfiguration config = app.Configuration;

if (app.Environment.IsDevelopment())
{
    app.MapOpenApi();
    app.UseSwagger();
    app.UseSwaggerUI(c => c.SwaggerEndpoint("/swagger/v1/swagger.json", "My 
    microservice for map information."));
}
// rest of code not shown for brevity
```

CHAPTER 5   FIRST MICROSERVICE

Now, when you run the application, you can go to this URL in your browser: `https://localhost:7274/swagger/index.html`.

Note that the port number is likely to be different. The port number in use can be found in the launchSettings.json file.

You will see a page showing the multiple available action methods. In this application, there are two ways of calling our single action method "GetDistanceInfo." One way is without specifying the action method name. The other is for when specifying that action method. Now, select one of the methods and then select the "Try it out" button. The page shows the two parameters "originAddress" and "destinationAddress." For the request body put in

```
{
  "OriginAddress":"101 S. Main St. Chicago, IL",
  "DestinationAddress":"500 S. Main St. Los Angeles, CA"
}
```

Select the button "Execute." The page will call your application and then show the result.

Using Swagger is a great way to test your microservice while you are developing it. It also helps you see the structure of the HTTP call for when you modify the monolith to call the microservice.

Leveraging gRPC

The previous way of communicating with the microservice was with REST and JSON. You can also leverage a binary transport mechanism for faster communication. With gRPC, communication may be faster depending on the type of data sent. It takes some time to convert an instance of a class to a message. For small, simple message payloads, you may be better off with JSON. However, as soon as the message payload size is more than tiny, the time to convert to binary is quickly justified. And with the high-performance nature of binary communication, gRPC is used for large message payloads and even streaming. gRPC is also platform agnostic, so it can be running on anything that can use HTTP/2.

gRPC uses HTTP/2 for transport and Protocol Buffers for the Interface Definition Language (IDL). With JSON, converting an instance of a class to a stream of text relies on many rules and uses reflection. Since gRPC is a binary representation of data, the conversion effort is not as straightforward. Developers must use customizations even on simplistic data types. In this section, you will modify the microservice to leverage gRPC to learn how to trim latency with the network calls.

gRPC uses an IDL definition file, or "contract," to define the message data and must be shared on both the sender and receiver. A quick example of a "proto" file is

```
syntax = "proto3";
service SubscribeToEvent {
  rpc Subscribe (EventSubscription) returns (Subscribed)
}
message EventSubscription {
  int32 eventId = 1;
  string name = 2;
}
message Subscribed {
  string message = 1;
}
```

In this example, a service "SubscribeToEvent" is defined with the method "Subscribe." The "Subscribe" method takes in a parameter type "EventSubscription," which returns the type "Subscribed."

Incorporating gRPC

Let's now create another project of type Console Application. Then, create a project reference to the GoogleRouteService project. In the appSettings.json file, include the API key and URL that you used in the DistanceMicroservice project.

Create a new folder called Protos. Inside that folder create a new file called DistanceInfo.proto and put the following code inside.

```
syntax = "proto3";

option csharp_namespace = "GrpcDistanceMicroservice";

package distance;
```

CHAPTER 5 FIRST MICROSERVICE

```
service DistanceInfoSvc {
  // Sends a greeting
  rpc GetDistance (Addresses) returns (DistanceInformation);
}

message Addresses {
  string OriginAddress = 1;
  string DestinationAddress = 2;
}

message DistanceInformation {
  string OriginAddress = 1;
  string DestinationAddress = 2;
  string Message = 3;
  repeated Route routes = 4;
}

message Route {
  int32 DistanceMeters = 1;
  string Duration = 2;
}
```

Create a file called Usings.cs and insert the following.

```
global using Grpc.Core;
global using GoogleRouteService;
global using GrpcDistanceMicroservice;
global using GrpcDistance.Services;
global using Addresses = GoogleRouteService.Addresses;
```

Create a folder from the project called Services. In the Services folder, create a new Class called gRpcDistanceService.cs and replace the template code with this:

```
namespace GrpcDistance.Services;

public class gRpcDistanceService(GoogleRouteServices googleRouteService,
IConfiguration config) : DistanceInfoSvc.DistanceInfoSvcBase
```

```csharp
{
    public override async Task<DistanceInformation> GetDistance(Grpc
    DistanceMicroservice.Addresses request, ServerCallContext context)
    {
        var apiUrl = config["googleRoutesApi:apiUrl"]
                    ?? throw new InvalidOperationException("URL key,
                    googleRouteApiUrl, not found.");
        var apiKey = config["googleRoutesApi:apiKey"]
            ?? throw new InvalidOperationException("API key,
            googleRouteApiKey, not found in user secrets.");

        var addresses = new Addresses(request.OriginAddress, request.
        DestinationAddress);

        var distanceResponse = await googleRouteService.
        GetRouteInfo(addresses, apiUrl, apiKey);

        var response = new DistanceInformation()
        {
            OriginAddress = request.OriginAddress,
            DestinationAddress = request.DestinationAddress,
            Message = distanceResponse.Message
        };

        foreach (var routeInfo in distanceResponse.Routes)
        {
            response.Routes.Add(new GrpcDistanceMicroservice.Route()
            { DistanceMeters = routeInfo.DistanceMeters, Duration =
            routeInfo.Duration });
        }

        return response;
    }
}
```

CHAPTER 5 FIRST MICROSERVICE

In the Program.cs file, replace any existing lines with the following.

```
var builder = WebApplication.CreateBuilder(args);

builder.Services.AddGrpc();

var app = builder.Build();

app.MapGrpcService<gRpcDistanceService>();

app.MapGet("/", () => "Communication with gRPC endpoints must be made through a gRPC client. To learn how to create a client, visit: https://go.microsoft.com/fwlink/?linkid=2086909");

app.Run();
```

NuGet Packages

You need to install the gRPC NuGet packages to work with the proto files and code it generates. Add the following NuGet packages.

```
Grpc.AspNetCore
Grpc.Tools
```

Project File

Modify the project file by left-clicking the project. It will open the file in the editor. Modify the project file to include this:

```xml
<ItemGroup>
  <Protobuf Include="Protos\DistanceInfo.proto" GrpcServices="Server" />
</ItemGroup>
<ItemGroup>
  <Folder Include="Protos\" />
</ItemGroup>
```

With modifications completed, build the project. The gRPC Tools NuGet package will build supportive class files based on the proto file. This allows the gRpcDistanceService to reference the information defined in the proto file. These supportive class files are re-created every time the project is built, and they are located in the obj folder.

CHAPTER 5   FIRST MICROSERVICE

Testing gRPC Endpoint

Until now, you can test the connection to the REST API, but how can you test the gRPC service endpoint? You can test with a simple console application.

In this new console application, create a folder called Protos and place a copy of the DistanceInfo.proto file. Then add the following NuGet packages.

Google.Protobuf
Grpc.Net.Client
Grpc.Tools

In the program.cs file, replace any existing lines with the following.

```
using Grpc.Net.Client;
using GrpcDistanceMicroserviceClient;

// The port number must match the port of the gRPC server.
using var channel = GrpcChannel.ForAddress("https://localhost:7005");
var client = new DistanceInfoSvc.DistanceInfoSvcClient(channel);

var address = new Addresses() {
  OriginAddress = "101 S. Main St, Chicago, IL",
  DestinationAddress = "123 S. Main St., Los Angeles, CA"
};

Console.WriteLine("Getting distance");

var reply = await client.GetDistanceAsync(address);

Console.WriteLine("Message: " + reply.Message);

var routeCount = 1;
foreach(var r in reply.Routes)
{
  var miles = Math.Round(r.DistanceMeters / 1609.34, 2);
  Console.WriteLine($"Route {routeCount} distance in meters:
  {r.DistanceMeters.ToString("N0")}; Miles {miles.ToString("N2")}");
  routeCount++;
}
```

103

```
Console.WriteLine();
Console.WriteLine("Press any key to exit...");
Console.ReadKey();
```

At this point, you can build our new gRPC endpoint tester. But before you can run it, you will need to note one more detail. Notice the URL is set to https://localhost:7005. This path needs to match that of the DistanceMicroservice. Looking in the microservice project, in the launchSettings.json file, you see that when running with Kestrel, for HTTPS, the URL is https://localhost:7005. Kestrel is a web server included by default in ASP.NET Core.

Our microservice can now accept REST-based requests using JSON as well as gRPC-based requests using binary. You will have to judge when to REST vs. gRPC as it largely depends on the size of the message payload needed in your architecture design. You will have runtime decisions based on the payload size. Instead, your architectural design, governed by your business requirements, helps shape the use of one transport method vs. another.

Modify the Monolith

To enable your monolithic application to communicate with a microservice, you'll need to update the sections of code that require data provided by a microservice. Identify the areas in the monolith where information from the microservice is needed and refactor those parts to issue a request to the microservice instead of handling the logic internally. If multiple parts of the monolith need to interact with the microservice, consider encapsulating the call logic within a service inside the monolith. By implementing this change, the monolith becomes capable of leveraging microservices without duplicating connection logic throughout the codebase. This in turn makes the changes to the monolith easier to implement and to maintain.

Service Discovery

So far, the caller (monolith in our case) requires knowing the URL of where the microservice instance is hosted. Even if there was only one microservice instance, the caller should not have the IP because another instance could replace the microservice with a new IP address. However, there should never be just one microservice instance in production. You might have one microservice but with multiple instances for high availability. Each microservice instance has an IP address. Should the caller (monolith in our case) know the IP address of each microservice instance? If one instance dies or another is created, how will you update the monolith?

Callers of a microservice should not have the responsibility to know about every instance of microservice. That creates a tightly coupled architecture. Instead, the caller should only know about one IP address, which is a load balancer. Using a load balancer, you have a separation of concerns between the caller and the microservice instances.

The ability for a load balancer to know about the multiple microservice instances is service discovery. For this purpose, many products are available, such as Azure's API Management service (APIM), Apache's ZooKeeper, HashiCorp's Consul, Eureka by Netflix, and even Nginx.

Summary

We went over interprocess communication methods for calling a microservice. Specifically, in this chapter, we covered the RPC communication style. We also covered the need to design the API first to better understand how the microservice is called and the payload structure. We then went over transport mechanisms and the details of REST and gRPC. Then we built the first microservice that leveraged Google's Route API. Then we modified the microservice to leverage gRPC for binary payload. Finally, we noted how service discovery is an additional part of the architecture to prevent hard-coding IP addresses and handle multiple microservice instances.

CHAPTER 6

Microservice Messaging

In the last chapter, you learned how to create microservices using RPC communication. You also learned how synchronous communication requires a request and a response. In this chapter, you will create two microservices using messaging's asynchronous communication method to fulfill some business needs regarding invoice management.

Issues with Synchronous Communication

Before we dive into messaging communication, let's first understand why messaging is a viable option. Imagine this scenario: you are a coach of a sports team for kids. An issue comes up that causes the rescheduling of a game. You start down a list of people and call them one by one. You call the other coaches, plus the umpires/judges and *all* the parents.

Now imagine that you call one of the parents that oversee the concession stands. That parent then calls the owner of the concession stands and discovers they cannot attend on the proposed date. You called the parent, and the parent called the owner. Each step in the communication chain has transitive latency. This transitive latency is problematic for you, who never intended to spend so much time trying to communicate with others.

Other issues exist for you and the other coaches. The list of people to contact varies. They also vary by purpose. Just because a coach is contacted does not mean all the parents must be contacted as well. And it is never known who has the correct list of contact information.

This direct communication is extremely inefficient. It allows for all sorts of communication issues. What would happen if anyone were not notified of the schedule change? What if the chain of communication involved other downstream pieces? And what if there is a failure to notify them? This allows for cascading failures.

This way of contacting others is a huge drain on you and the other coaches. You agreed to be the coach to help the kids, not worry about communication issues. Each call has the potential of not being answered and information failing to be sent and understood. Also, each call takes the coaches' time because they are synchronous. Each caller must wait for someone to answer, receive the message, and acknowledge what needs to happen next.

Limits of RPC

The preceding real-life scenario is an example of RPC communication. Each call you and the coaches made required waiting for a response. This shows the biggest drawback of RPC with microservices; processes must wait for a response.

Another issue with this type of communication is handling the number of simultaneous calls. For example, if more calls are coming in than the microservice can handle, the caller will see either severe latency or no contact at all. This forces the caller to use retry policies or the circuit breaker pattern.

Scaling microservices horizontally requires a load balancer to distribute traffic evenly. These load balancers must be high-performance to avoid introducing latency. However, when a new instance of a microservice is created, it isn't automatically available to handle requests – it must first be registered with the load balancer.

Then there is the other issue of adding other microservices to a business process. If the caller is only aware of one microservice, then the caller must be alerted to know about the additional microservices. This means more code changes to each caller that must be aware of the others. And how is versioning to be handled? There are even more code changes to handle adapting to a different version.

Messaging

With the scenario of you as the coach, what if there was a way to broadcast the information once? Perhaps a group text or an email would suffice. Then everyone receives that information independently, and each recipient reacts accordingly. That is the purpose of asynchronous messaging.

Using messaging in the microservices architecture allows independent pieces to communicate without knowing the location of each other. In the preceding scenario, each coach would have to have a list of the other coaches and how to reach them. Also, they each need to know how to reach the parents and anyone else involved in a game.

Messaging solves many of the problems identified in the preceding example story. If the coach had a messaging system in place, contacting some people or everyone would be easier. Also, adding, removing, and updating contact information would be simpler. So, where does messaging fit in an architecture?

Architecture

With messaging, there is a shift in the way of thinking about microservices. You can use simple messaging architecture to reach a microservice in a disconnected way. But moreover, using messaging with microservices allows for a dynamic and reactive architecture. With event-driven architecture, the microservices react to messages sent as a response to an event. Perhaps a user has committed to the creation of an order. Or maybe there is a change to the inventory of an item.

Reasons to Use Messaging

There are multiple reasons to use the messaging communication style over the RPC style. The list of reasons includes

- Loosely coupled
- Buffering
- Scaling
- Independent processing

Loosely Coupled

By using messaging, the sender and the receivers (message consumers) are loosely coupled. The sender of a message does not need to know anything about the microservices receiving the message. This means that microservices do not need to know the endpoints of others. It allows for the swapping and scaling of microservices without any code changes.

This provides autonomy for microservices. With autonomy, microservices can evolve independently. This allows for microservices to only be tied together where they fit to fulfill business processes and not at the network layer.

Buffering

With the microservice architecture, there are opportunities for downtime or intermittent network connection issues for both the sender and receiver. Message brokers utilize queues that provide a buffer of the messages. During times of issues, the undeliverable messages are stored. Once the consumers are available again, the messages are delivered. This buffering also retains sequencing. The messages are delivered in the order they were sent. Maintaining the message order is known as First In, First Out (FIFO).

Scaling

The ability to scale a microservice architecture is paramount. For any production applications or distributed processing, you will have multiple instances of your microservices. This is not just for high availability but allows messages to be processed with higher throughput.

Independent Processing

Messaging allows a microservice architecture solution to change over time. You can have a solution to generate orders and manage the shipping of the products. Later, you can add other microservices to perform additional business processes by having them become message consumers. The ability to add microservices to business processes as consumers allows them to be independent information processors.

Message Types

There are multiple types of messages, depending on the need for communication. These message types play a role in fulfilling various responsibilities in business processes. They are query, command, and event.

Query

Consider the scenario of contacting your favorite store to see if they have the latest game in stock. (Pretend they don't yet have a site to sell online.) You want to purchase three copies quickly, but the store is not open. You send them an email or perhaps fill out an inquiry form on their website for that information. This is using a query message type in an asynchronous communication style. Although the query could be done synchronously, like a phone call, it does not have to be done that way.

When the store opens, they reply that they do have the game in stock. The reply also includes how many are currently in stock and suggestions on other similar games. A reply to a query is the Document message type. The document contains the information requested and any supporting information.

Command

You reply confirming you want to secure those three copies, and you are on your way to the store. The message to the store letting them know that they are to hold the items aside for you is a command. The command message type instructs what the consumer is to do without explicitly requiring a reply.

Event

You arrive at the store and purchase the games. Later, you receive an email about the purchase. The store thanks you for the purchase and includes a digital receipt. That email was sent due to an event in their system. An order was created for you, and as a result, you received the email.

When you purchased the games, the system notified other areas of the system about the order. The event kicked off processes in other parts of the store's system. Each independent process received that event and reacted. For example, the system processed the payment and took the item out of inventory.

The architecture of having multiple consumers listening to the same event is called Publish/Subscribe (Pub/Sub). The publisher of the event sends out messages for others to process. The consumers subscribe to the event and process the incoming messages differently. For example, the payment processor consumer will act on the message differently than an inventory management consumer.

CHAPTER 6   MICROSERVICE MESSAGING

Message Routing

For messages to go from a publisher to the consumers, there must be a system to handle the messages and the routing. This system provides message routing to the consumers that have subscribed to the different messages. There are two types of these systems: brokered and broker-less.

Broker-less

A broker-less system, like ZeroMQ, sends messages directly from the publisher to the consumer. This requires each microservice to have the broker-less engine installed. It also requires each endpoint to know how to reach others. As you scale your microservices, it quickly becomes harder to manage the endpoint list.

Because there is no central message system, it can have lower latency than a brokered system. This also causes a temporal coupling of the publisher to the consumer. This means that the consumer must be live and ready to handle the traffic. One way to handle the chance of a consumer not being available is to use a distributor. A distributor is a load balancer to share the load when you have multiple instances of a microservice. The distributor also handles when a consumer is unavailable, sending a message to another instance of your microservice.

Brokered

Brokered systems like ActiveMQ, Kafka, and RabbitMQ provide a centralized set of queues that hold messages until they are consumed. Because the messages are stored and then sent to consumers, it provides a loosely coupled architecture. The storing of messages until they are consumed is not a high latency task. It simply means the publisher does not have to store the messages but can rely on the broker.

Designing the use of a broker is about first understanding the business needs of each application and microservice. This topology will consist of various producers and consumers, each with their own messaging needs. Some producers only need to send messages and are not subscribing to other messages. Other producers will send messages for one business while also subscribing to other messages. As you will see in the code examples, our test client sends commands regarding invoices. It also subscribes to the message that the invoice was created. This means that although you can use a broker, the applications are not totally unaware of other applications, so there is still a topological coupling.

An advantage of using a broker is that if a message fails in the processing by a consumer, the message stays in queue until it can pick it up again or another process is ready to process it.

Consumption Models

There are multiple models for receiving messages you will see with multiple consumers. You will use one or both models. Two models are described in the following sections.

Competing Consumers

Various business processes need to have a message processed by only one consumer. For example, a *create invoice* message should only be processed once. If multiple instances of a consumer processed it, duplicate information could be stored and sent out to other microservices. Figure 6-1 depicts competing consumers.

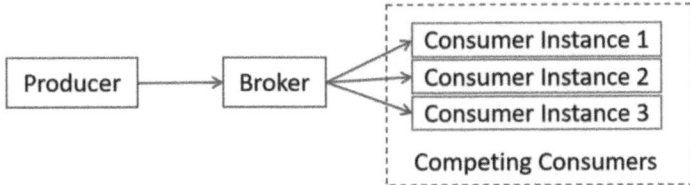

Figure 6-1. Competing consumers

An example of a competing consumer, Figure 6-2, is the Invoice Microservice. When you create multiple instances of the Invoice Microservice, they each become a competing consumer.

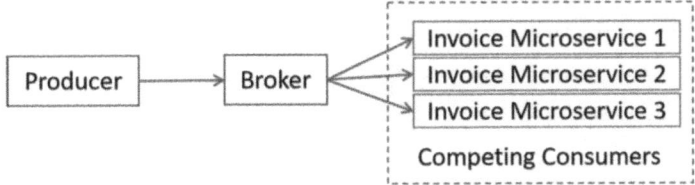

Figure 6-2. Invoice Microservice instances as competing consumers

CHAPTER 6   MICROSERVICE MESSAGING

You should have multiple instances of a microservice for scaling, availability, and distribution of load. A microservice is designed to subscribe to a specific queue and message type. But when there are multiple instances of that microservice, you have a competing consumer scenario. When a message is sent, only one of the microservice instances receives the message. If that instance of the microservice that has the message fails to process it, the broker will attempt to send it to another instance for processing.

Independent Consumers

There are times when other microservices must also consume the message. This means that these microservices do not compete with other consumers. They receive a copy of the message no matter which competing consumer processes the message.

These independent consumers process the messages for their specific business processing needs. In the preceding example, Figure 6-3, a message is sent from the Order Microservice. The message needs to be received by one instance of the Payment Microservice and one instance of the Shipping Microservice. Here the Payment and Shipping microservices are not competing with each other. Instead, they are independent consumers. Also, note that each instance of a Payment Microservice is a competing consumer to itself. The same is true for the Shipping Microservice instances.

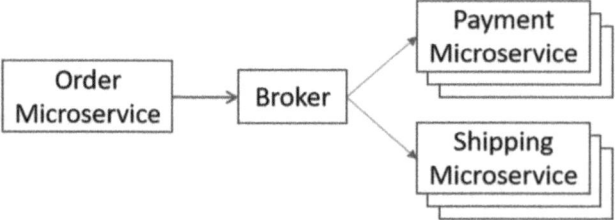

Figure 6-3. *Independent consumers*

Having independent consumers allows for a Wire Tap pattern (see Figure 6-4). An example of this has a front-end component that sends a command to the Order Microservice to revise an order. In RabbitMQ, you can have an exchange that is bound to another exchange. This allows copies of messages to be sent to another consumer, even though the exchange is set up with direct topology.

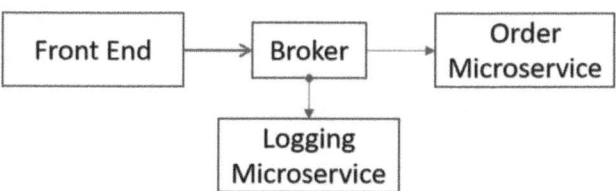

Figure 6-4. Wire Tap pattern

Delivery Guarantees

As we evaluate our business needs and design a messaging topology solution, we must consider that there will be times when messages either cannot be delivered or are delivered again. Message delivery disruption can allow for the possibility of causing duplication of data or other side effects. There are many reasons why messages fail delivery. Network failures/interruptions happen often enough that we must take them into account. Also, there can be issues with hardware, bugs in our code, or even timeouts. As great as brokers are, they cannot solve all of the problems. So, we must design for those issues when we build our applications.

When issues occur, there is a chance of duplicate messages being sent, so our consumers must handle the messages in an idempotent manner. That is, treat every message with the possibility that it has already been processed before. Exactly how to do that is per message type and business needs. Some messages may include a timestamp, and as they are processed, only messages with later timestamps are processed. And the latest timestamp is stored by the consumers to compare the timestamp in the next message. This also means that competing consumers must have a way for all instances to know the latest timestamp.

There are a few patterns regarding the delivery of messages that apply per message type we design. As each consumer may consume multiple message types, consider how these patterns apply to their needs.

At Most Once

This delivery guarantee is for when your system can tolerate the cases when messages fail to be processed. An example is when receiving temperature readings every second. If the broker delivers the message, but the consumer fails to process it, the message is not re-sent. The broker considers it delivered regardless of the consumer's ability to complete any processing of the message.

Another term for this delivery guarantee is "Fire-and-Forget." The principle is the same. The publisher sends a message without any assumption it is delivered or processed. This also offers the highest performance since there is no state management required.

At Least Once

The "at least once" delivery guarantee is where you will spend the most effort designing the consumers to handle messages in an idempotent manner. If a message fails to be given to a consumer, it is tried again. If a consumer receives a message but fails during the process, the broker will resend that message to another consumer instance.

An example scenario: you have a consumer that creates a database entry for a new order, then that instance dies. It did not send an acknowledgment to the broker that it was done with the message. So, the broker sends that message to another consumer instance. There the message is processed and inadvertently creates a duplicate database entry.

Although most broker systems have a flag that is set when it sends a message again, you are safer to assume the message is a duplicate anyway and process accordingly. For example, if the message is to create an order, search the database of another order by that customer on that date for those same items. Then if an order exists, you have confidence that the previous attempt got that far in the business operation.

Because microservices architecture is an implementation of distributed computing, there is a lot to consider. Here we are referring to how messages are handled. There is also much to understand with distributed transactions which is outside the scope of this book. I highly recommend a book, *The Art of Immutable Architecture* by Michael Perry, published by Apress. In Perry's book, there is a specific section on Idempotence and Commutativity applicable to handling messages.

Once and Only Once

Another name for this delivery guarantee is "Exactly Once," which is the hardest to accomplish. Many argue it does not exist. When you need a message to be processed only once, how do you know it was only processed once? How do you know the message is not a duplicate? Essentially, how do you know the intended state has not already succeeded?

The point here is that guaranteeing a message was only delivered and processed once requires state management involving the consumers and the broker system. This addition of state management may be far more trouble than designing for the other delivery guarantees.

Message Ordering

If the entire message system were single threaded, then there would be a guarantee of the order of messages. However, that would be an extremely inefficient system and quickly discarded. Instead, we use messaging systems that process messages as efficiently as possible. But this puts the onus on developers to build an architecture that can tolerate the reception of out-of-order messages.

An example scenario is that of a message sent to an Order Microservice to create a new order. Another message to a different instance of the same microservice is sent with an update to the order. During the processing of the first message, an error occurs, and the message is not acknowledged. The broker then sends that message to the next microservice instance that is available. Meanwhile, the message with the update to the order is being processed. The microservice code must decide how to update an order that does not exist yet.

One suggestion is for each instance of the microservice to share the same data store. Then messages received out of order could be stored temporarily and then reassembled when the order's creation message is processed. Of course, there is a lot to manage to do this successfully. Thankfully there is an easier way.

In the book *The Art of Immutable Architecture*, Perry notes that operations should be commutative as it applies here. This means that if the messages do not arrive in the correct order, the result should be the same as if they arrived in the correct order. So, how is our code supposed to handle the information commutative?

We cannot force the order of the messages, but we can design for handling messages out of order. In our scenario, the message with the order update can include all the information that was in the message to create the order. Since the order has not yet been created, there is no order number. So, the update message was sent knowing that it was an update to an order not yet created. Including the original information in the update message allows a consumer to create the order and apply the update in cases where the order does not exist. When the message to create the order is received, it is ignored as it now already exists.

CHAPTER 6   MICROSERVICE MESSAGING

Building the Examples

Since the microservice we will create in this chapter is meant to process invoices for the company, we need to understand the various states of an invoice. Those listed here are simple examples. You should get with your subject matter experts or domain experts to understand the applicable "real world" invoice states during processing.

- New
- Late
- Modified
- Paid
- Closed

The invoice microservice we will build in this chapter will first have the responsibility of creating an invoice. It may seem like the monolith would be responsible for creating the invoice. But since a microservice is responsible for persisting data, then it should own that data. So, this microservice will receive a request to create an invoice. And part of that process will persist it to a database.

Of course, the microservice we will build here is only an example of a fully featured microservice for processing invoices. This microservice will provide a starting point for you to build more business functionality as you deem necessary.

Building the Messaging Microservices

To demonstrate microservice messaging, we'll create four projects. The first project has class models that will be shared with the other three projects. The first demonstration will use the competing consumer pattern. Then we'll modify the code slightly to show the publish-subscribe pattern.

Disclaimer   The code examples are not meant to be production worthy. They are just enough to help demonstrate concepts.

Running RabbitMQ

You have some options when running RabbitMQ. It can run on a server, on your computer, in a Docker container, or an alternative like Podman or Minikube. If you would like to install RabbitMQ, go to https://rabbitmq.com/download.html. In our examples, we will run RabbitMQ from a Docker container. Docker Desktop is required to be installed. To install Docker Desktop, go to https://docker.com/products/docker-desktop.

With Docker Desktop installed, go to a command prompt and enter

```
docker run -p 5672:5672 -p 15672:15672 rabbitmq:3-management
```

If you prefer to run the RabbitMQ instance detached from the console:

```
docker run -d -p 5672:5672 -p 15672:15672 rabbitmq:3-management
```

You can look at the RabbitMQ Management site by going to http://localhost:15672. The default username and password for RabbitMQ are *guest* and *guest*.

With RabbitMQ running, now we will create the microservices. We will start with the microservice for invoices.

First Project

For the first project, we will create a class library on which the other projects will depend. This project will contain the classes that become the payload in the messages.

Create a new class library project named MessageContracts and insert the following code.

```
namespace MessageContracts;
public class InvoiceCreated
{
  public int InvoiceNumber { get; set; }
  public InvoiceToCreate? InvoiceData { get; set; }
}
public class InvoiceToCreate
{
  public int CustomerNumber { get; set; }
```

```
  public List<InvoiceItems>? InvoiceItems { get; set; }
}
public class InvoiceItems
{
  public required string Description { get; set; }
  public double Price { get; set; }
  public double ActualMileage { get; set; }
  public double BaseRate { get; set; }
  public bool IsOversized { get; set; }
  public bool IsRefrigerated { get; set; }
  public bool IsHazardousMaterial { get; set; }
}
```

Building the Invoice Microservice

Now let's create an application that will publish invoice messages. As this is just a demo, it will create invoices with randomly generated numbers. In production, this would be a microservice receiving a trigger to create an invoice. This trigger would likely be from a monolith or another domain event message. The idea here is that the microservice responsible for generating an invoice would also be responsible for persisting to a database. This way it can protect the data integrity of invoices.

Create a console application named InvoiceMicroservice. Then create a project reference to the MessageContracts project you recently made. Install the latest RabbitMQ NuGet package. Now replace existing code with the following:

```
using MessageContracts;
using RabbitMQ.Client;
using System.Text;
using System.Text.Json;

var factory = new ConnectionFactory { HostName = "localhost" };
using var connection = await factory.CreateConnectionAsync();
using var channel = await connection.CreateChannelAsync();

await channel.QueueDeclareAsync(queue: "invoice-service", durable: false,
    exclusive: false, autoDelete: false, arguments: null);
```

```csharp
//await channel.ExchangeDeclareAsync(exchange: "invoice-service",
ExchangeType.Fanout);

var exit = false;
while (!exit)
{
  Console.WriteLine("Press 'q' to exit or any other key to create an
  invoice.");
  var key = Console.ReadKey(true).Key;
  if (key == ConsoleKey.Q)
  {
    exit = true;
    continue;
  }

  var newInvoiceNumber = new Random().Next(10000, 99999);
  Console.WriteLine($"Created invoice with number:{newInvoiceNumber}");

  InvoiceCreated invoiceCreated = new()
  {
    InvoiceNumber = newInvoiceNumber,
    InvoiceData = new InvoiceToCreate()
    {
      CustomerNumber = 12345,
      InvoiceItems =
          [
             new InvoiceItems
    {
      Description = "Item 1",
      Price = 100.0,
      ActualMileage = 50.0,
      BaseRate = 10.0,
      IsOversized = false,
      IsRefrigerated = false,
      IsHazardousMaterial = false
    },
```

CHAPTER 6 MICROSERVICE MESSAGING

```
      new InvoiceItems
      {
        Description = "Item 2",
        Price = 200.0,
        ActualMileage = 75.0,
        BaseRate = 15.0,
        IsOversized = true,
        IsRefrigerated = false,
        IsHazardousMaterial = true
      }
          ]
        }
      };

    var message = JsonSerializer.Serialize(invoiceCreated);
    var body = Encoding.UTF8.GetBytes(message);

      await channel.BasicPublishAsync(exchange: string.Empty,
        routingKey: "invoice-service", body: body);
};
```

Building the Payment Microservice

For the consumer, we'll create a Payment Microservice. This project will serve as an example of a downstream microservice that reacts to creating an invoice. Create a new console application named PaymentMicroservice. Add a project reference to the MessageContract application. You'll also need to add the latest RabbitMQ NuGet package.

In the program.cs file replace existing code with the following:

```
using MessageContracts;
using RabbitMQ.Client;
using RabbitMQ.Client.Events;
using System.Text.Json;

var factory = new ConnectionFactory { HostName = "localhost" };
//replace HostName with your RabbitMQ server address if not running locally
```

```csharp
using var connection = await factory.CreateConnectionAsync();
using (var channel = await connection.CreateChannelAsync())
{
    await channel.QueueDeclareAsync(queue: "invoice-service",
    durable: false,
    exclusive: false, autoDelete: false, arguments: null);

    Console.WriteLine($" [*] Waiting for messages. - {DateTime.Now}");

    var consumer = new AsyncEventingBasicConsumer(channel);
    consumer.ReceivedAsync += (model, ea) =>
    {
      var body = ea.Body.ToArray();
      var message = JsonSerializer.Deserialize<InvoiceCreated>(body);
        Console.WriteLine($" [x] Received invoice number: " +
    $"{message?.InvoiceNumber}");
        return Task.CompletedTask;
    };

    //for competing consumers
    await channel.BasicConsumeAsync("invoice-service",
    autoAck: true, consumer: consumer);

    Console.WriteLine(" Press [enter] to exit.");
    Console.ReadLine();
};
```

Testing the Competing Consumers

Now configure the startup projects to run both the InvoiceMicroservice project and the PaymentMicroservice project. When you run this, you'll see two screens appear. If you send a message, the PaymentMicroservice will receive it. But that's only a single consumer. Now right-click on the PaymentMicroservice project in the Solution Explorer. Select Debug ➤ Start New Instance. Another window will appear. Now send more messages. You should see each Payment Microservice instance receiving a message but taking turns on what they receive.

CHAPTER 6 MICROSERVICE MESSAGING

The instances of the Payment Microservice work as competing consumers because of the queue that was set up to send messages. With the publish-subscribe pattern, we'll use an exchange.

Building a PubSub Demo

In the Invoice Microservice code, find the code declaring a queue:

```
await channel.QueueDeclareAsync(queue: "invoice-service", durable: false, exclusive: false, autoDelete: false, arguments: null);
```

and replace with

```
await channel.ExchangeDeclareAsync(exchange: "invoice-service", ExchangeType.Fanout);
```

Now find the code that publishes the message, and we'll swap the exchange and routing key values to look like this:

```
await channel.BasicPublishAsync(exchange: "invoice-service", routingKey: string.Empty, body: body);
```

Now in the Payment Microservice code, find the line

```
await channel.QueueDeclareAsync(queue: "invoice-service", durable: false, exclusive: false, autoDelete: false, arguments: null);
```

and replace with

```
await channel.ExchangeDeclareAsync(exchange: "invoice-service", ExchangeType.Fanout);

QueueDeclareOk queueDeclareResult = await channel.QueueDeclareAsync();

string queueName = queueDeclareResult.QueueName;

await channel.QueueBindAsync(queue: queueName, exchange: "invoice-service", routingKey: string.Empty);
```

CHAPTER 6   MICROSERVICE MESSAGING

For the code to publish the message, find the code

```
await channel.BasicConsumeAsync("invoice-service",
autoAck: true, consumer: consumer);
```

and replace it with

```
await channel.BasicConsumeAsync(queueName,
autoAck: true, consumer: consumer);
```

Now, the code is using an exchange to send messages to one or more consumers or "subscribers."

To test this, compile and run the code. As like before, create other instances of the Payment Microservice by right-clicking the PaymentMicroservice project and select Debug ➤ Start New Instance. You should have three screens, one being the invoice message publisher and the other two being invoice subscribers. Each subscriber receives a duplicate message.

In production, you're not likely to have multiple instances of a subscriber reacting the same to every message. Instead, you can have other subscribers in other microservices receiving the same message but with different behaviors. You might have one subscriber receiving the invoice message to prepare payment information while another subscriber is journaling for accounting and compliance purposes.

Drawbacks of Messaging

Although there are numerous reasons for implementing messaging, it is not without drawbacks. Messaging solutions require effort and time to understand the many pieces that must be decided. Expect to create several proofs of concept to try out the many designs. You will need to judge each design based on complexity, ease of implementation, and manageability variations.

After a messaging solution has been chosen, you then have the infrastructure to create and manage. The messaging product, RabbitMQ, for example, must run on a server someplace. Then for high availability, you must create a cluster on multiple servers. With the additional servers, you have more infrastructure to maintain.

Troubleshooting is also much harder. Since microservices can reside on numerous servers, there may be many log files to comb through when there is an error. You will have to understand if only one microservice failed to receive and process a message and which microservice instance failed.

Since messages can end up in a Dead Letter Queue, you may have to replay that message or decide to delete it. Then, decide if the timeout setting for the DLQ is sufficient. You will also need to verify the messaging system of choice is fully functioning.

Summary

We covered a lot in this chapter. There is so much more to learn with messaging, even if not used with microservices. This chapter provided a high-level overview of messaging with a couple of example microservices.

You learned about the reasons to use messaging. Messaging is a communication style that helps keep microservices loosely coupled. It also provides buffering, scaling, and independent processing of messages. Each microservice can stay as an independent application, written in the best language for business needs.

In this chapter, you also learned about message types Query, Command, and Event. Commands are for when a microservice is being directed to execute a specific business operation. Queries are for retrieving data, and Events are for alerting subscribers about the fact something has occurred. In our code examples, a command was used to have the Invoice Microservice create an invoice. When that invoice was created, it published a Queue. Subscribers like Payment Microservice received the published message and reacted independently with that information.

You also learned that message routing could be done by brokered or broker-less systems. They each have pros and cons that must be evaluated depending on the various business needs you will have. And note, depending on what business needs you are trying to solve, you may have a mix of solutions. Just because a broker-less system solves one aspect of your needs does not mean it will solve them all.

With messaging, you learned about different types of consumers. When you have a consumer subscribed to a queue and scale-out that consumer, multiple consumers compete for the message. Competing consumers help to ensure that only one microservice is processing a specific message. Using independent consumers means that differing microservices can receive the same message. You saw this with the Payment

Microservice demo. They each receive the message when an invoice is created. Using independent consumers is useful when another subscriber should receive a copy of the message. Another example could be logging or a data warehouse solution where they need a copy of the message regardless of what other business processes are doing.

You also learned about delivery guarantees and that you must consider that message delivery is not easy. Many circumstances can cause a message to fail to be delivered or processed. As much as we want a message to be delivered once and processed every time, the real world has factors that require developers to build more robust consumers. We must have our consumers be idempotent in case a duplicate message is sent. And our consumers must handle commutative messages as they can be delivered out of expected order.

CHAPTER 7

Decentralizing Data

Microservices architecture is an implementation of a distributed system. This means that we may need to separate computational load across multiple systems for reasons like governance, performance, scalability, etc. Now that microservices exist to handle business functionality across systems, we need to discuss how to handle the data. In this chapter, we will go over decentralizing data and suggestions for implementing different ways to handle data across multiple microservices.

The developer, Kathy at Code Whiz, has now made multiple microservices. She made microservices for retrieving distance information to increase quote accuracy. Kathy also made microservices for handling invoices and other related functionality. But now is the time for Kathy to consider if the database system that the client, Hyp-Log, uses is sufficient or if other databases should be created.

Current State

Most monolithic applications' code has grown over time, and this usually includes the centralized database. Considering one of the most common database types is relational, multiple tables in one database make it easy to serve several business processes. Queries can join tables, making it relatively easy to gather data. This type of database works very well until business process changes require a different way of handling data. There are relational database systems like Microsoft's SQL Server and Oracle. There are also nonrelational database systems, some of which are called No-SQL. Azure Cosmos DB and AWS DynamoDB are two examples. The database of choice is largely dependent on the data model you choose.

Businesses must change and adapt over time to stay relevant. Some adapt to new requirements in regulations and compliance mandates. Many businesses change because the industry changes, and they cannot be left behind. Perhaps a new product line can help supply income that supports them for the next set of changes. To stay competitive, businesses and their processes must change.

CHAPTER 7   DECENTRALIZING DATA

You have been learning how microservices may help with the endeavors for a business to handle change. Just as applications evolve as the business changes, so must the data models and schemas. You may be knowledgeable about how data is modeled in your monolith. Developing microservices allows for data modeling changes as you understand the needs of the changing business processes applied to microservices and the monolith. There are several database types to choose from, and their pros/cons help the success of microservices.

Most monolithic applications have data models that store changes by searching for the record and applying the update. The current state is the only thing stored. There might be a history table, and they generally include changes across multiple tables and have little if any query performance. While this way of storing records is still valid for many scenarios, with microservices, there are other data models to consider.

The Rule

There is a general "rule" stating that if a microservice persists data, it should own that database. This could be a database or a data store. The difference is that a database is a system with the sole purpose of housing and managing data. A data store could be a database but could also be a file, a messaging system like Kafka, Redis, or anything else that can house data. These two terms may be interchangeable in this chapter depending on the use case.

So, must we adhere to the rule that a microservice should own its own database? Many organizations have dedicated database administrators (DBAs), and they are not usually excited about another database to manage. It is not easy for a database to simply exist when dealing with availability, patching, logging, backups, capacity planning, security, and many other details. Adding more databases also adds to additional possibilities of failures and support calls.

Depending on the size of your architecture, you may be able to have microservices without decentralizing your database. But if this is true, why does the rule even exist? The reason is that at some point in the growth of microservices, you may be in a position where the schema needs of one microservice impact the needs of another microservice. Just as a monolith has grown over time with additional functionality and bug fixes, so do the data schemas. Code to handle the processing of an order must rely on the database and schema to properly manage that data. Over time, with changes to functionality, you may create new columns or additional tables. Consider also the changes to any stored procedures or functions. It can also be difficult to coordinate these changes across dev teams or maybe even third-party companies. If these changes impact the evolution of other microservices, then it becomes a clear indicator of the need to separate data to their respective microservices.

Each microservice exists to be the processor of their business functionality, their domain. Each microservice also needs to be the sole manager of the single source of truth, the data. This simplifies communication between teams to the microservice's API and frees the microservice developers to quickly evolve the data store to match the speed of developing the code.

Without the ability to manage the single source of truth, you risk losing data integrity. This means that if more than one application uses a database, you risk having incomplete data in various tables because the requirements and validations may not be the same in each application.

Database Choices

There is a huge advantage of having a separate database for a microservice. If, for example, your monolithic application uses SQL Server, and you build a new microservice for handling incoming telemetry data from field sensors. Having a separate database than what the monolithic application uses allows you to pick a different database type depending on the data modeling needs. You may consider using a time series database geared for temporal queries like Azure Table Storage for telemetry data processing because it stores nonrelational structured data.

For order data, it is possible to use a database system like Azure Cosmos DB. Azure Synapse or AWS Redshift might be preferred for a high volume of data with microservices that perform data analysis. The point is that you can choose different database types that best fit the processing needs of the data.

Availability

Every microservice has a chance of failure. This could be from a server host rebooting, a container rebooting, a bug in the code, network outage, or when the database becomes unreachable. No microservice can have 100% availability. We measure the availability of our system using "nines." If a system has four nines, it is 99.99% available as it uses four nines in the percentage description. Considering how many minutes are in a year – 525,600 – a system that has four nines of availability means it may have up to 52.56 minutes of downtime per year.

With microservices relying on other microservices, we get an understanding of the availability (see Figure 7-1). To get an overall calculation of the availability, multiply the percentage of each microservice. Here we would get 99.98% × 99.95% × 99.99% which equals 99.92% of availability.

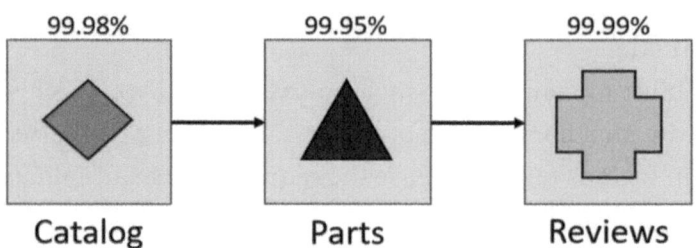

Figure 7-1. Example of availability

With microservices that are called in parallel, the method of calculation does not change (see Figure 7-2). Looking at the following microservices, we take the percent of availability of each microservice to 99.98% × 99.95% × 99.99% × 99.94%. This gives us a total availability of 99.86%.

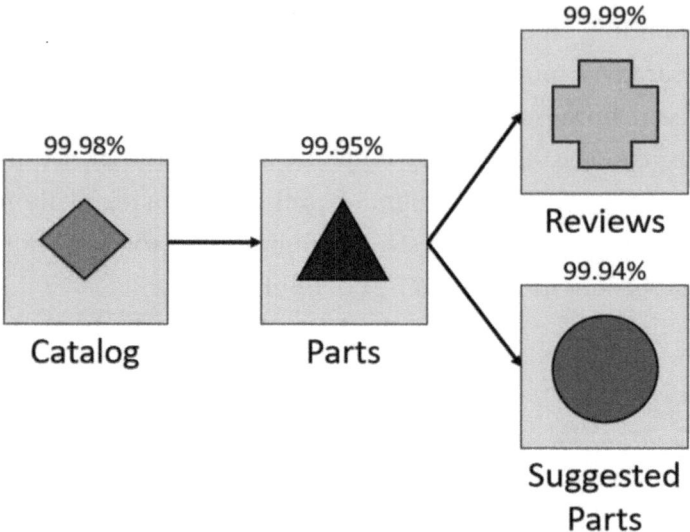

Figure 7-2. Example of availability with parallel execution

The opportunity of downtime must consider how and where you are hosting your microservices. Downtime occurring in data centers may take down more than one microservice and other dependent systems like databases and storage accounts. Systems like Kubernetes can help with some downtime issues. When a pod fails, Kubernetes attempts to create a new instance of that pod for resiliency.

Sharing Data

As we explore decentralizing the data to different databases, we quickly see a new issue.

There are other processes fulfilled by other microservices that still need data, but now from other microservices. Perhaps you have a shipping microservice that needs information about the order. How does it get that data?

One option is to simply have the shipping microservice call the order microservice to retrieve the necessary data (see Figure 7-3). This is a reasonable solution but not without its challenges. As microservices are calling each other to retrieve data, it is possible to have a rather chatty network. As the network calls increase, so could the latency. As the requests for data increase, so does the load on the related databases.

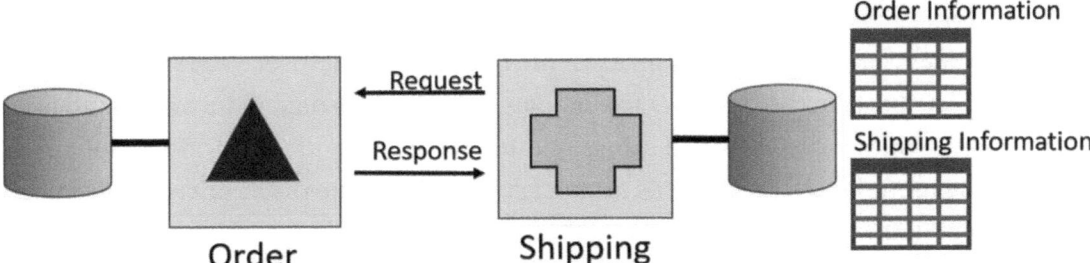

Figure 7-3. *Sharing data*

Consider one microservice that calls another microservice that must also call another. Each microservice call only adds to the latency, and the business processes have an increased opportunity of failing. Looking at Figure 7-4, if the call to the Reviews microservice takes 1.5 seconds, the Part microservice takes 2.1 seconds, and the Catalog microservice takes 2.4 seconds to execute, you have a total latency of six seconds. This should challenge your architectural decisions. Do the calls really need to be synchronous? Can the calls be done asynchronously?

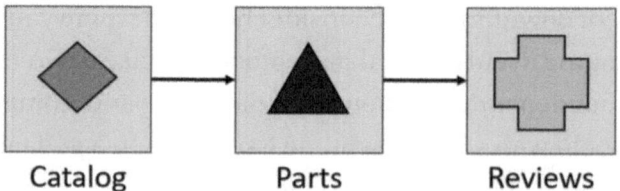

Figure 7-4. *Inline microservice calls*

Latency is not the biggest issue we have. It is something to consider, but what about handling the fact that now data is in two or more databases? How is that data kept in sync? Or perhaps we ask this differently. With business processes needing data to be in multiple databases, how do we keep the data consistent? When downtime occurs in one microservice but not another, what happens to the data consistency? We will cover this topic in the section for transactional consistency.

Duplicate Data

The other option is to duplicate data. That may sound absurd. It sounds absurd because database normalization rules suggest avoiding data duplication to reduce storage size and thus storage cost. So, why separate databases just to duplicate data later? This is not as bad as it seems at first. Consider an example of having a microservice for parts you sell online. The parts microservice is the manager of the parts data in its own database. It is the single source of truth for all things related to parts. As new parts are added or updated, the requests go through this microservice. What if the order microservice needs a copy of that data?

With the need for the order microservice to have a copy of the parts data, you also notice that it does not need every detail of the part. The following list is to convey the idea of a lot of detail that makes up a part of the parts microservice, which is the single source of truth database:

- Id
- Part number
- Name
- Description
- Category

- Classification
- Size description
- Color
- Container
- Manufacturer
- Manufacturer's part number
- Manufactured date
- Replaces part number
- Discontinued date

The order microservice needs a copy of the part information **but** only enough information to fulfill the requirements of an order. It does not need a copy of when a part was discontinued or when it was replaced. The order microservice only needs details about a part, such as a name and some description details. Now, in the order microservice database, there is a table for the part information. This list is an example of what details could be in this parts table to fulfill the needs of processing orders:

- Part Id
- Part number
- Name
- Description
- Size description
- Color

Now that there are some duplicate data across microservices, the next challenge is keeping the data in sync. For example, what if the application administrator fixes a typo in the description of a part? How does the duplicate information in the order microservice get updated? This is where using messaging helps (see Figure 7-5).

CHAPTER 7   DECENTRALIZING DATA

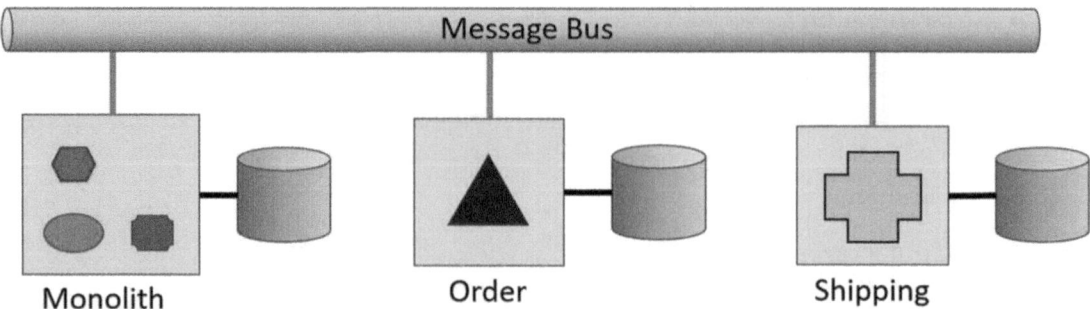

Figure 7-5. Example of an order system with messaging

A message of *OrderShippingAddressUpdated* is sent from the product microservice or in this case the monolith and processed by the shipping microservice as well as the order microservice (see Figure 7-6). The shipping microservice processes the update by finding the shipping address for the specified order in the database and applying the change. The order microservice can also process the message by searching its database for the specified order and correct the address.

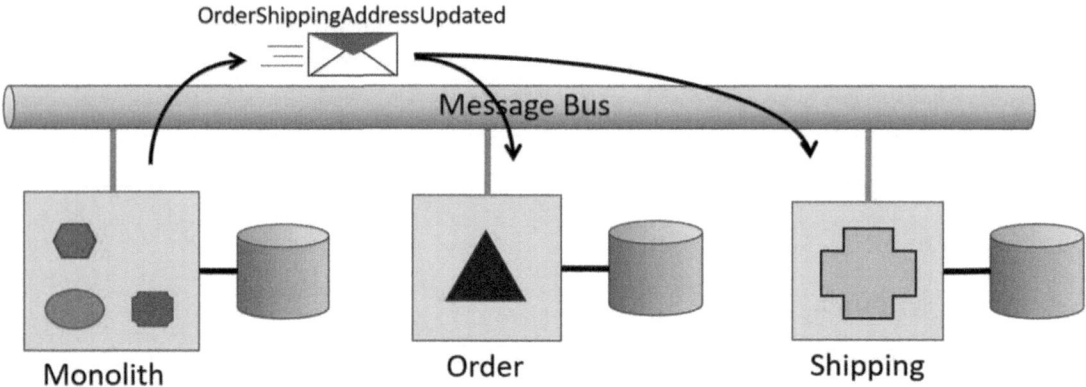

Figure 7-6. Messaging example

This is a simple way of keeping multiple microservices with some duplicate data in sync without requiring the microservices to be aware of each other. By keeping microservices unaware of each other, your architecture is loosely coupled and allows the microservices to continue to evolve independently.

Transactional Consistency

With a microservice architecture and decentralized data, we have big decisions to make on how to handle transactions. Monolithic applications with a central database generally rely on the database for handling how transactions are committed. These transactions have properties that are handled by the database to help ensure reliability. These are known as the ACID properties. ACID stands for Atomic, Consistent, Isolated, and Durable.

Transactions that are atomic will either commit the change completely or not at all. This helps ensure that the intended change is not partially committed. Consistency guarantees the intended change is not altered during the transaction. Isolation requires the transaction to not be altered by other transactions. The durability guarantee is so that the committed change remains in the system until another transaction occurs to change that data. This is for handling times when there is a system failure right after a transaction commits. For example, the committed change is saved and can survive a reboot.

With distributed systems like microservices, there is an increased chance of failures. Attempting to do distributed transactions across multiple microservices is difficult and adds transactional latency and many failure scenarios. With each possible type of failure, you have to build in compensating transactions. This complicates the architecture.

CAP Theorem

With data decentralized, we need to understand how to handle times when the database is unavailable for the related microservice. Eric Brewer created the CAP theorem that states it is impossible to provide more than two guarantees during a time of failure. The CAP theorem has three guarantees: **C**onsistency, **A**vailability, and **P**artition tolerance. Because microservices communicate over a network, we design them to handle the times when there is an issue on the network, known as partition tolerance. This means that if a microservice communication fails, it must handle that condition, such as using retry policies. Because network interruptions are easily possible, we must decide the behavior of microservices during those times.

This leaves us with the choice of Availability or Consistency. When we decide that a microservice should favor Availability, we are saying that it will continue being available for callers when the microservice cannot reach its database. When receiving a request for data, it will return the last known data even if it is out of date from what is in the database. Changes to data are cached, and when the connection is re-established to the database, it will sync up any changes.

The option of Consistency is for when the microservice must either return up-to-date information or an error. Consistency here is not the same as the consistency in the ACID guarantees. Consistency in ACID is about trusting the data is not altered during a transaction. The Consistency in CAP is about the data returned in a query during a network partition.

Consider a game application on a mobile device. If the application favors consistency, then when there is a network communication issue, the application does not continue working. However, if it favors availability, then it continues to operate with the last known information it has and synchronizes the data when the connection is restored.

Transactions Across Microservices

With the data decentralized, we need to analyze our business processes to understand their data needs and how best to keep the data in the various microservices consistent. We start by understanding the roles the microservice fulfills in these business processes. Some processes have activities that are sequential because of their dependency on a flow of committed transactions (see Figure 7-7). An example of a sequential process is an eCommerce purchase, billing, and shipping process. Shipping can't begin until the order is paid for.

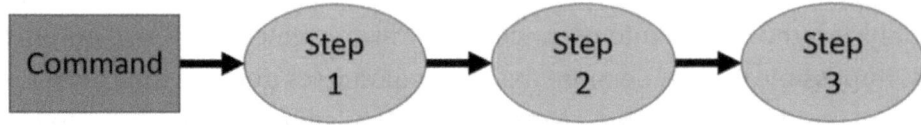

Figure 7-7. *Sequential business processes*

Other processes can be done in parallel, or a fan-out design, as their activities are not dependent on other transactions (see Figure 7-8). An example of a parallel process is a product page that also loads recommended products and advertising. The page can still load if these extra services are unavailable.

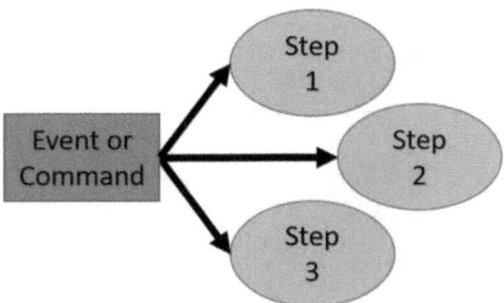

Figure 7-8. *Parallel activity*

The individual processes covered by the microservices still need to complete before the business process as a whole is considered complete. Regardless of choice to use sequential or fan-out design, the collection of transactions needs to be managed, so we understand when the business process is complete and, just as important, when they fail to complete. This maintainable collection of transactions is called a saga.

Sagas

A saga is a mechanism for managing potentially long-lived transactions in a distributed system. Depending on the processing needs of the transactions, you may choose one of three saga patterns to manage the transactions. The three patterns are Routing Slip, Choreography, and Orchestration.

Note that sagas do not provide atomicity across the transactions. Each microservice included in a saga has atomicity to their database but not across other databases (see Figure 7-9).

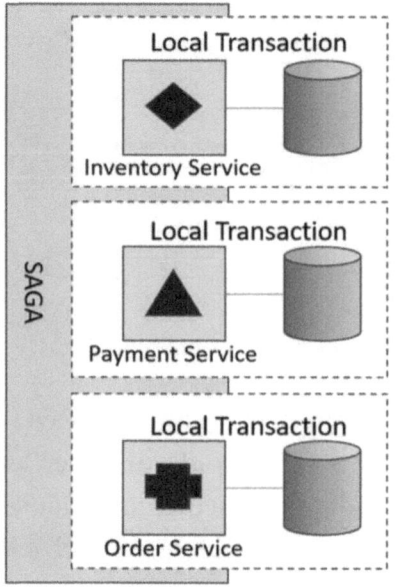

Figure 7-9. *Example of saga with local transactions*

A saga is not a distributed transaction. A distributed transaction holds a lock on resources across microservices and has a lot of issues when dealing with failure cases. Also, distributed transactions cannot tolerate a large time span like sagas. A saga is for coordinating a set of local transactions that may take fractions of a second to complete or potentially days depending on the business process needs and availability of microservices.

Routing Slip

When using the routing slip pattern, information passes from one microservice to another. As a microservice receives the routing slip, it acts accordingly based on the information provided, including storing information in its database. For an example of information in a routing slip, consider what it would take to make flight and cruise reservations. This approach is with the premise that you will make a cruise line reservation only after a flight reservation has successfully been completed. Consider the following questions that need to be answered to make these reservations:

CHAPTER 7 DECENTRALIZING DATA

- What day does the cruise leave the port?
- What time do you need to arrive at the port?
- When are you expected back?
- What flight arrangements need to be made?

Your application will obtain those answers and attempt to make those reservations. The routing slip contains information that is passed to each microservice. Each microservice contacts independent systems to create the reservations. The routing slip has those answers and includes what microservice is next in the call chain (see Figure 7-10).

Figure 7-10. Routing slip activities

If a microservice has an error, it updates the routing slip based on its information and sends it to the previous microservice. This way, each microservice knows if it is performing actions based on the forward progression or performing a compensating transaction (see Figure 7-11). The error condition could be from a required reservation not being made or an issue with the microservice itself. Each state of the transactions is kept with the routing slip.

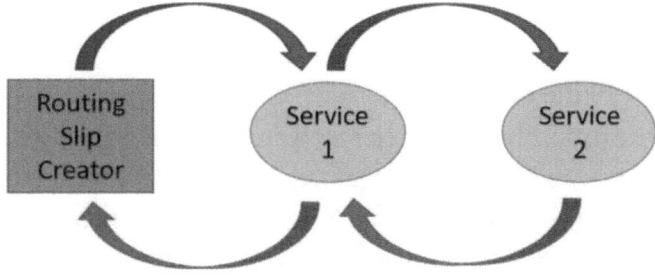

Figure 7-11. Routing slip error condition handling

CHAPTER 7   DECENTRALIZING DATA

The routing slip pattern is useful for sequential operations that require preconditions to be met. Although this example assumes the order of reservations, you should challenge if this pattern is the right one to use. Do you require a cruise ship reservation to be made before the flight reservation? What if the flight reservation comes first? Or can the operations be done in parallel? The next two patterns discuss how to handle operational needs in parallel.

Choreography

With choreography, the microservices communicate using events. As the operations complete, they send events with information about the succeeded transaction. Other microservices receive the events they subscribe to so they can perform their actions (see Figure 7-12).

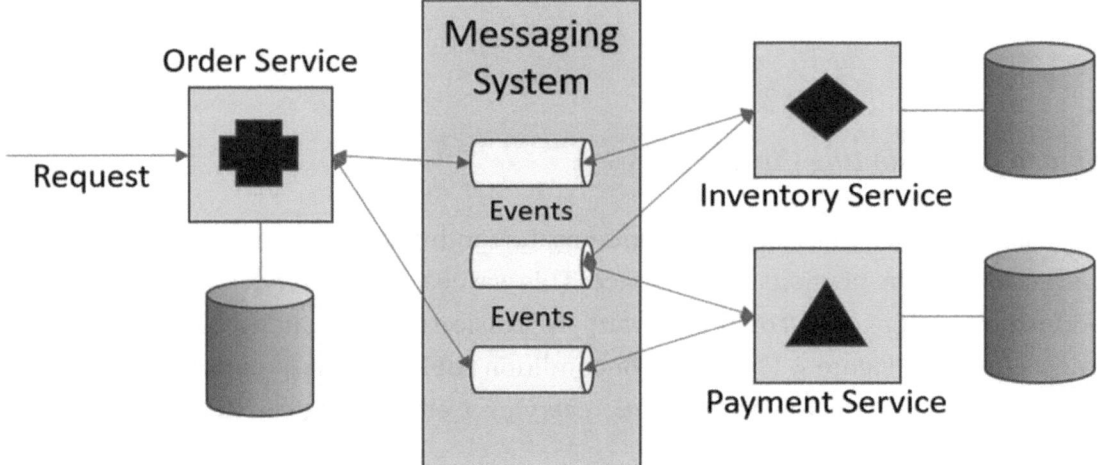

Figure 7-12. Choreography

With the example of the online order system, consider this flow of activity (see Figure 7-13). After the order microservice receives a command, it creates an order and saves it to its local database with Pending status. It then publishes an *OrderCreated* event. The inventory microservice consumes that event. If the inventory microservice validates the number of items on hand and successfully places a reserve on those items, it publishes an *ItemsReserved* event. The payment microservice consumes that message and attempts to process a payment. If the payment succeeds, the payment microservice publishes a *PaymentProcessed* event. The order microservice consumes that event and updates the status of the order accordingly.

CHAPTER 7 DECENTRALIZING DATA

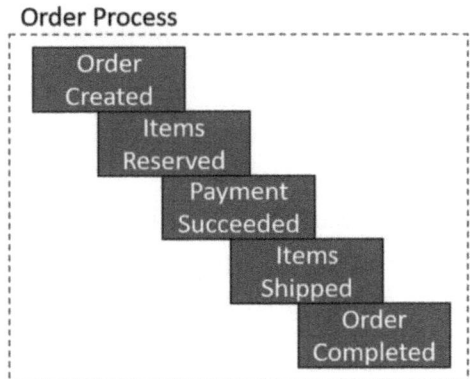

Figure 7-13. *Order creation process*

But what if there is a failure someplace in the process? Each microservice that plays a part in the business process may also need to have compensating transactions. Depending on the process and the reason for the need to revert a previous transaction, you might simply undo a change (see Figure 7-14). When payment has already been applied to a customer's credit card, you cannot undo the transaction. And it is best to leave a record that it occurred in the system. The compensating transaction then is to refund the charge amount. It is a new transaction but is also a record of history for audit needs.

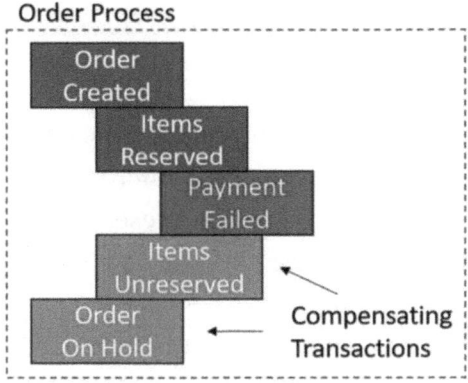

Figure 7-14. *Order process with compensating transactions*

Some processes may not need compensating transactions, nor are they required to restore data to a previous state. If there is a compensating transaction to change the count of an item in stock, it could be wrong as there could have been another transaction on the items during the processing of this order.

143

CHAPTER 7   DECENTRALIZING DATA

Orchestration

With orchestration, microservices are contacted using commands directly from the central process manager. Just like with choreographed sagas, the manager maintains the state of the saga.

Using the online order system example, the order microservice acts as the central controller, sometimes called the orchestrator (see Figure 7-15). As a request comes in, the order microservice issues a command directly to other microservices in turn as they process and complete their steps.

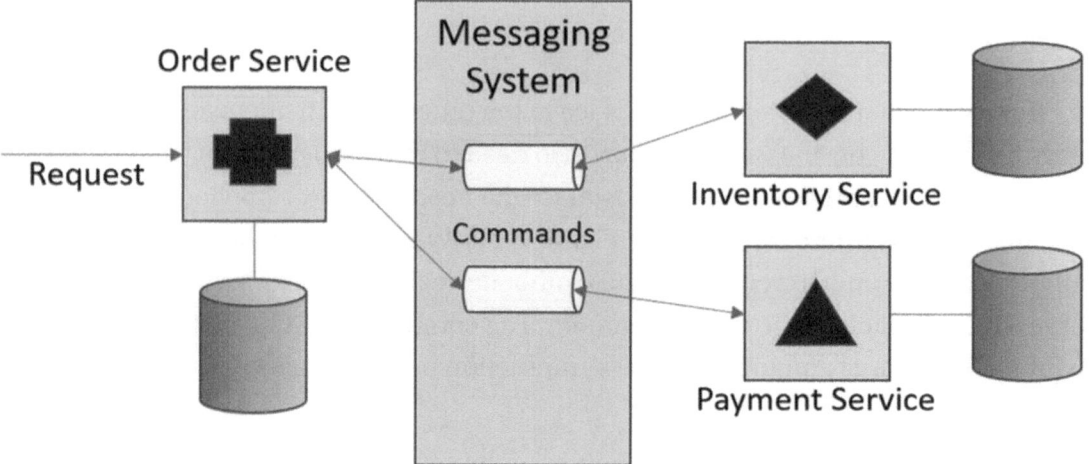

Figure 7-15. *Orchestration*

After creating and saving the order information to its database, the order microservice issues a command to the inventory microservice. The inventory microservice receives the command and places a reservation for the items. The order microservice then issues another command to the payment microservice. Payment is processed, and the order goes to shipping.

The ability to create compensating transactions also needs to be applied here. If the payment fails to process, a different reply is sent back to the order microservice. The order microservice then sends another command to the inventory microservice to release the reservation on the items. Then the order status is set to PaymentCorrectionNeeded.

CHAPTER 7 DECENTRALIZING DATA

CQRS

Some business processes have different data models for the writing vs. the reading. Consider the scenario of a system that receives telemetry data from devices in the field (see Figure 7-16). This data comes in from many devices several times per second. The data model used to write the data to a database is simple. It contains fields like pressure values of different sensors, battery voltage, and temperature. The data model also has properties like device Id, sensor Id, and a date/timestamp.

Retrieving the data is for a different purpose, so the read data model is vastly different than the write data model. The read data model includes computed values based on values from other fields as well as a rolling average. It also includes value offsets for calibration based on the Id of the device sending data. What is queried is different than what is written to the database. Because the write and read use vastly different data models, the design pattern Command Query Responsibility Segregation (CQRS) can be leveraged.

By splitting the microservice into two, you can have more dedicated resources for the data models. One microservice handles all the commands to insert data and stores them in a dedicated database. Another microservice is dedicated to the responsibilities of querying the data and computations needed, all from a different database. A very interesting piece to this pattern is that there are two databases.

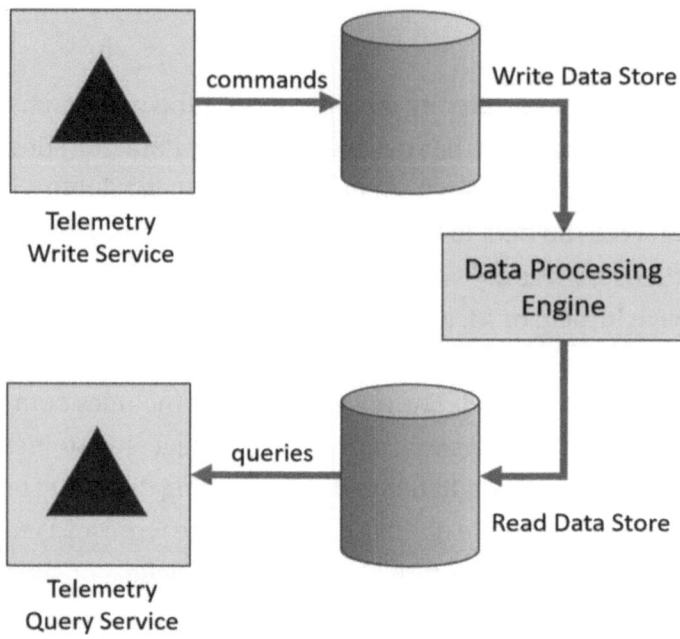

***Figure 7-16.** Example of CQRS with telemetry data*

Having two databases, you can have the database for writes be tuned for handling volumes of incoming data. The read database can be tuned with indexes to support retrieving the necessary data. It also does not have to be the same database type as the write database. Commands may come in as JSON documents, but the read database can be relational to store a materialized view of a cumulation of data.

There are a few benefits of using CQRS. Security is applied differently for the data models. You can scale the microservices independently. And there is a separation of complexity between the microservices.

The challenge now is getting data from the write database to the read database. There are multiple ways of doing this. Depending on your needs, this can be done with log shipping, data streams, messaging, or even another microservice. Because the read database is separate from the write database, the data may be behind or stale. You must be able to handle eventual consistency. With eventual consistency, the data in a database or database cluster will become consistent at a later time. Business processes are affected by this and will need to have procedures to handle those conditions.

The CQRS pattern, much like the event sourcing pattern, should not be everywhere. It should not be used if your data model or business processing needs are simple. If CRUD-like operations will suffice, then that is more likely the better option.

CHAPTER 7 DECENTRALIZING DATA

Event Sourcing

Most relational database designs only store the current value. Updates occur to replace data, and the previous value is not automatically retained (see Figure 7-17). Building on the previous example, a typo is fixed in a record for the shipping address (see Figure 7-18). The new value replaces the current value. For most applications, this model of operations is fine. But for some business processes, this model of handling data lacks required additional details.

Order Id	Customer Id	Creation Date Stamp	Payment Terms	Shipping Address	...
24156	10232	20170531163456	30 Days	123 Any Sreet ...	

Figure 7-17. Example of record with typo in shipping address

Order Id	Customer Id	Creation Date Stamp	Payment Terms	Shipping Address	...
24156	10232	20170531163456	30 Days	123 Any Street ...	

Figure 7-18. Example of record after typo fixed

Event sourcing is a design pattern for persisting data changes instead of data state. In relational terms, we're storing the transaction log instead of the data rows. It can be used to store the events that affect items like an order, invoice, or a customer's account. Events like *OrderCreated* and *OrderStatusUpdated* are stored so that the events can be replayed to get the current value. This allows for history to be kept with objects at all times. This is not just a history of changes to an order but is also proof of how an order got to the latest state. By using event sourcing, you have the records needed for processes that must adhere to regulation and compliance mandates. Data should never be directly updated or deleted. Instead, to delete a record, use a "soft delete" that sets a property in your data to signal that is to be considered by your application as a deleted record. This way, you still have the history of events.

The entries stored are the events that have happened to the state of the objects. The events are essentially domain events. In Domain-Driven Design (DDD), the domain events are noted as past tense. This is because they are events as opposed to commands.

The event payload is the key to each change of state. As each event occurs, you store the payload. That payload could be a simple JSON document that has just enough detail to support the event. For example, this JSON document has an event type of *OrderCreated*. It also has the details about the initial state of the order.

```
{
  "Event":{
    "Type":"OrderCreated",
    "Details":{
      "OrderId":1234,
      "CustomerId":98765,
      "Items":[
      "Item1":{
         "ProductId":"ABC123",
         "Description":"WhizBang Thing",
         "UnitPrice":35.99
          }
       ]
     }
   }
}
```

Before the customer pays for their order, they add another item.

```
{
  "Event":{
    "Type":"ItemsAdded",
    "Details":{
      "Items":[
       {
        "ProductId":"FOO837",
         "Description":"Underwater Basket Weaving Kit",
         "UnitPrice":125.99
         }
        ]
      }
    }
}
```

The event payload of the new item does not contain the other item in the order. It only has the details of an item to add to the order. The shipping and taxes can also be applied.

```
{
  "Event":{
    "Type":"ShippingAmountApplied",
    "Details":{
      "OrderId":1234,
      "Amount":15.00
    }
  }
}
{
  "Event":{
    "Type":"TaxAmountApplied",
    "Details":{
      "OrderId":1234,
      "Amount":7.58
    }
  }
}
```

Now the customer attempts to make a payment, but it fails. The event is also captured.

```
{
  "Event":{
    "Type":"PaymentFailed",
    "Details":{
      "OrderId":1234,
      "TransactionId":837539
    }
  }
}
```

Perhaps the customer makes a partial payment. They could pay from a gift card that does not have enough balance to pay the whole amount.

```
{
  "Event":{
    "Type":"PartialPaymentApplied",
    "Details":{
      "OrderId":1234,
      "Amount":10.00,
      "TransactionId":837987
    }
  }
}
```

Then the customer applies another payment.

```
{
  "Event":{
    "Type":"PartialPaymentApplied",
    "Details":{
      "OrderId":1234,
      "Amount":174.56,
      "TransactionId":838128
    }
  }
}
```

Figure 7-19 shows an example of a table that stores events on orders. The details and amount fields are data pulled from the event body. Separating data like this can help the read process when calculating a total. Notice that the order ID is used as a correlation ID. This allows you to query for the order ID and get all related change entries.

Event	Order ID	Details	Amount
OrderCreated	1234	Order	0.00
ItemsAdded	1234	Items...	35.99
ItemsAdded	1234	Items...	125.99
ShippingAmountApplied	1234	Shipping	15.00
TaxAmountApplied	1234	Tax	7.58
PaymentFailed	1234	Payment	184.56
PartialPaymentApplied	1234	Payment	10.00
PartialPaymentApplied	1234	Payment	174.56
ItemsShipped	1234	Inventory	
OrderCompleted	1234	Order	

Figure 7-19. Records of order activity

Event sourcing is great for processes handling financial transactions, medical records, and even information for lawsuits. Anything that needs a track record of change might be a candidate for this pattern of data handling. However, this pattern is not for everything, and you may be headed toward overengineering. If a process does not need state change tracking, then the event sourcing pattern may not serve you as well as you would like. Also, you may see an increase in data storage cost with event sourcing.

Scenarios

Another benefit of event sourcing is how it can offset the role of the system. It is no longer in charge of the state of the data. Instead, a person is in charge. The system receives all events and also provides a report noting missing events. The following scenarios help explain some uses of event sourcing.

Scenario 1

Using an inventory management system, a person loading a truck scans a box before putting it on a truck. The system says the box does not exist. The person has to stop what they are doing and find a way to have the box entered into the system. The state of the object must be corrected before it can be placed on the truck. But the box does exist!

With event sourcing, the event of scanning the box and placing it on a truck continues even if the box is believed not to exist. The event is still captured in the system, and an additional entry is sent to an exception report. This allows people to manage the state of an object without stopping the flow of business.

This also shows another condition. You may have an event of a box being scanned before the event that it exists. Now that an administrator has added the item to the system, an event is created. That event of creation is in the database after the event of the box being placed on a truck. Having a creation event after an activity event is tolerable. For one, it shows that there was an issue that a person had to fix. You could also have specific events to have a sequence number prior to other events. Then your timestamps are in order for evidence tracking. And queries will show the order based on a sequence number.

Scenario 2

The items in the box from scenario 1 are for an order on an online system. The online system sold the items to the customer, but the items were not in stock. The order was able to take place without the inventory in stock. The order event triggered a process to get the items to fulfill the order. The order system did not need to act on a true count of the items in inventory.

The idea of selling an item that could be out of stock is a matter of policy and not architecture. This allows people to decide how to handle such events. For example, one policy could be to alert the customer that the items are delayed, and they can cancel the order. Another option is to expedite shipping from a different warehouse to the customer. The business gets to decide how to handle the events.

Eventual Consistency

So many things in the world around us are eventually consistent. Actions like deposits and debits to our bank accounts, to sports scores as the changes are sent to scorekeepers and reporters, etc., are examples of events that are eventually made consistent over time. As much as we may want a deposit made immediately available once it hits the account, most systems do operate with the emphasis on availability over consistency. If we design our microservices architecture with the expectation of strong consistency, then we risk terrible latency. This is because the microservices are independent applications communicating over a network. Most of the time, everything is working fine, and there are no delays in achieving consistency. We must design our systems for when those times of delay occur.

What does it mean to have eventual consistency instead of strong consistency? A microservice using a transaction to its own database may use strong consistency. This means that every node in the database cluster must meet a quorum and agree on the change. Again, most of the time, this is fine. However, because some database systems use nodes, there is a chance of issues. Then, a quorum may not be met, and the transaction is rejected. What if you are using a database in the cloud and it is multiregional? Using strong consistency may require a quorum to be met on multiple nodes in different regions. This only adds latency.

Must the changed data be immediately readable? This is the challenge. Writing data to multiregional systems is allowed to take the time it needs when the changed data is not expected to be read immediately. When the need to read the changed data is a bit relaxed, you are better off with eventual consistency. Going back to the example of the bank account, it uses eventual consistency. You may be able to query the database and see the deposit. But other systems related to the transaction may not see the change immediately.

If you queried the order database directly with an online order system, you would see the new order. But the report microservice may not have that data yet. So, some reports and dashboards are seconds or minutes behind. Depending on some processes, it may be the following day before a report is created reflecting the previous day's events.

For microservices to attempt strong consistency, they have to make synchronous API calls to each other. This requires each microservice to complete its steps before the next microservice can proceed. This not only increases latency but also has a higher failure rate. Anything that stops a microservice instance from completing a task will cause a failure the caller must handle. This also includes error conditions such as invalid data, bugs in code, or an unknown condition.

Leveraging the asynchronous messaging patterns mentioned earlier, you can provide eventual consistency across microservices. This allows microservices to process as soon as they can without the dependency of another service. By allowing eventual consistency, microservices can stay loosely coupled without demanding unnecessary restraints.

CHAPTER 7   DECENTRALIZING DATA

Data Warehouse

Some companies use a data warehouse, sometimes referred to as Data Lake, to store massive amounts of data, or "Big Data." This data comes from many different sources and allows for differing data models to be stored for varied purposes. A data warehouse is a collection of data stores for storing massive amounts of data that do not have to be the same type (see Figure 7-20).

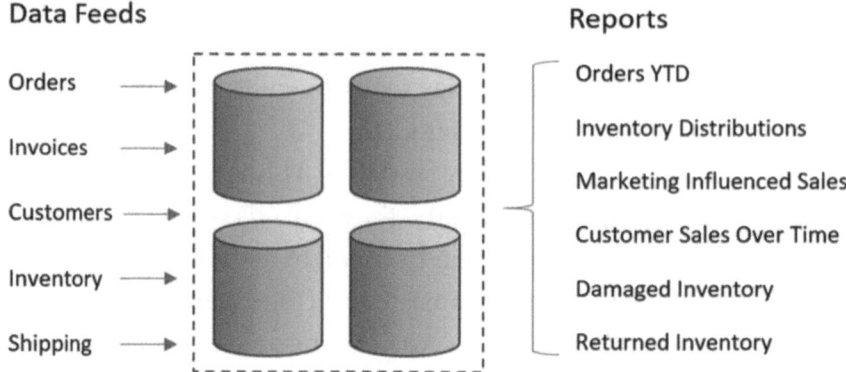

Figure 7-20. *Example of multiple data feeds*

Data warehouses allow companies to collect data both for historical compliances and for reporting. SQL Server is an Online Transactional Processing (OLTP) type database system. The main purpose is for handling normalized data in transactions using ACID properties. The Online Analytical Processing (OLAP) type database system stores denormalized data for analytics, data mining, and business intelligence applications.

With the locking nature of most OLTP database systems, it is best never to use them as a source for reports. The massive reads on those databases have locks that can interfere with write activities. Instead, the data should be copied and any conversions applied in an OLAP database system. This allows for data processing to be done on other servers without impeding transactions. It also allows for data to be retrieved and utilized with different data models than what was used when the data was written.

You can use Extract, Transform, Load (ETL) tools such as Azure Data Factory, Microsoft SQL Server Integration Services (SSIS), and Informatica PowerCenter for moving and transforming data to an OLAP database.

CHAPTER 7 DECENTRALIZING DATA

ETL tools can be used for pulling data into a data warehouse, but it is also possible for data to be sent instead. As a microservice is writing data to a database, it can also send that data on a message bus that is received by an endpoint in the data warehouse.

Patterns like CQRS can be used to feed data warehouse solutions. Having a data warehouse provides a separation of databases used by microservices (see Figure 7-21). The data in the data warehouse can now be leveraged in many various ways. One of which is a way of combining data from multiple sources into a materialized view.

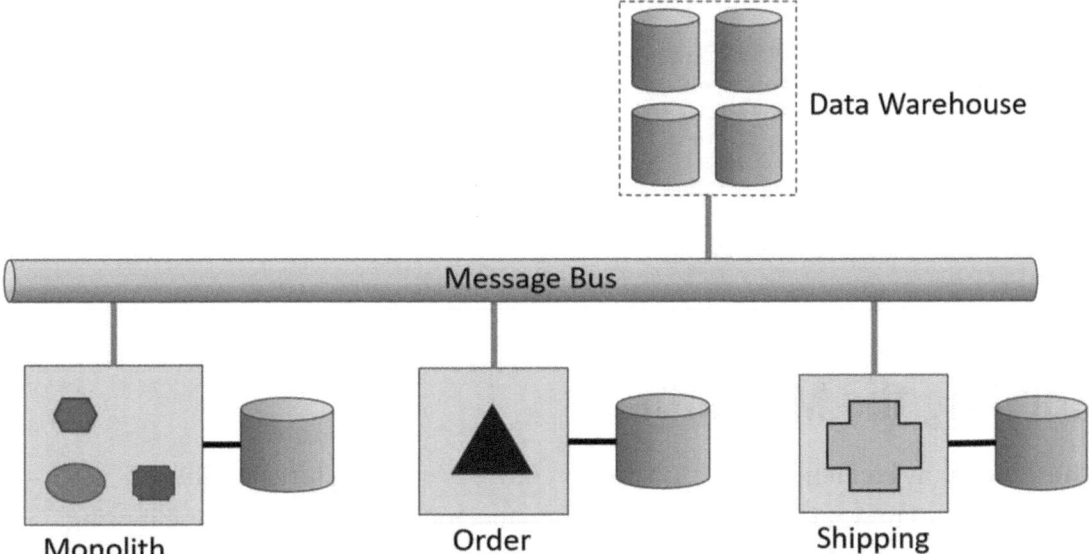

Figure 7-21. *Microservices architecture using a data warehouse*

Materialized View

A materialized view is a way of viewing data that differs from the way it is stored. But it is more than a way of viewing data. Using materialized views allows for showing raw data as well as any computed data based on those values. Materialized views are meant to be rebuilt from a data source and never modified by the applications.

Materialized views allow applications to retrieve predefined views of data (see Figure 7-22). This helps with performance and adaptability. These materialized views can be used for reporting and dashboards. The data could be sales vs. forecasted sales for the month or year. It can help see sales trend lines. Even the ability to how well customers are able to use your application can benefit future changes.

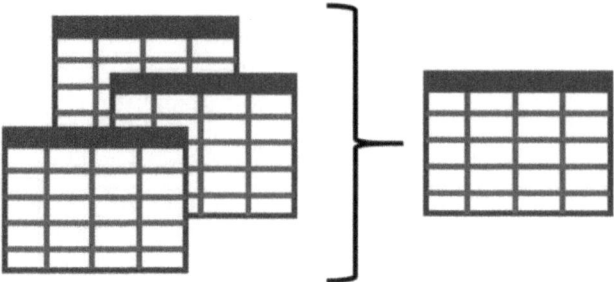

Figure 7-22. Materialized view

Splitting the Monolith

There are many challenging details when it comes to splitting functionality out of a monolith to a new microservice. Every challenge may make you question if using microservices is the right approach. So, where should we begin?

Let us start with the approach that the code has not yet separated from a monolith. With so much infrastructure to put in place for even the smallest code base to be a microservice, start small. You should consider putting in place a Continuous Integration/Continuous Deployment (CI/CD) pipeline for code releases. A team of developers dedicated to managing the requirements, coding standards, tests, and bugs should also be in place first. Even testing strategies (discussed in Chapter 8) need to be thought out and implemented. No matter the size of the code you intend to pull from a monolith without infrastructure in place, you will have a much harder time developing and managing the microservice. If you find that even with the smallest code things are not working for you, reconsider if microservices is the correct approach.

CHAPTER 7 DECENTRALIZING DATA

Moving Code

One approach to developing a microservice from a monolith is starting with code. You do some analysis to find what code really needs to be pulled out. If you are pulling out the functionality for accounting, you must find where other code in the monolith is using that domain functionality. By identifying what other code is using accounting functionality, you can list the areas where refactoring is required. Instead of calling the accounting code in memory, it must now call the microservice by either an HTTP API or with messaging. For the examples here, we will assume the use of HTTP API.

The monolith now calls the accounting microservice by the API. This is in the right direction, but the microservice is still tied to the same database used by the monolith (see Figure 7-23). As discussed earlier in this chapter, staying in this position will allow for contention of the schema changes and challenge data integrity. And there are likely other parts of the monolith that are using tables that the accounting microservice will need once extracted. The accounting microservice needs to be the single source of truth of the accounting data.

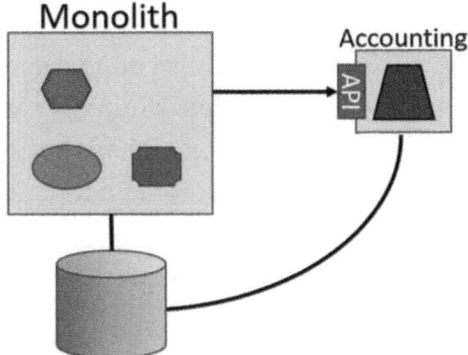

Figure 7-23. Monolith sharing database with single microservice

Another problem is also presented here. The accounting functionality may require contacting other domain functionality that is still in the monolith (see Figure 7-24). In this case, we add an API to the monolith for the accounting microservice to call. We now have a circular reference that should otherwise be avoided. However, this is one of those migration steps that can buy you time. Having this circular reference helps to get the accounting microservice developed as well as highlighting areas for change that might otherwise never be identified. This position is tolerable **if** this is not the final state. Do not go to production with this position unless you have a solid plan to continue the migration in the next sprint.

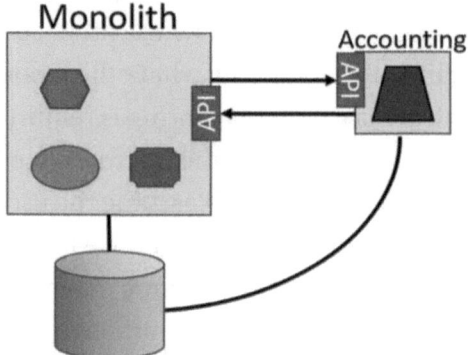

Figure 7-24. Accounting microservice calls back to monolith

Having a new API to the monolith only adds complexity to the architecture and is more to manage. And circular dependencies should always be avoided. It is only mentioned here as it is a reasonable migration step to get you to a solid architecture. Going through this development highlights tightly coupled code and allows you to attempt to refactor to be more loosely coupled. Ultimately, you want to be in a position where the accounting microservice is not reliant on code in the monolith (see Figure 7-25). You may have to further segregate domain functionality and leave some in the monolith. For example, if functionality for accounts payable cannot be refactored well, then split the microservice even further. Perhaps you have a microservice just for handling accounts receivable business processes.

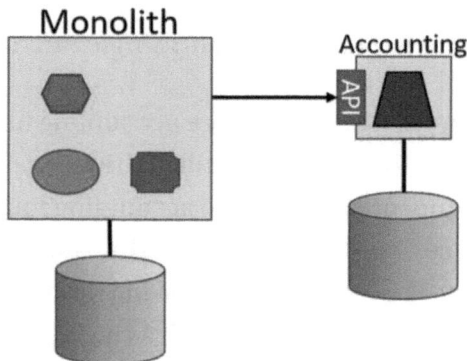

Figure 7-25. Accounting microservice with its own database

Strangler Pattern

The strangler pattern is useful for refactoring code to a microservice. You start by adding an interception layer between the caller and the accounting code (see Figure 7-26). The interception layer you create can direct the calls to either the functionality still in the monolith or redirect to call the microservice. As you migrate additional functionality to the accounting microservice, the interception layer code is updated to redirect calls accordingly.

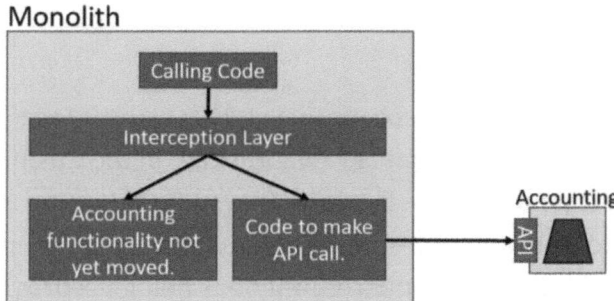

Figure 7-26. *Strangler pattern using interception layer*

Feature Flags

An option to consider that controls the flow of processes is feature flags (also known as feature toggle). With feature flags, the execution of code in the monolith is governed by the settings of the individual flags you set up. The settings for the flags are usually in configuration files. They can also be set using values you place in a database. One product of feature flags to check out is LaunchDarkly.[1]

Splitting the Database

We went over several details about how to handle data transactions and different data storage models. Now for another challenge, splitting apart a database. For this section, we are going to assume the monolith is using a relational database like SQL Server. Looking at Figure 7-27, there is a table for shipments and another table for accounting that has a final amount for a round-trip shipment.

---

[1] https://launchdarkly.com

CHAPTER 7 DECENTRALIZING DATA

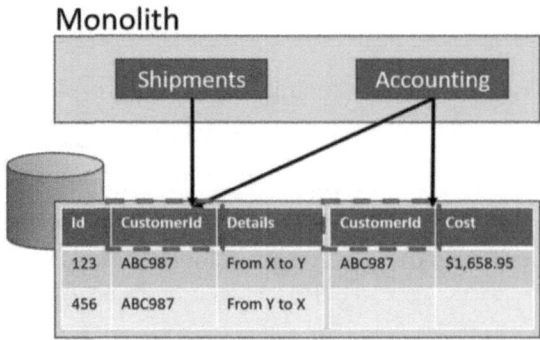

Figure 7-27. *Analyzing data*

From the image, we can see the accounting code is using information from two tables. These two tables have a foreign key relationship on the CustomerId column. The accounting department may use this information for reporting current sales per customer or month-to-date and year-to-date reports. What is not shown is how the data is managed. Are there stored procedures or functions being used? What about an Object Relational Mapper (ORM) like Entity Framework? Since the attempt is going to be to move accounting functionality to a microservice, that code needs to have the accounting data under its control. This helps with data integrity management.

We know the accounting table will move to the database for the accounting microservice. We need to identify the foreign key constraints, stored procedures, and functions using the connected tables. To find the stored procedures that use a table by name, use the following command:

```
SELECT Name
FROM sys.procedures
WHERE OBJECT_DEFINITION(OBJECT_ID) LIKE '%TableNameToFind%'
```

To find functions that include the table name:

```
SELECT
    ROUTINE_NAME,
    ROUTINE_DEFINITION ,
    ROUTINE_SCHEMA,
    DATA_TYPE,
    CREATED
```

```
FROM INFORMATION_SCHEMA.ROUTINES
WHERE ROUTINE_TYPE = 'FUNCTION'
AND ROUTINE_DEFINITION LIKE '%TableNameToFind%'
```

To find tables that have a foreign key relationship to a specified table:

```
SELECT
    OBJECT_NAME(f1.parent_object_id) TableName,
    COL_NAME(fc1.parent_object_id,fc1.parent_column_id) ColName
FROM
    sys.foreign_keys AS f1
INNER JOIN
    sys.foreign_key_columns AS fc1
        ON f1.OBJECT_ID = fc1.constraint_object_id
INNER JOIN
    sys.tables t
        ON t.OBJECT_ID = fc1.referenced_object_id
WHERE
    OBJECT_NAME (f1.referenced_object_id) = 'TableNameHere'
```

Kathy, the Code Whiz developer, has been hard at work understanding the existing database structure and data models. She used the queries shown earlier to help identify the connected resources to determine if there are supporting tables that need to move with the accounting table. Kathy created a map of the tables specific to the accounting functionality. She then added to the map the resources that had a relationship to the accounting tables.

Kathy noted the direction of the dependencies (see Figure 7-28). Some tables need information from accounting objects. Some tables were used by the accounting objects. As Kathy identifies the dependencies, she is able to analyze further if there is data that should be copied to the database for the accounting microservice. This is possible using the knowledge you learned in the previous section on sharing and duplicating data.

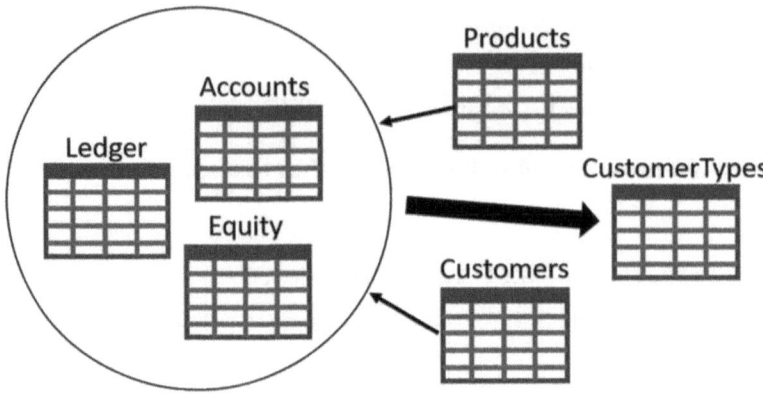

Figure 7-28. *Direction of data dependencies*

Much more information can be found on splitting monoliths to microservices at https://www.amazon.com/gp/product/B081TKSSNN.

Summary

Decentralizing data is far from easy and plays a critical role in the evolution of architecture. As you learned in this chapter, there may be a point where applications using the same tables and schema need to have their own databases. This does not mean separate database servers though. By having separate databases, the applications are in more control of the data integrity. Also, it allows you to choose a different database type based on your needs.

You also learned that it is permissible to have duplicate data in various databases. This allows for microservices to work autonomously with just enough information to fulfill the needs of business processes.

We also went over handling data transactions distributed across microservices. As business processes span microservices, local transactions are used to manage changes in data. Managing a collection of transactions may involve the patterns like routing slip and sagas.

You learned about using the CQRS pattern when the write model differs greatly from the read model. This model difference and processing needs may impact performance, so splitting the responsibilities into a write microservice and another for reads provides a clean way of handling the data requirements.

Event sourcing was shown as a pattern of storing data where you do not store the current value but a collection of events. The collection of events can be queried, and the values computed to obtain the latest known values up to that time. This is useful when processes need to keep proof of how the state of data changed over time.

We also went over how eventual consistency is used instead of strong consistency. Allowing different systems to get the latest state change at a later time provides systems with more availability.

Then we touched on how some companies use data warehouses and materialized views based on data that came from other sources. This allows the growing changes to how data is read and reported on from impacting the performance of the microservices.

You also learned some ideas to split code from a monolith with the strangler pattern and feature flags. The best way for you is only known after you try them to which pattern best fits your scenarios. Splitting up a database to allow data to move to another database to be owned by a microservice is just as tedious as splitting code. So, you learned ways of looking for stored procedures and functions that use a table by name. Also, you learned how to identify foreign key constraints.

CHAPTER 8

Testing Microservices

Kathy, the developer at Code Whiz, has made a few microservices and is concerned with proving they work as expected. She knows that the microservices are crucial for their client Hyp-Log, our hypothetical company in this book. Kathy looks at the various ways of testing microservices.

This chapter will go over why testing is important, what to test and what not to test, and various approaches to testing. We will also build an example of contract testing for REST-based communication. Then we build tests for messaging-based microservices.

Remember that each microservice is an independent application deserving of all the attention as any other application. A microservice has a focus on domain functionality. And they are pieces of a larger architectural solution. As such, these microservices have testing requirements just like any other application. However, they have more testing requirements because they are interconnected to form a bigger picture of that architectural solution.

The development of microservices adds complexity to the architecture. It allows bugs not to be found until much later in the development process or after deploying to the production environment. And these bugs are costly.

Cost of Errors

Testing plays a crucial and often underrated role in software development. Too often, we are required to rush code development only to have errors in understanding what the business/users need and how we implement those needs. For Kathy and the other developers at Code Whiz, this is no exception.

> **Note** You should build tests throughout the development of any application. Test-Driven Development (TDD) is a highly recommended methodology to consider.

Numerous studies prove that the cost of fixing a bug grows exponentially from time of gathering requirements to when found in production. It is cheaper to identify and fix bugs as early as possible in the software development life cycle.

The cost of fixing bugs is not only monetary but also in the loss of confidence. If you hire a contractor to add an electrical outlet and it randomly functions, you would be rather upset. If you buy a new car and it breaks down after a month, you would be upset as well. We require quality effort from others. That requirement applies to software development as well. Does that mean perfection every time? No, but it does mean we are to give our best attempt.

The role of microservices in a distributed architecture increases the likelihood of bugs inadvertently getting into the code. Given the additional complexity of a microservices architecture, the cost of these bugs is much more than an N-tier style application. The cost only adds the need for not only more testing but also more types of testing. Before we talk about testing details, let us first go over some items that do not need testing.

What Not to Test

There is so much to test with any system to verify accuracy, performance, and overall quality. However, there are some things that testing would be a waste of time. Instead of creating a test to verify an external system/dependency exists, write tests that prove your code is handling the times when a connection to a system is expected but fails.

Other things you should not test are items like the .NET Framework. The .NET Framework is already well tested before release. Though that does not make it bug-free, it removes the need for you to test it. Testing the .NET Framework is like testing the frame of a new car before buying. Generally, we test the car operates well without proving it will hold on to all the tires. The caveat to this is that when you are learning something about a framework or library, testing is a fantastic way to learn.

What to Test

As important as it is for us to test our code, we must test in appropriate ways and at the right time. A microservice does not exist alone. It is part of an architecture for specific business purposes, meaning testing is required at multiple layers of code and from multiple perspectives. Testing microservices includes not only testing the code but also performance as well as handling failures.

Code

In the book *Succeeding with Agile,* Mike Cohn presents a test pyramid (see Figure 8-1). The pyramid depicts various layers of testing with an emphasis on the number of tests. The bottom of the pyramid is the widest part, suggesting more unit tests than other test types. Above that is the service test and at the top is User Interface (UI) test. These are sometimes called end-to-end (E-to-E) tests and usually require human execution.

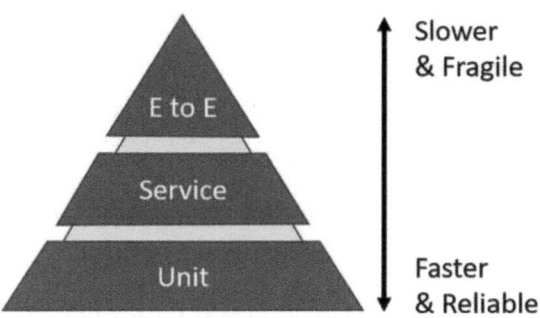

Figure 8-1. Testing pyramid

Others have added to the pyramid, noting that not only are there more unit tests than service tests and E-to-E tests, but they also expect the cheapest execution cost. That is, they are easier to automate and can be run repeatedly throughout the day. The tests at the top of the pyramid are the most expensive. They are hard to automate and generally take a lot of time and resources of people.

Performance

Each microservice is purpose built to solve various problems with business processes. So, knowing how they fulfill their responsibilities for those business processes is as important as knowing they are stable and performant.

After the microservices are working and accurate, then consider making them performant. It does not matter how fast any code runs to a wrong answer. Make it work, make it accurate, and then make it fast.

There are several metrics to consider when evaluating the performance of microservices architecture. The following list provides a few metrics to consider when gauging the health of the microservices. More details are in Chapter 10 addressing cross-cutting concerns.

- CPU/RAM – Is the microservice showing signs there is a need to scale the number of instances? Perhaps you need to provide more CPU or RAM for the microservice instance.

- Network connections – Is the microservice handling new requests and responsive?

- Messaging – How many messages can be processed in a given time period?

- Rate limiting – You may need to consider rate-limiting access to the microservices. Products like Azure API Management and AWS API Gateway provide rate-limiting options.

- The number of errors/exceptions/retries – Ensure you are logging information and seeing the error count over time.

- Capturing metrics to bill a customer – You may need to add another microservice to receive custom information about business processes that you can use to bill your customers.

System Failure Handling

During the transition from a monolithic architecture to a full microservices architecture, Netflix created some Open Source Software (OSS) packages. One of which is Chaos Monkey (https://github.com/Netflix/chaosmonkey). Chaos Monkey can be used to randomly turn off virtual machines or containers, which provides the challenge of making sure you add in resilience handling protective measures. You can run Chaos Monkey in your test environment, but you can also run it in your production environment. Because there is always a chance of a virtual machine or container going away, the architecture must handle those scenarios. Running Chaos Monkey in your production environment guarantees those system-level failures will occur. Have you prepared for those situations? How well are you expecting the unexpected?

Security

Imagine that you have developed a microservice to process payroll functionality. And further, imagine that this microservice will process your paycheck. Attention to detail increases, and you strive for the best code development. But what about security?

Assumedly, the microservices will exist on a private network. And you are sure that no public traffic can get to the microservice. However, incoming traffic is not the only problem here. It is common to use third-party public NuGet packages, but do we ever review the code in that package? We must protect microservices from the traffic coming into the network and traffic going out that is not warranted. Unwanted code can sniff the network and attempt to send information to an external site. And that code could be in another microservice. Consider reviewing the recommendations by the OWASP organization (https://owasp.org/www-project-top-ten).

Using a service mesh like Istio (https://istio.io) provides a way to secure traffic between microservices. A service mesh may help keep the communication encrypted/secure and should be used even on a private network. Now that you have made a microservice that processes your paycheck, you need also to control who can call it. Just having a microservice available on the network allows it to be callable by anyone. But by using Istio, you can also control the authorization on microservices. Now, only the permitted caller can reach sensitive information provided by a microservice.

Testing Levels

A modified test pyramid shows more explicit layers where microservices interact (see Figure 8-2). The following image is the pyramid revised for use with testing microservices. It has six levels as opposed to the original three levels. The pyramid test levels are Unit, Integration, Component, Contract, Service, and End-to-End (E to E).

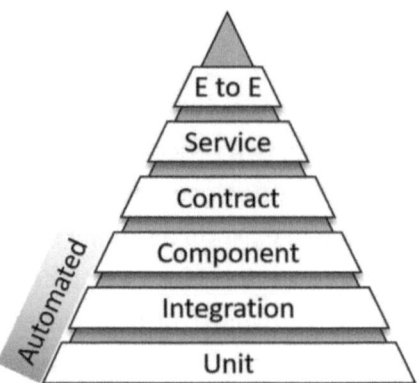

Figure 8-2. Extended testing pyramid

Unit Testing

The unit tests should be automated and run against code that is the smallest piece of independent business logic (see Figure 8-3). These tests are for verifying the accuracy of an algorithm, for example, a method that takes in various information and returns a tax rate. Is the tax rate correct? Is the calculation correct every time with the same information? If not, then you probably have a factor, like time, that is changing.

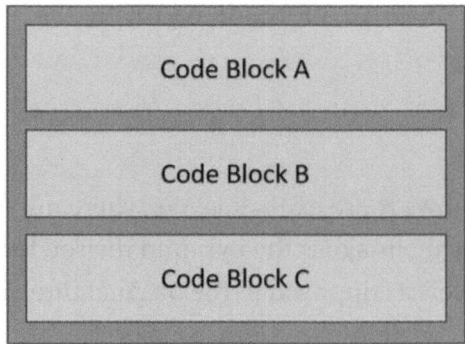

Figure 8-3. Code blocks

Unit tests have fast execution time compared to the other testing types on the pyramid. And unit tests should not connect to any other code module or third-party systems like a database, file, or messaging system.

You can prove that the code at the most basic level is performing accurately by having unit tests. It also helps to prove your understanding of the business requirements. If you have misunderstood a requirement, then the tests will help show that given certain conditions, the answer is wrong, and something needs to change.

Unit tests should not test logic that resides outside of the boundary of the algorithm. For example, testing an algorithm for tax rates does not test for connections to a database or other outside systems. Testing processes that rely on code external to itself are integration tests.

Integration Testing

Integration tests are for code blocks connected to a resource either in another module or an external system like a database, file, or messaging system (see Figure 8-4). Tests here are for algorithms that work with other algorithms. These other methods may be in another class. In those cases, you see class dependencies.

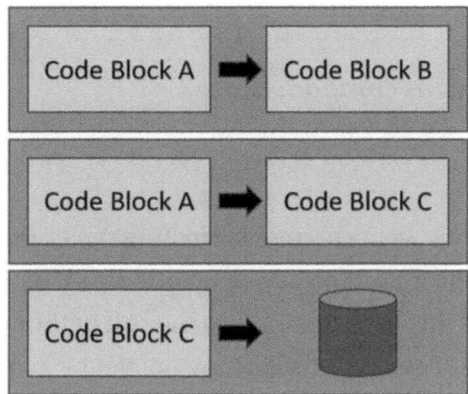

Figure 8-4. *Code blocks calling outside of boundary*

Integration tests also help to prove dependency injection is working with the registered classes. Because of the dependencies of other classes and sometimes third-party systems, you usually find there to be fewer integration tests than unit tests. However, these tests are usually more involved and have more setup and teardown code.

CHAPTER 8   TESTING MICROSERVICES

Component Testing

With a microservice architecture, you can think of microservices as components (see Figure 8-5). And code in a monolith that calls a microservice is also a component. These components are the pieces that are communicating to each other to distribute computational needs. This level of testing is about testing these components in isolation. We are not ready to have them talking to each other just yet.

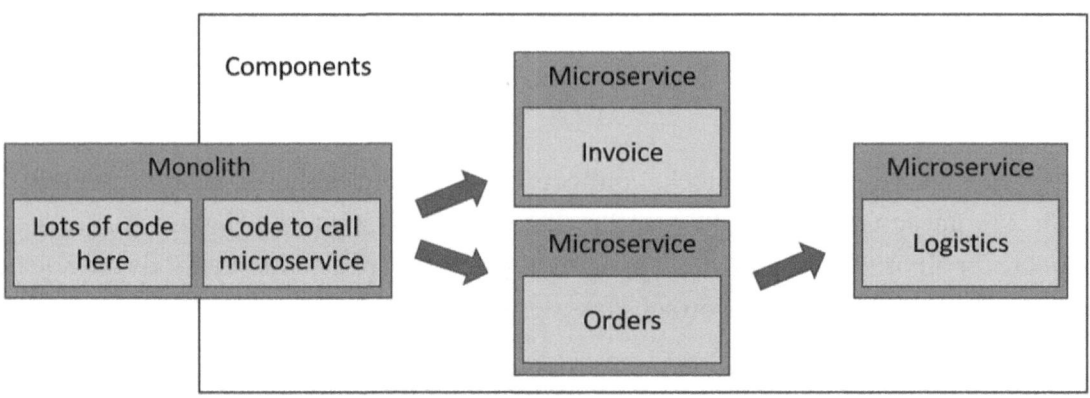

Figure 8-5. *Microservices as components*

Mocking

There are a couple of options we have here for testing the components. Consider a scenario where code is calling a microservice owned by a different development team. The purpose here is to test the code that makes the call without the other microservice being available. That provider microservice may not yet be available or may require resources of its own not ready for testing without preparation. Mocking is the type of testing that is useful in the cases.

A mock object is code that simulates an external resource like a database or simply another dependency. The main purpose of a mock object is to allow tests to provide a replica of a dependency to isolate the code under test better.

For testing microservices, a mock may represent a database or another microservice. It replaces the object on the other end of a call and allows testing a microservice without specific dependencies (see Figure 8-6). A mocking framework that works well is called "moq" at https://github.com/moq/moq.

CHAPTER 8   TESTING MICROSERVICES

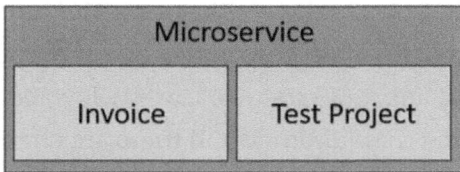

Figure 8-6. Test project as a mock

Stub

Having a mock object will only get you so far with the testing. There is still the need to make sure a microservice correctly reacts when sending or receiving data. A stub is custom application you make to serve various purposes with predefined responses (see Figure 8-7).

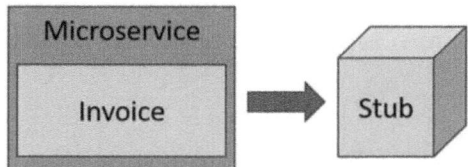

Figure 8-7. Stub testing object

The use of a stub is to receive calls made by your microservice. In this case, the stub is a stand-in for another microservice. You create stubs to behave in predefined ways. For example, if the stub receives certain parameter values, then it returns a specific value. The parameter value may trigger a valid response to test the happy path. You could have another value that triggers a reply of a random HTTP 400 or 500 code.

Using expectations of requests and responses prove how the code handles conditions, and that code changes have not broken anything. Another idea is to have the stub wait an extremely long time before replying to test the microservice's ability to handle timeout issues.

Contract Testing

Microservices receive a payload of data by either an API call or messaging. Either way, the data needs to be in the expected format. This format is the contract. Contract testing is about verifying that calls from components to microservice are communicating with the agreed-upon data format.

173

Each microservice plays a part in the architecture. Therefore, it must be known as early as possible the format of the data. Of course, requirements change, and so must the code, data format, tests, and any mocks/stubs. During development, it can be malleable as needed to fulfill the business requirements. If there are changes to the contract of a microservice already in production, you will handle the change by versioning the API or the contract itself.

Consumer-Driven Contract Testing

When creating code that calls or "consumes" a microservice, you test the code that works with the contract. This type of testing is called consumer-driven contract testing. The test verifies your code that handles the data in the contract.

By leveraging consumer-driven contract testing, the developers of the consumer can both define the contract and code to that definition. For the developers working on the provider microservice, they too can code and test using the same tests defined by the developers of the consumer.

Service Testing

At this level, you are testing the interaction to a microservice. The components are now talking to each other without mocks or stubs. Automating tests here is possible but hard to accomplish. If you are the developer of both the calling and the receiving sides, then automating is easier. However, with microservices developed by other teams, testing is usually manual. These tests are also more expensive in time and money because they involve people doing more test preparations. With service testing, you are verifying conditions like

- Use of network
- API interaction
- Sending or receiving messages
- Failure from network or CPU/memory exhaustion

End-to-End Testing

End-to-end testing is the most expensive level. It requires people to test the system as a whole. Here administrators might create users for the system and perhaps making new customer accounts, load requests, invoices, etc. End-to-end testing is about exercising the business logic from a user's perspective. The users do not care about what the system does to process an invoice. They just need to have the confidence that it does and that the system handles not only when correct data is used but also with invalid data. Does your new microservice handle network issues like partitioning and latency and incorrect data by a user?

End-to-End Testing Microservices

ASP.NET has great systems to test an entire microservice at once. This system includes tools to make it easy to stand up a complete microservice, and even replace dependencies with mocks if needed. Let's explore building a test with these tools.

The first step is to build a fixture that can be used in tests. Create a new xUnit test project in the code you created for Chapter 5. In your test project, create a new file named *DistanceApp.cs*. In it put this code:

```
public class DistanceApp(string environment = "Development") :
WebApplicationFactory<Program>
{
  protected override IHost CreateHost(IHostBuilder builder)
  {
    builder.UseEnvironment(environment);

    builder.ConfigureServices(services =>
    {
      // Add mock/test services to the builder here
    });

    return base.CreateHost(builder);
  }
}
```

CHAPTER 8   TESTING MICROSERVICES

Compiling this code will give us a compile time error. Our microservice uses top-level statements, and the compiler magic builds the class and method definition. Unfortunately, the Program class is private by default. Let's change that. In the *DistanceMicroservice* project, open Program.cs and put this at the bottom:

```
// For testing:
public partial class Program { }
```

This works perfectly for making the *Program* class public. The compiler generated code for top-level statements happens to make the class a partial class, so we can easily implement the other half, marking the class public. It's helpful to mark this line with a comment so future developers don't wonder the purpose of this line and delete it.

Now the test project compiles correctly. Let's write a test to use the fixture. Create a new test in a convenient test project and add this code:

```
[Fact] // using xUnit here. If using NUnit or MSTest, use [Test]
public async Task CallDistanceAPI_ReturnsResults()
{
  // Arrange
  Addresses addresses = new Addresses(
    OriginAddress: "123 Main St, Anytown, CA",
    DestinationAddress: "456 Lincoln Ave, Anytown, CA"
  );

  using var siteApp = new DistanceApp();
  using HttpClient httpClient = siteApp.CreateClient();

  // Act
  var res = await httpClient.PostAsJsonAsync("/getdistanceinfo",
  addresses);
  res.EnsureSuccessStatusCode();
  var body = await res.Content.ReadAsStringAsync();
  var result = JsonSerializer.Deserialize<DiscoveredRoutes>(body, new
  JsonSerializerOptions
  {
    PropertyNameCaseInsensitive = true
  });
```

CHAPTER 8   TESTING MICROSERVICES

```
  // Assert
  result.ShouldNotBeNull();
  // TODO: validate results
}
```

Notice how in this test, we're instantiating the *DistanceApp* fixture, then creating an *HttpClient* from it. Although the fixture creates the *HttpClient* for us, we use it just like we would in any other application.

In this case, we did a POST request and deserialized the response as JSON. We could also make a GET request to an ASP.NET MVC app, and use a tool like the HTML Agility Pack[1] to look for details in the HTML response.

In the fixture, it can be easy to swap out dependencies or inject configuration. Perhaps we want to swap out the connection string to an in-memory database. Or override the configuration for service discovery so it could locate another microservice container we might have started with GitHub Actions Services.[2]

In the fixture, we could also swap out an interface for a mock implementation. Maybe we want to replace the *GoogleRouteService* with one that returns mocked results. Consider this code inside the *DistanceApp* fixture's *ConfigureServices* override:

```
builder.ConfigureServices(services =>
{
  // Add mock/test services to the builder

  var oldDb = services.FirstOrDefault(s => s.ServiceType ==
  typeof(MyDbContext));
  if (oldDb != null)
  {
    services.Remove(oldDb);
  }

  services.AddDbContext<MyDbContext>(options =>
    options.UseInMemoryDatabase(databaseName: "MyDb"));

});
```

---

[1] https://html-agility-pack.net/
[2] https://docs.github.com/en/actions/tutorials/use-containerized-services/create-redis-service-containers

177

In the example above, we remove the Entity Framework Data Context, and replace it with an in-memory version. We could just as easily replace any interface with a different implementation. For more examples of this technique, see the GitHub repository companion to this book.

The critical piece of this technique is creating a fixture by deriving from `WebApplicationFactory<Program>`. This allows us to easily create an `HttpClient` that we can use like any `HttpClient` in C#. But under the hood is a great level of elegant engineering.

When we use `WebApplicationFactory<Program>`, we get an in-memory Kestrel server. There is no check for an available port, there is no trying to connect to it over HTTP, there is no TLS certificate chain. Under the hood, the Kestrel server runs in memory, and the `HttpClient` is rigged to connect in-memory to the server.

By comparison, if we started our microservice in a container within our DevOps pipeline, we'd need to do port detection, service discovery, TLS termination, a certificate trust chain, and we'd have no opportunity to mock out parts of the microservice during testing.

Consumer-Driven Contract Testing Deep Dive

In this section, we will create examples of consumer-driven contract testing. The provider will be the microservice you built in Chapter 5 used to retrieve route and distance information from Google's Route API.

The consumer will be a new microservice. The idea here is this new microservice could be called by a monolith or something else but receives the route information from the provider microservice. With the discovered route information, we can apply any transformations and analysis before returning that data to the caller. So, for this example, the consumer will be our Route Analysis microservice.

Like mentioned earlier, the purpose of this type of testing allows microservices to be developed simultaneously and possibly by different development teams. The payload is expected information required by the consumer of the provider. To help with this testing, we will use the NuGet package PactNet from `https://pact.io`. With the consumer, it will generate a file that is used to test both the consumer and the provider. The consumer must create the file first, thus why it's called consumer-drive contract testing.

CHAPTER 8   TESTING MICROSERVICES

Consumer Project

Let's create a new project of type ASP.NET Core Web API named RouteAnalysis. In the Program.cs file, replace contents with the following code.

```
var builder = WebApplication.CreateBuilder(args);

builder.Services.AddOpenApi();
builder.Services.AddSwaggerGen();
builder.Services.AddHttpClient();

var app = builder.Build();

IConfigurationRoot config = new ConfigurationBuilder()
    .SetBasePath(Directory.GetCurrentDirectory())
    .AddJsonFile("appsettings.json", optional: false, reloadOnChange: true)
    .AddUserSecrets<Program>()
    .Build();

// Configure the HTTP request pipeline.
if (app.Environment.IsDevelopment())
{
    app.MapOpenApi();
    app.UseSwagger();
    app.UseSwaggerUI(c => c.SwaggerEndpoint("/swagger/v1/swagger.json"
        , "My microservice for map information."));
}

app.UseHttpsRedirection();

app.MapPost("/getrouteanalysisinfo", async
    (Addresses addresses, HttpClient httpClient) =>
{
  var apiUrl = config["RouteServiceUrl"]
    ?? throw new InvalidOperationException
      ("URL key, Route Microservice, not found.");

  httpClient.BaseAddress = new Uri(apiUrl);
```

179

```csharp
  var response = await httpClient
    .PostAsJsonAsync("getdistanceinfo", addresses)
    .ContinueWith(async task =>
    {
      var result = await task;
      if (!result.IsSuccessStatusCode)
      {
          throw new HttpRequestException
          ($"Request failed with status code {result.StatusCode}");
      }
        return await result.Content
            .ReadFromJsonAsync<DiscoveredRoutes>();
    }).Result;

    return new ReturnedRoute(addresses.OriginAddress
    , addresses.DestinationAddress, BestRoute:
      response?.Routes?.MinBy(r => r.DistanceMeters)
        ?? new Route(DistanceMeters: 0, Duration: "0 seconds"));
})
.WithName("GetRouteAnalysisInfo");

app.Run();

public record ReturnedRoute(string OriginAddress, string
DestinationAddress, Route BestRoute);

public record Addresses(string OriginAddress, string DestinationAddress);

public class DiscoveredRoutes(string OriginAddress, string
DestinationAddress, string Message, Route[] Routes)
{
    public string OriginAddress { get; } = OriginAddress;
    public string DestinationAddress { get; } = DestinationAddress;
    public string Message { get; set; } = Message;
    public Route[] Routes { get; set; } = Routes;
}
```

```
public record Routes(Route[] routes);

/// <param name="distanceMeters"> Distance in meters. </param>
/// <param name="duration"> Duration in seconds. </param>
public class Route(int DistanceMeters, string Duration)
{
    public string Duration { get; } = Duration;
    public int DistanceMeters { get; } = DistanceMeters;

    // Convert meters to miles
    public double DistanceInMiles =>
        Math.Round(DistanceMeters / 1609.34, 2);
}
```

In the appsettings.json file, add an entry for the URL of the provider microservice created in Chapter 5.

```
"RouteServiceUrl": "https://localhost:7250"
```

There should be another file called RouteAnalysis.http. Modify the file to look like this:

```
@RouteAnalysis_HostAddress = http://localhost:5076
POST {{RouteAnalysis_HostAddress}}/getrouteanalysisinfo
Content-Type: application/json
{
  "OriginAddress":"101 S. Main St. Chicago, IL",
  "DestinationAddress":"500 S. Main St. Los Angeles, CA"
}
###
```

The port number, 7250, should be replaced with the port number in the launchSettings.json file.

Now, you should be able to select the "Send request" or "Debug" links and it sends a request to your microservice. Do notice that "Debug" will start the application whereas "Send request" expects it to already be running. Without the application running, you'll receive the following message.

```
No connection could be made because the target machine actively refused it.
```

CHAPTER 8   TESTING MICROSERVICES

Consumer Test Project

Now let's add a test project. Create a new project of type xUnit Test Project named ConsumerTests. Add the NuGet package PactNet. Create a new file called Usings.cs and place in the following code.

```
global using PactNet;
global using PactNet.Matchers;
global using System.Net;
global using System.Net.Http.Json;
global using System.Text.Json;
```

In the UnitTest1.cs file, replace any contents with the following code.

```
namespace ConsumerTester;

public class RouteApiClient
{
  private readonly HttpClient _httpClient;

  public RouteApiClient(string baseUri)
  {
    _httpClient = new HttpClient { BaseAddress = new Uri(baseUri) };
  }

  public async Task<DiscoveredRoutes?> GetDistanceInfo(Addresses addresses)
  {
    JsonSerializerOptions jsonSerializerOptions = new()
      { PropertyNameCaseInsensitive = true };
    var response = await _httpClient.PostAsJsonAsync("getdistanceinfo"
    , addresses
    , jsonSerializerOptions);

    response.EnsureSuccessStatusCode();
    var result = await response.Content
      .ReadAsStringAsync();
```

```csharp
      return JsonSerializer
        .Deserialize<DiscoveredRoutes>(result
        , jsonSerializerOptions);
  }
}

public class DiscountSvcTests
{
  private readonly IPactBuilderV4 pactBuilder;

  public DiscountSvcTests()
  {
    var pact = Pact.V4("RouteAnalysisConsumer"
    ,"RouteServiceProvider"
    , new PactConfig
      {
        PactDir = Path.Combine("C:\\temp", "pacts", "RouteAnalysis-
        RouteInformation"),
        LogLevel = PactLogLevel.Debug
      });
    pactBuilder = pact.WithHttpInteractions();
  }

[Fact]
public async Task GetRoutesBasedOnLocations_ReturnsDiscoveredRoutes()
{
  var testAddresses =
    new Addresses("101 S. Main St. Chicago, IL"
    , "500 S. Main St. Los Angeles, CA");

  pactBuilder
    .UponReceiving("A POST request to retrieve the route analysis
      information")
        .WithRequest(HttpMethod.Post, "/getdistanceinfo")
        .WithHeader("Content-Type"
          , "application/json; charset=utf-8")
```

```csharp
            .WithJsonBody(new
            {
                OriginAddress = Match.Type(testAddresses.OriginAddress),
                DestinationAddress = Match.Type(testAddresses.DestinationAddress)
            })
        .WillRespond()
          .WithStatus(HttpStatusCode.OK)
          .WithHeader("Content-Type"
            , "application/json; charset=utf-8")
          .WithJsonBody(new
          {
            originAddress = Match.Type(testAddresses.OriginAddress),
            destinationAddress = Match.Type(testAddresses.DestinationAddress),
            message = Match.Type("Number of routes found: 3"),
            routes = new[]
              {
                new { distanceMeters = 3217611,
                  distanceInMiles = 1999.34
                },
                new { distanceMeters = 3421492,
                  distanceInMiles = 2126.02
                },
                new { distanceMeters = 3398574,
                  distanceInMiles = 2111.78
                }
              }
          });

  Await pactBuilder.VerifyAsync(async ctx =>
  {
    var client = new RouteApiClient(ctx.MockServerUri.ToString());

    var result = await client.GetDistanceInfo(testAddresses);
```

```
      Assert.NotNull(result);
      Assert.Equal(3, result?.Routes.Length);
      });
  }
}

public record Addresses(string OriginAddress
  , string DestinationAddress);

public record ReturnedRoute(string OriginAddress
  , string DestinationAddress, Route BestRoute);

public class DiscoveredRoutes(string OriginAddress
  , string DestinationAddress, string Message, Route[] Routes)
{
  public string OriginAddress { get; } = OriginAddress;
  public string DestinationAddress { get; } = DestinationAddress;
  public string Message { get; set; } = Message;
  public Route[] Routes { get; set; } = Routes;
}

public record Routes(Route[] routes);

/// <param name="distanceMeters"> Distance in meters. </param>
/// <param name="duration"> Duration in seconds. </param>
public record Route(int distanceMeters, string duration)
{
  public required int DistanceMeters = distanceMeters;
  public required string Duration = duration;

  // Convert meters to miles
  public double DistanceInMiles =>
    Math.Round(distanceMeters / 1609.34, 2);
}
```

Let's go over a few details before we run the test. Notice the RouteApiClient. This is a class that uses HttpClient to make a REST-based call. The address it calls is controlled by the PactNet mock server. It opens a port on localhost to receive the calls. This helps prove the call will succeed.

In the method WithJsonBody, there is a new object being defined. The property names here are case sensitive and must match those in the pact contract file it creates.

Also in the file is the expected HTTP status code response of 200. This allows testing to be done using other codes like 201 for when creating items, or 404 when an item is not found.

Now to generate the pact file, execute the test GetRoutesBasedOnLocations_ReturnsDiscoveredRoutes. This can be done using the dotnet test command.

```
dotnet test –filter "GetRoutesBasedOnLocations_ReturnsDiscoveredRoutes"
```

The Pact Builder creates a pact contract file based on the directory and name specified. The directory is `C:\temp\pacts\RouteAnalysis-RouteInformation` with filename `RouteAnalysisConsumer-RouteServiceProvider.json`. The name and location of this file is used in the provider test.

Provider Test Project

Now that we have made a consumer-driven contract integration test with PactNet, we will create a test project for the provider microservice that was created in Chapter 5. Create a new xUnit Test Project named ProviderTests. Create a new class file named Usings.cs and place in the following code.

```
global using PactNet;
global using PactNet.Infrastructure.Outputters;
global using PactNet.Output.Xunit;
global using PactNet.Verifier;
global using Xunit.Abstractions;
```

In the UnitTest1.cs file, replace any contents with the following code.

```
namespace ProducerTests;

public class ProducerPactProviderTests(ITestOutputHelper output)
{
  private const string ProviderUri = "https://localhost:7250";
  private readonly string _pactFile =
    Path.Combine("C:\\temp", "pacts", "RouteAnalysis-RouteInformation",
    "RouteAnalysisConsumer-RouteServiceProvider.json");
```

```csharp
    public ITestOutputHelper Output { get; } = output;

    [Fact]
    public void EnsureProviderMeetsPactWithConsumer()
    {
      var config = new PactVerifierConfig
      {
        Outputters = [new ConsoleOutput() , new XunitOutput(Output)],
        LogLevel = PactLogLevel.Debug
      };

      IPactVerifier verifier =
        new PactVerifier("RouteServiceProvider", config);
      verifier
        .WithHttpEndpoint(new Uri(ProviderUri))
        .WithFileSource(new FileInfo(_pactFile))
        .Verify();
    }
}
```

There is a detail in that code worth mentioning. The Provider URI is the location on which the Route Information microservice is listening. The test will not succeed unless that project is running. We will need to start that application before running the test. With the Route Information microservice, start the application using the IDE or the dotnet command. Be sure to double-check the port number.

```
dotnet run --urls "https://localhost:7250"
```

In the provider test project, execute the test.

```
dotnet test –filter "EnsureProviderMeetsPactWithConsumer"
```

Great! It succeeded. But, what if it didn't? In the pact output there is rather verbose information to help you troubleshoot. The following is a truncated output I used to discover the JSON body in the pact file must also match the case of the properties that were returned from the provider. Notice the "- OriginAddress" and the lower-case version a few lines down. This also applies to "Routes".

```
-   "OriginAddress": "101 S. Main St. Chicago, IL",
        "Routes": [
        +   "destinationAddress": "500 S. Main St. Los Angeles, CA",
        "message": "Number of routes found: 3",
        "originAddress": "101 S. Main St. Chicago, IL",
        "routes": [
```

Summary

In this chapter, we went over how testing plays a critical role in developing any software application. You learned that the cost of errors rises as the project continues development and certainly after deployment to production. So, testing must be considered in the early stages of development and reviewed constantly. Methodologies like Test-Driven Development should be considered as it helps reduce opportunities in a lot of cases. Also, tests should evolve just as the code and architecture change.

You also learned that knowing what to test is as important as knowing how to test them. And knowing what not to test saves time and keeps you focused on error or system failure scenario handling.

We went over the testing pyramid by Mike Cohn and the modified one as it applies to microservices architecture. The modified pyramid shows different types of tests based on what you are testing and why.

Then you learned how to do contract testing for microservices that work together via REST communication. You also created code that uses the Pact library to test the contract between microservices.

CHAPTER 9

Deploying Microservices

This chapter discusses containerized deployment options for .NET microservices. Though it's possible to deploy ASP.NET to IIS, we specifically don't discuss that here because it's a legacy deployment system. Instead, we focus on all the places Linux containers can run in Azure, nodding to other cloud providers and other Azure container hosting platforms. We containerize a .NET app into a Docker container, run in various Azure resources that run containers, then discuss reverse proxies that allow a single URL to all the microservices.

When we finish building the microservice, it's time to deploy it to production. In the past that meant purchasing hardware, installing the OS, and configuring the web server. Now-a-days, we can leverage containers to make it really easy to deploy .NET. Once the microservice is in a container, the hosting options are plentiful. Though it's still possible to run ASP.NET in IIS or Windows containers, that's really not the way it's done today. Linux container hosting is much more versatile.

In this chapter, we'll begin by putting the ASP.NET microservice into a Linux container. Once in a container, we can look at various cloud hosting options for running containers. Though the authors are most familiar with Azure and Kubernetes, the same principles apply to other cloud providers as well. You could definitely run an ASP.NET container on AWS, GCP, Oracle cloud, CloudFoundry, or locally in your development environment using Docker Compose.

Containerize a .NET Microservice

Our first stop is to get our ASP.NET microservice into a Docker container. From there, we can host it on Kubernetes, run it in various Azure services, or anywhere else Linux containers can run. When we containerize an ASP.NET app, there are a few techniques we can use. We'll look at two of the most popular: a Dockerfile and using the built-in containerization built into the .NET SDK.

CHAPTER 9   DEPLOYING MICROSERVICES

Containerize .NET with a Dockerfile

Let's build a Dockerfile that'll containerize an ASP.NET web property.

Add a new file to the website project and name it *Dockerfile*, without a file extension. It's important it be named *Dockerfile* and not ~~Dockerfile.txt~~. If your editor added the .txt extension, it's easy enough to remove the extension.

In the Dockerfile, place this content:

```
FROM mcr.microsoft.com/dotnet/sdk:10.0-alpine

WORKDIR /src

COPY . .
RUN dotnet restore
RUN dotnet build -c Release
RUN dotnet test -c Release
RUN dotnet publish -c Release -o /dist MyProject.csproj

ENV ASPNETCORE_URLS=http://+:8080
EXPOSE 8080
ENV ASPNETCORE_ENVIRONMENT=Production

WORKDIR /app
COPY /dist .
CMD ["dotnet", "MyProject.dll"]
```

This Dockerfile is a good start, but we're not done. Let's take a look at the finer points of this Dockerfile.

In this example, we're using the Alpine variant of the .NET SDK image. Alpine Linux is known for being exceedingly small, so the resulting image created here will be easy to push to a container registry and quick to download to Kubernetes or another container runtime. Alpine isn't without its challenges though. Because Alpine isn't Ubuntu-based (or RedHat-based), installing Linux packages is a little weird. We're not doing that here, but it's something to keep in mind.

We could combine each of the *dotnet* commands into a single Docker layer, but with them as separate Docker layers, it's easier to see which command failed. We'll play with layers more carefully later in this exercise.

Technically, the .NET CLI will build in Release mode by default if it notices it is running inside a Docker image. But it's always more descriptive to carefully call out the Release build. This avoids the ambiguity and ensures the configuration choice is easily discoverable.

There are a few problems with this Dockerfile that we should address:

1. We're including build tools in the production image. Imagine if an attacker compromised this container. They could upload their own source code, compile it into place, and take over the running process. (Granted, the best way to avoid this is to not let the attacker compromise the container.) In addition, having build tools and source code in the image makes it significantly larger than necessary. Let's separate this into a multi-stage build.

```
# build "server" image
FROM mcr.microsoft.com/dotnet/sdk:10.0-alpine AS build

WORKDIR /src

COPY . .
RUN dotnet restore
RUN dotnet build -c Release
RUN dotnet test -c Release
RUN dotnet publish -c Release -o /dist MyProject.csproj

# production runtime "server" image
FROM mcr.microsoft.com/dotnet/aspnet:10.0-alpine

ENV ASPNETCORE_URLS=http://+:8080
EXPOSE 8080
ENV ASPNETCORE_ENVIRONMENT=Production

WORKDIR /app
COPY --from=build /dist .
CMD ["dotnet", "MyProject.dll"]
```

We added a new *FROM* line in the middle. This splits the image in half. Now the new image only includes the built, published content, and doesn't include build tools or source code. This makes the image significantly smaller and more secure.

In the last *COPY* line, we need to specify where we're copying from. Without the *--from=build* we'd try to copy from the host machine. We also modified the top *FROM* line to specify the name of this stage – in this case "build". There's nothing magical about this name. We could have called it anything.

Now we have a smaller resulting image, but there's one more best practice we can leverage. Right now, if we changed any file in the project, we'd re-restore the NuGet libraries because we invalidate the *COPY* line right above it. Instead, let's restore NuGet packages first, and copy source code second. Of course we need to know which NuGet packages to restore, so we also copy in the csproj file(s) and sln or slnx file. Here's an updated Dockerfile:

```
# build "server" image
FROM mcr.microsoft.com/dotnet/sdk:10.0-alpine AS build

WORKDIR /src

COPY MyProject.csproj .
RUN dotnet restore
COPY . .
RUN dotnet build -c Release
RUN dotnet test -c Release
RUN dotnet publish -c Release -o /dist MyProject.csproj

# production runtime "server" image
FROM mcr.microsoft.com/dotnet/aspnet:10.0-alpine

ENV ASPNETCORE_URLS=http://+:8080
EXPOSE 8080
ENV ASPNETCORE_ENVIRONMENT=Production

WORKDIR /app
COPY --from=build /dist .
CMD ["dotnet", "MyProject.dll"]
```

In this final Dockerfile, we first copy in the csproj file, then restore NuGet packages, then copy in everything else. This pattern leverages Docker's caching mechanisms. If we only change C# files, we don't invalidate the cached NuGet dependencies, but if we update a package version or add a new package, we'll correctly load the new dependencies. This can make local builds significantly faster.

Now that we have a Dockerfile in place, let's add a *.dockerignore* file. This specifies everything we don't want to copy into the production container. It almost mirrors a *.gitignore* file.

Create a new text file named *.dockerfile*. (Note the leading dot and no file extension.)

```
# downloaded files
packages
# built files
**/bin
**/obj
# temp files
**/*.tmp
**/*.log
**/*.orig
# user-specific files
*.suo
.vs
**/*.user
**/.DS_Store
# secrets
.env
# non-production files
appsettings.*.json
**/launchSettings.json
```

In this *.dockerignore* file, we have the standard five sections from the *.gitignore* file:

- Downloaded files
- Built files
- Temp files
- User-specific files
- Secrets

193

Depending on the *.gitignore* file you used, these five sections may include many other elements or be combined and mixed together. In this *.dockerignore* file, we add a sixth section: nonproduction files. Of course, we don't need *appsettings.Development.json* in production. We can also exclude *launchSettings.json* since this file contains debugging configuration.

Unlike a *.gitignore* file which looks recursively through every directory for a match, the *.dockerignore* file looks only in the root directory by default. So, when one copies a *.gitignore* file into a *.dockerignore* file, we add **/ to the front of each entry. "**" is the signal for "recursively through any directory", thus restoring the behavior in a *.gitignore* file.

With both the *Dockerfile* and *.dockerignore* file in place, we can run standard Docker commands to build and publish the container image.

In a terminal in the directory with the *Dockerfile*, run these commands:

```
docker build -t myaccount.azurecr.io/myimage:v0.1 .
docker push myaccount.azurecr.io/myimage:v0.1
```

You may need to tag this differently to match your container registry information. In this case, we're using Azure Container Registry (ACR). You could also use Docker Hub or AWS Elastic Container Registry (ECR) or Artifactory or any other container registry.

In this section, we built up a *Dockerfile* using industry best-practices that ensure the container image is lean and tailored exactly to the needs of the application. Not shown here, we could install Linux dependencies and configure other environment variables that could override configuration details.

With a *Dockerfile*, we gain the most control over the resulting image. We can easily tune the image to exactly the specifications we need. The site is built inside the container, preserving the rule of build servers: always build in a neutral environment. Adding a *.dockerignore* file ensures we don't copy files into the container image that aren't needed. Though the SDK method is easier, the Dockerfile method is the most powerful.

Containerize .NET with the .NET SDK

New in .NET 8, and refined in each release since, we can leverage the .NET SDK to produce a Docker image. This option is definitely significantly easier than the Dockerfile method described above. Provided we can live with the opinions in the SDK, it can work great.

To produce an image with the .NET SDK, we don't need Docker or Podman installed to build the image. We may choose to install a container runtime to leverage Aspire or test out the image we're building, but we won't need it installed or running to build. However, to publish to a local registry, we will need either Docker Desktop or Podman installed. Though there are many other container runtimes, only these two are supported by the .NET SDK.

To publish a container image, open a terminal in the project directory and run these commands:

```
dotnet restore
dotnet build -c Release
dotnet test -c Release
dotnet publish --os linux --arch x64 /t:PublishContainer -p ContainerRegistry=myaccount.azurecr.io
```

These commands look an awful lot like the commands we ran in the Dockerfile example above. In this case, we're not running them from inside a Dockerfile but instead from a local terminal.

There are optional flags you can set to take control of the image name or base image. None are required, but each could be helpful in certain circumstances. By default, the image will be named to match the assembly name. You can control the image name by adding a *<ContainerRepository>* attribute in the csproj file or *-p ContainerRepository=myimage* on the command line. If you don't change the base image, you'll use the standard ASP.NET base image, but if you need to specify a different base image, add the *<ContainerBaseImage>* tag in the csproj file or *-p ContainerBaseImage=...* in the terminal. By default, the image label will be *latest*, but you can change that to a label of your choice by setting *-p ContainerImageTag=v0.1* on the command line or setting *<ContainerImageTag>* in the csproj. To set all three, we could use this command:

```
dotnet publish --os linux --arch x64 /t:PublishContainer -p ContainerRegistry=myaccount.azurecr.io -p ContainerRepository=myimage -p ContainerImageTag=v0.1
```

This command would produce this image: *myaccount.azurecr.io/myimage:v0.1*. See https://learn.microsoft.com/en-us/dotnet/core/containers/sdk-publish for instructions on using these flags and https://learn.microsoft.com/en-us/dotnet/core/containers/publish-configuration to see all the flags available to control containers during the publishing process.

This method was far easier, but comes with a lot of downsides. In this technique, we can control the base image and resulting tag, but we really can't configure much more. Need to apt-get install a Linux package? You can't do that here. Instead, you must flip to the Dockerfile technique.

One of the core principles of CI/CD is that we build in a neutral environment, a machine that isn't used for other purposes or cluttered with other software. In this technique, we're not building in an isolated environment, we're building on the build agent, or more likely on a developer's workstation. With the Dockerfile method, we built inside the container, ensuring a virtual clean-room to build and publish the solution identically every time. In this SDK method, we're building outside the container. Therefore, we must take great care to ensure only containers produced on the build agent can be published to the container registry, and that the build agent is cleaned and reset between runs.

Producing a container image using the .NET SDK is definitely significantly easier than the Dockerfile method described above. However, we must accept a lot of conventions and opinions in the .NET build system. If we fit into the typical use-case, this is perfect. If we need more control, we should use the Dockerfile method instead.

Deploy a Containerized .NET Microservice

We now have the ASP.NET microservice inside a Linux container and pushed to a container registry. Either technique is sufficient for getting to this point. Our next step is to host the microservice in a container runtime. In this section, we'll compare and contrast various container hosting mechanisms available in Azure. See these options summarized in Table 9-1.

Table 9-1. *Microservice Deployment Options*

Technology	Pros	Cons	Best use-case
Kubernetes	Industry standard container runtime	Complex configuration	Run many microservices with maximum configurability
Azure Container Apps	Easy configuration	Only on Azure Complex configuration isn't possible	Run many microservices with a simpler abstraction than Kubernetes
Azure Web Apps	Drop-dead simple	Heavy setup for multiple microservices	Run few or one microservice

Deploy to Azure Kubernetes Service (AKS)

Kubernetes (k8s) is an industry standard platform for running containers at scale. Almost every cloud has an easy-to-deploy Kubernetes cluster available. Kubernetes is known for easily running a large collection of microservices, making it easy to upgrade and scale services to meet demand.

To deploy a microservice to Kubernetes, we need a pod, a deployment, a service, and an ingress. The pod wraps a container and is the unit of scale in Kubernetes. If we want more instances of the container, we scale up the number of pods. A deployment is the recipe for creating pods, and includes the number of pods to create. (Though outside the scope of this book, we could also use a horizontal pod autoscaler to adjust the pod quantity based on changing cluster conditions.) A Kubernetes service acts as a round-robin load balancer in front of all the pods, creating a single point of entry for the suite of pods. An ingress often terminates the TLS connection, and maps a DNS endpoint to a service. See Figure 9-1.

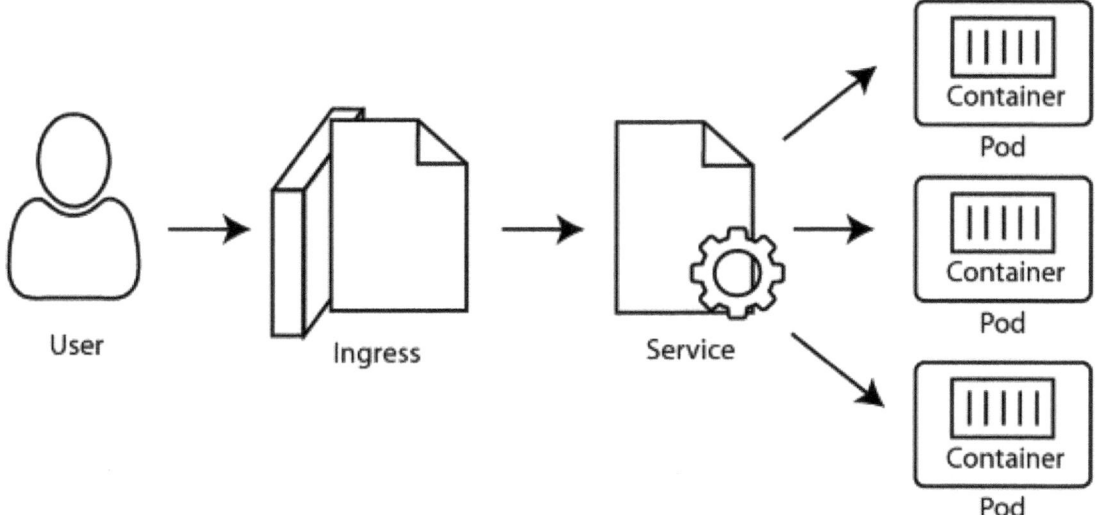

Figure 9-1. Kubernetes elements: Ingress, Service, Pod, and Deployment

These Kubernetes elements are created in a YAML configuration file. Here's a YAML file that defines all these elements:

```
apiVersion: apps/v1
kind: Deployment
metadata:
```

```yaml
  name: my-microservice
spec:
  replicas: 3
  selector:
    matchLabels:
      app: my-microservice
  template:
    metadata:
      labels:
        app: my-microservice
        version: v0.1
    spec:
      containers:
      - name: my-microservice
        image: myaccount.azurecr.io/myimage:v0.1
        resources:
          limits:
            memory: "128Mi"
            cpu: "500m"
          requests:
            memory: "64Mi"
            cpu: "250m"
        ports:
        - containerPort: 8080
        env:
        - name: ASPNETCORE_ENVIRONMENT
          value: "Production"
---
apiVersion: v1
kind: Service
metadata:
  name: my-microservice
spec:
  type: NodePort
```

```yaml
  selector:
    app: my-microservice
  ports:
  - port: 8080
    targetPort: 8080
---
apiVersion: networking.k8s.io/v1
kind: Ingress
metadata:
  name: my-microservice
  labels:
    name: my-microservice
  annotations:
    cert-manager.io/cluster-issuer: letsencrypt
    acme.cert-manager.io/http01-edit-in-place: "true"
spec:
  ingressClassName: nginx
  tls:
  - hosts:
    - my-microservice.example.com
    secretName: tls-secret
  rules:
  - host: my-microservice.example.com
    http:
      paths:
      - pathType: Prefix
        path: "/"
        backend:
          service:
            name: my-microservice
            port:
              number: 8080
```

In this Kubernetes yaml file, we define a deployment, a service, and an ingress. Inside the deployment's template section is the pod definition.

CHAPTER 9   DEPLOYING MICROSERVICES

In this example, we also use cert-manager[1] to hook up a Let's Encrypt TLS certificate into a Kubernetes secret.

Run these on the Kubernetes cluster like this:

```
kubectl apply -f k8s.yaml
```

The beauty of using the apply command is it's an upsert – either a create or an update. It's easy to get k8s resources into place with YAML files.

Unlike other hosting options we'll look at, a Kubernetes Ingress can act as a great API gateway, mapping URL segments to various microservices. We don't need API Gateway or YARP to map a single domain to a suite of microservices. Instead, the Kubernetes Ingress can do it. Look at this example:

```yaml
apiVersion: networking.k8s.io/v1
kind: Ingress
metadata:
  name: microservice-ingress
  labels:
    name: microservice-ingress
  annotations:
    cert-manager.io/cluster-issuer: letsencrypt
    acme.cert-manager.io/http01-edit-in-place: "true"
spec:
  ingressClassName: nginx
  tls:
  - hosts:
    - api.example.com
    secretName: tls-secret
  rules:
  - host: api.example.com
    http:
      paths:
      - pathType: Prefix
        path: "/api/customer"
        backend:
```

---

[1] https://cert-manager.io/

```
        service:
          name: customers
          port:
            number: 8080
    - pathType: Prefix
      path: "/api/order"
      backend:
        service:
          name: orders
          port:
            number: 8080
    - pathType: Prefix
      path: "/api/product"
      backend:
        service:
          name: products
          port:
            number: 8080
    - pathType: Prefix
      path: "/"
      backend:
        service:
          name: frontend
          port:
            number: 80
```

With this Ingress configuration, we have four microservices all running on the same subdomain, running from different paths. With this approach, we avoid the need for complex Cross-Origin Request Header (CORS) setup on the server and on the client, complex configuration to enumerate the other services' domains. The browser may not even realize it's communicating with a suite of microservices.

Kubernetes is great when we have many microservices that form the solution. Kubernetes is the industry standard platform for running containers at scale. However, Kubernetes configuration can get complex and cumbersome. If you prefer open source solutions, Kubernetes is an excellent choice for hosting lots of services.

CHAPTER 9   DEPLOYING MICROSERVICES

Deploy to Azure Container Apps

Azure Container Apps (ACA) is an Azure-specific opinionated abstraction over top of Kubernetes. If you squint hard, you'll see a few of the Kubernetes (k8s) principles emerging. Azure Container Apps works well if you have many microservices, you're overwhelmed by the complexity of Kubernetes, and you're ok with the vendor lock-in.

An ACA container environment is the fully managed Kubernetes cluster. Within this cluster, you provision various containers, specifying the ingress (if needed), and container details. The particulars of pods, deployments, and services melt away into a single "container" concept in ACA.

It's easy to get started by configuring an ACA container environment and container via the Azure Portal. First create the container environment so you can carefully name it. Then as you create the container, pick the image we pushed to Azure Container Registry previously.

You can also build an ACA container environment and container using the Azure CLI. Here's a shell script that will build all these resources. Because line breaks are removed, this script will work in Linux shells and in PowerShell. If you get a syntax error, you may have added a carriage return.

```
# Variables - customize these
RESOURCE_GROUP="pro-microservices"
LOCATION="canadacentral"
ACR_NAME="my-registry"  # ACR name only (no .azurecr.io)
CONTAINERAPP_ENV="pro-microservices"
CONTAINERAPP_NAME="my-container"
IMAGE_NAME="myimage:v0.1"
IDENTITY_NAME="${CONTAINERAPP_NAME}-identity"
TARGET_PORT=8080
SETTING="ASPNETCORE_ENVIRONMENT=Production"

# if not already, `az login` and `az account set --subscription "..."`
az group create --name $RESOURCE_GROUP --location $LOCATION
az containerapp env create --name $CONTAINERAPP_ENV --resource-group $RESOURCE_GROUP --location $LOCATION
az identity create --name $IDENTITY_NAME --resource-group $RESOURCE_GROUP --location $LOCATION
```

```
PRINCIPAL_ID=$(az identity show --name $IDENTITY_NAME --resource-group 
$RESOURCE_GROUP --query 'principalId' -o tsv)
az role assignment create --assignee $PRINCIPAL_ID --role "AcrPull" --scope 
$(az acr show --name $ACR_NAME --query id -o tsv)
az containerapp create --name $CONTAINERAPP_NAME --resource-group 
$RESOURCE_GROUP --environment $CONTAINERAPP_ENV --image "$ACR_NAME.azurecr.
io/$IMAGE_NAME" --target-port $TARGET_PORT --ingress 'external' --registry-
server "$ACR_NAME.azurecr.io" --user-assigned $IDENTITY_NAME --min-replicas 
1 --max-replicas 3 --env-vars $SETTING
az containerapp show --name $CONTAINERAPP_NAME --resource-group $RESOURCE_
GROUP --query
# now open this URL in a browser and view the newly deployed web app
```

In this script, we create the ACA environment, rig a service principal to pull from Azure Container Registry, create the container with scaling details and settings, and finally show the URL of the container.

ACA isn't without its limitations. Current limitations in ACA prohibit mapping one ingress to more than one container. To accomplish this, we'll need to use a reverse proxy such as API Gateway or YARP. We'll configure this later in this chapter. Though we can configure additional ports, it isn't intuitive how to call other containers in the ACA environment.

With Azure Container Apps, it's easy to provision a collection of microservices. ACA is perfect if you're less familiar with Kubernetes, don't want to take on the burden of Kubernetes administration, and want to get going with a large collection of microservices quickly. Alternatively, if you need more customization beyond the opinions baked into ACA, upgrading to Kubernetes might be a better choice.

Deploy to Azure App Service

Azure App Service is one of the earliest services in Azure. It's ideal for provisioning a single monolithic website. App Service now supports hosting both Linux and Windows sites, and in particular, both Linux and Windows containers.

Configuring a Web App in the Azure portal is quite straightforward. As you create the App Service, you can create the App Service Plan and the link to Azure Container Registry at the same time.

CHAPTER 9   DEPLOYING MICROSERVICES

You can also configure all these details through the Azure CLI. Here's a shell script that will deploy a web app to Azure App Service:

```
RESOURCE_GROUP="pro-microservices"
LOCATION="canadacentral"
PRICE_TIER="F1"
ACR_NAME="my-registry"  # Just the name, not full URL
ACR_LOGIN_SERVER="$ACR_NAME.azurecr.io"
APP_SERVICE_PLAN="app-plan"
WEBAPP_NAME="my-webapp"
IMAGE_NAME="myimage:v0.1"
SETTING="ASPNETCORE_ENVIRONMENT=Production"

# if not already, `az login` and `az account set --subscription "..."`
az group create --name "$RESOURCE_GROUP" --location "$LOCATION"
az appservice plan create --name "$APP_SERVICE_PLAN" --resource-group "$RESOURCE_GROUP" --is-linux --sku "$PRICE_TIER"
az appservice plan show --name "$APP_SERVICE_PLAN" --resource-group "$RESOURCE_GROUP" -o table
# create an empty webapp to avoid chicken-and-egg problem between ACR and webapp
az webapp create --resource-group "$RESOURCE_GROUP" --plan "$APP_SERVICE_PLAN" --name "$WEBAPP_NAME" --runtime "DOTNETCORE:8.0"
az webapp identity assign --name "$WEBAPP_NAME" --resource-group "$RESOURCE_GROUP"
ACR_ID=$(az acr show --name "$ACR_NAME" --query id --output tsv)
WEBAPP_IDENTITY=$(az webapp show --name "$WEBAPP_NAME" --resource-group "$RESOURCE_GROUP" --query identity.principalId --output tsv)
az role assignment create --assignee "$WEBAPP_IDENTITY" --role AcrPull --scope "$ACR_ID"
az webapp config container set --name "$WEBAPP_NAME" --resource-group "$RESOURCE_GROUP" --docker-custom-image-name "$ACR_LOGIN_SERVER/$IMAGE_NAME" --docker-registry-server-url "https://$ACR_LOGIN_SERVER"
az webapp config appsettings set --name "$WEBAPP_NAME" --resource-group "$RESOURCE_GROUP" --settings "$SETTING"
```

```
az webapp config appsettings list --name "$WEBAPP_NAME" --resource-group
"$RESOURCE_GROUP"
az webapp show --name "$WEBAPP_NAME" --resource-group "$RESOURCE_GROUP"
--query defaultHostName --output tsv
# now open this URL in a browser and view the newly deployed web app
```

In this shell script, we create the resource group, create the app plan, create the web app, configure ACR and the web app to allow pulling the image, set the container details in place, set an app setting, and finally show the website's URL.

If we look carefully, we can see IIS details leaking through the Azure App Service configuration. Even when running on Linux, the paradigm is like IIS. An App Service Plan is like the IIS server. One or more app services can live inside the app plan much like websites and app pools live inside the IIS server.

On the upside, configuring an Azure App Service is quite simple. Even scaling up to multiple instances or very large instances is only a slider away. On the downside, one web app is one microservice. If we have a suite of microservices, we could easily exhaust the app service plan or require multiple app service plans, leading to a large compute bill.

Though we could tie all the App Services together in a private network, this is quite the task to configure. Service discovery almost certainly requires some fancy configuration or referencing public URLs. Later in this chapter, we'll tuck everything behind an API Gateway to ensure a single public API surface for a suite of microservices.

Azure App Service is definitely the easy button when it comes to hosting. App Service is ideal for hosting a single monolith. However, if we have a suite of microservices, the hosting and configuration gets complex quickly as we need one App Service per microservice.

Other Deployment Options

We've looked at a few options for deploying containers to Azure. But we've barely scratched the surface for deployment options. The authors are most familiar with Azure, so we've leaned into our knowledge. But there's lots of other great deployment options for containers on Azure and other clouds.

One could host containers in Azure Container Instance (ACI). ACI is a REST API for hosting containers as a cloud-native primitive. ACI is an ideal place to build a custom platform to spin up containers on-demand, and decommission them when no longer needed.

Azure App Fabric is a completely managed container orchestrator. The particulars of VMs and patching just melts away. Install a container image, and App Fabric will take care of the rest. App Fabric can be great if you want to outsource container deployment and management concerns to Azure.

On AWS, we can host containers in Fargate, Elastic Container Service (ECS), or in Elastic Beanstalk. Fargate is a completely managed container runtime built on top of either Kubernetes or ECS. Where Kubernetes focuses on industry standards and maximum flexibility, ECS focuses on developer simplicity. There's no VMs to manage or complex YAML to learn.

On Azure, AWS, or many other clouds, one could spin up virtual machines, and install Kubernetes, Docker Swarm, or another container runtime. This scenario is perfect for very large deployments where an enterprise is looking for consistency across clouds. With many of the managed services, the underlying Kubernetes version isn't as easy to control. By comparison, if we install Kubernetes ourselves on VMs, we can ensure it is configured exactly the way we want.

Reverse Proxy

In most of the hosting options we've discussed, we can configure a microservice to a unique subdomain, but they don't support configuring a single subdomain to host a suite of microservices. In this section, we'll look at techniques for hosting multiple microservices behind a single reverse proxy. This allows a suite of services to appear as a single website to consuming applications.

If each microservice is on a separate domain, consumers have a dizzying array of URLs to keep track of. What's the URL for the customer service? For the order service? For the product catalog? An API design like this is really confusing to use.

In this scenario where each is on a separate subdomain, the React app will need to call out to separate domains for each service. This means the React app needs a collection of URLs. Each server app also needs a CORS header matching the browser's domain for the browser to complete the call.

CHAPTER 9   DEPLOYING MICROSERVICES

This additional configuration means we must carefully configure both the browser app and the server microservices to be able to complete the call. This is a lot of work.

Instead, let's build a thing in front of the fleet of microservices that can forward different paths to different microservices. The customer service is at */customer*, the order service is at */order*, and the product catalog is at */product*. This reverse proxy setup greatly simplifies consumer setup to consume the fleet of microservices.

If we also add the front-end React app hosting to the same reverse proxy, we can avoid complex CORS setup. React doesn't need to know the services' subdomain as it's the same subdomain where the browser is running. Now even client API requests need only begin with */*.

The reverse proxy allows a suite of microservices to appear like a single, unified API surface. This elegant design makes APIs really easy and fun to consume.

To properly protect the microservices, it's best practice to put all microservices on a private network, and use the reverse proxy as a bridge from the outside world. This setup ensures ingenious clients can't call internal URLs on the services or circumnavigate authentication or rate limits managed by the reverse proxy.

Now let's look at a few reverse proxy setups in Azure.

Kubernetes Ingress

If all of our microservices are running as pods inside Kubernetes, we can use a k8s ingress as a reverse proxy. This ensures service discovery stays within Kubernetes, simplifying the cloud infrastructure required. To the rest of the cloud services and to consuming applications, the entire fleet of microservices is exposed through a single, scaled URL.

In the AKS section above, we looked at an example of an ingress YAML file. Let's look at it again:

```
apiVersion: networking.k8s.io/v1
kind: Ingress
metadata:
  name: microservice-ingress
  labels:
    name: microservice-ingress
  annotations:
    cert-manager.io/cluster-issuer: letsencrypt
```

```yaml
      acme.cert-manager.io/http01-edit-in-place: "true"
spec:
  ingressClassName: nginx
  tls:
  - hosts:
    - api.example.com
    secretName: tls-secret
  rules:
  - host: api.example.com
    http:
      paths:
      - pathType: Prefix
        path: "/api/customer"
        backend:
          service:
            name: customers
            port:
              number: 8080
      - pathType: Prefix
        path: "/api/order"
        backend:
          service:
            name: orders
            port:
              number: 8080
      - pathType: Prefix
        path: "/api/product"
        backend:
          service:
            name: products
            port:
              number: 8080
      - pathType: Prefix
        path: "/"
        backend:
```

```
    service:
      name: frontend
      port:
        number: 80
```

With this Ingress configuration, we have four microservices all running on the same subdomain, running from different paths. In fact, we have the React or Vue.js frontend running within Kubernetes as well. Perhaps the static files are hosted in Nginx or an SSR setup runs inside a Node.js container.

As the browser hits `https://example.com/` it loads the React static index.html page and other JavaScript and CSS resources. When the React app wants to look up the product catalog, it calls `/api/product/...` and hits the products microservice. When the user pushes the place order button in the Vue.js app, it calls `/api/order/create` and hits the orders microservice.

The browser app doesn't need to know what subdomain hosts each microservice because they're on the same subdomain as the frontend. No complex CORS setup is necessary on the server, and no complex service configuration is necessary on the client.

When we deploy from dev to test to prod, the same containers can move across environments – there's no hard-coded cross-domain configuration baked into the Vite build.

Kubernetes is a great reverse proxy if all your services run inside Kubernetes. If Kubernetes is your hosting platform, this is the perfect solution. However, if you have other services called directly from browser apps that don't live inside Kubernetes, you'll have to look to other reverse proxy options.

Application Gateway

Azure Application Gateway is a light-weight layer 7[2] reverse proxy. It's a good fit for lightweight tasks where path-based routing is sufficient.

One can configure API Gateway as a Web Application Firewall (WAF) to protect from OWASP top-ten threats. Configuring the API Gateway as a WAF is considerably more expensive though.

---

[2] A discussion of the OSI Model is beyond the scope of this book. Typically, routers such as this operate either on layer 4 (TCP) or layer 7 (App layer, in this case HTTP). See `https://en.wikipedia.org/wiki/OSI_model` or `https://www.cloudflare.com/learning/ddos/glossary/open-systems-interconnection-model-osi/` for more details on the OSI Model.

CHAPTER 9   DEPLOYING MICROSERVICES

In App Gateway, we configure a frontend IP address. In our DNS provider, we can create an A record for our chosen domain. Then we configure "backend pools". We'd configure one for each microservice, pointing to the applicable VM, VM Scale Set (VMSS), or App Service. Then we configure routing rules that map a certain URL prefix to a specific backend within the virtual network.

The Azure Portal helps us be successful by providing wizards that help easily choose sensible defaults. In an App Gateway setup, there's a lot of knobs to set. Here's an example shell script that creates an App Gateway pointing to an App Service:

```
RESOURCE_GROUP="rg-pro-microservices"
LOCATION="eastus"
APP_SERVICE_PLAN="sp-pro-microservices"
WEB_APP_NAME="mywebapp$RANDOM"
APP_SKU="F1" # Free tier
ACR_NAME="myaccount"
IMAGE_NAME="$ACR_NAME.azurecr.io/myimage:latest"
VNET_NAME="myVNet"
SUBNET_NAME_APPGW="appgwSubnet"
SUBNET_NAME_APP="appSubnet"
APPGW_NAME="gw-pro-microservices"
PUBLIC_IP_NAME="myAppGwPublicIP"

# Create resource group
az group create --name $RESOURCE_GROUP --location $LOCATION

# Create ACR (optional if you already have one)
az acr create --resource-group $RESOURCE_GROUP --name $ACR_NAME --sku Basic
az acr login --name $ACR_NAME

# Create App Service Plan and Web App
az appservice plan create --name $APP_SERVICE_PLAN --resource-group
$RESOURCE_GROUP --is-linux --sku $APP_SKU
az webapp create --resource-group $RESOURCE_GROUP --plan $APP_SERVICE_
PLAN --name $WEB_APP_NAME --deployment-container-image-name $IMAGE_NAME

# Configure App Service to use ACR credentials
ACR_USERNAME=$(az acr credential show --name $ACR_NAME --query
username --output tsv)
```

CHAPTER 9 DEPLOYING MICROSERVICES

```
ACR_PASSWORD=$(az acr credential show --name $ACR_NAME --query
passwords[0].value --output tsv)
az webapp config container set --name $WEB_APP_NAME --resource-group
$RESOURCE_GROUP --docker-custom-image-name $IMAGE_NAME --docker-registry-
server-url https://$ACR_NAME.azurecr.io --docker-registry-server-user $ACR_
USERNAME --docker-registry-server-password $ACR_PASSWORD

# Set up networking for App Gateway
az network vnet create --resource-group $RESOURCE_GROUP --name
$VNET_NAME --subnet-name $SUBNET_NAME_APPGW
az network public-ip create --resource-group $RESOURCE_GROUP --name
$PUBLIC_IP_NAME --sku Standard

# Create and configure Application Gateway
az network application-gateway create --name $APPGW_NAME --location
$LOCATION --resource-group $RESOURCE_GROUP --sku Standard_v2 --capacity
1 --vnet-name $VNET_NAME --subnet $SUBNET_NAME_APPGW --public-ip-address
$PUBLIC_IP_NAME
az network application-gateway address-pool create --gateway-name $APPGW_
NAME --resource-group $RESOURCE_GROUP --name "appServicePool" --servers
"${WEB_APP_NAME}.azurewebsites.net"
az network application-gateway http-settings create --resource-group $RESOURCE_
GROUP --gateway-name $APPGW_NAME --name "appServiceHttpSetting" --port
80 --protocol Http --pick-hostname-from-backend-address
az network application-gateway frontend-port create --resource-group
$RESOURCE_GROUP --gateway-name $APPGW_NAME --name "httpPort" --port 80
az network application-gateway listener create --resource-group $RESOURCE_
GROUP --gateway-name $APPGW_NAME --name "httpListener" --frontend-port
"httpPort" --frontend-ip "appGatewayFrontend"
az network application-gateway rule create --resource-group $RESOURCE_
GROUP --gateway-name $APPGW_NAME --name "rule1" --rule-type Basic --http-
listener "httpListener" --backend-address-pool "appServicePool" --backend-
http-settings "appServiceHttpSetting"
```

In this example, we create an ACR, an Azure App Service, and build all the details for an Azure App Gateway: frontend, backend, routing rule, and other particulars like vnet, subnet, public ip, etc.

CHAPTER 9   DEPLOYING MICROSERVICES

If we chose to flee from Kubernetes because the configuration was too complex, this might be a good wake-up call. App Gateway setup can get involved.

App Gateway is a great reverse proxy choice when we want a basic layer 7 reverse proxy, we want to fill it full of configuration, and not have to manage any hardware. We can also choose to upgrade the reverse proxy to include a WAF that protects from OWASP top-ten threats. App Gateway isn't a good choice if we need authentication, rate limiting, or any advanced API features. After all, it's merely a layer 7 reverse proxy.

API Management

Azure API Management (APIM) is a feature-rich reverse proxy and API management suite. It boasts lots of capabilities to really take control of the traffic flowing into the fleet of microservices. Though we can use API Management as a simple reverse proxy, the real sweet spot is herding a suite of enterprise APIs.

With Azure API Management, we can make a front door for all the APIs. We can secure, authenticate, limit, govern, and even modify both request and response. In fact, where API Management really fits is enterprise API governance. Let's put not just one project or one team's APIs behind this service, but rather front a suite of teams' work into one unified API surface. This can centralize billing, security, and authentication for the enterprise.

When setting up API Management, we first create the API Management instance. Then create an API we'll put behind it, and finally register the API with API Management. The Azure Portal is the easiest way to get started. For the benefit of reproducibility, let's use the Azure CLI instead:

```
RESOURCE_GROUP="rg-pro-microservices"
LOCATION="canadacentral"
APP_SERVICE_PLAN="sp-pro-microservices"
APP_NAME="wa-pro-microservices"
CONTAINER_IMAGE="myaccount.azurecr.io/myimage:latest"
APIM_NAME="apim-pro-microservices"
SERVICE_PLAN_SKU="F1" # Free tier for testing

az group create --name $RESOURCE_GROUP --location $LOCATION
```

```
az apim create --name $APIM_NAME --resource-group $RESOURCE_GROUP --location
$LOCATION --publisher-email "admin@example.com" --publisher-name
"Admin" --sku-name Developer

az appservice plan create --name $APP_SERVICE_PLAN --resource-group
$RESOURCE_GROUP --is-linux --sku $SERVICE_PLAN_SKU
az webapp create --name $APP_NAME --resource-group $RESOURCE_GROUP --plan
$APP_SERVICE_PLAN --deployment-container-image-name $CONTAINER_IMAGE

APP_URL=$(az webapp show --name $APP_NAME --resource-group $RESOURCE_
GROUP --query defaultHostName --output tsv)

az apim api import --resource-group myResourceGroup --service-name
$APIM_NAME --path api/customer --api-id $APP_NAME --specification-format
OpenApi --specification-url "https://{$APP_URL}/swagger/v1/
swagger.json" --display-name "Customer" --protocols https
```

In this example, we first create the API Management resource, then create an App Service from a container, and finally register the web app with API Management using the site's swagger.json file.

Once we have the API running and registered with API Management, we can do lots of things with the API. Through the Azure portal, it's easy to publish the API as a product. Or we can test the API backends with the Swagger UI tester. Or transform the request or response. See `https://learn.microsoft.com/en-us/azure/api-management/transform-api` for specifics on configuring API Management details.

Azure API Management is definitely a great reverse proxy, but the typical use-case for API Management is so much bigger. With API Management, we can centralize an enterprise's worth of APIs into a common API surface area, centralizing authentication, security, and billing at the same time. We created a simple API Management resource here, but the potential is so much greater.

YARP

YARP stands for Yet Another Reverse Proxy. It's unique in this collection because it isn't an Azure service. Rather it's a NuGet package you can install into any ASP.NET application.

CHAPTER 9   DEPLOYING MICROSERVICES

YARP is used internally to power Azure App Service. In the article by Byron Tardif titled "A Heavy Lift: Bringing Kestrel + YARP to Azure App Services," he brags that moving from IIS to YARP + Kestrel yields an "almost 80% improvement in throughput in performance."

To set up YARP is quite simple. After adding the *Yarp.ReverseProxy* NuGet package, *Program.cs* looks like this:

```
var builder = WebApplication.CreateBuilder(args);
builder.Services.AddReverseProxy()
    .LoadFromConfig(builder.Configuration.GetSection("ReverseProxy"));
var app = builder.Build();
app.UseHttpsRedirection(); // <-- you can still use ASP.NET middleware
app.MapReverseProxy();
app.Run();
```

With Program.cs in place, we add an *appsettings.json* that tells YARP what services it will proxy to:

```
{
  "Logging": {
    "LogLevel": {
      "Default": "Information",
      "Microsoft.AspNetCore": "Warning"
    }
  },
  "AllowedHosts": "*",
  "ReverseProxy": {
    "Routes": {
      "customer": {
        "ClusterId": "customer",
        "Match": {
          "Path": "/api/customer/{**catch-all}"
        }
      },
```

```json
    "order": {
      "ClusterId": "order",
      "Match": {
        "Path": "/api/order/{**catch-all}"
      }
    },
    "product": {
      "ClusterId": "product",
      "Match": {
        "Path": "/api/product/{**catch-all}"
      }
    },
    "react": {
      "ClusterId": "react",
      "Match": {
        "Path": "{**catch-all}"
      }
    }
  },
  "Clusters": {
    "react": {
      "Destinations": {
        "destination1": {
          "Address": "https://react.azurewebsites.net/"
        }
      }
    },
    "customer": {
      "Destinations": {
        "destination1": {
          "Address": "https://customer.azurewebsites.net/"
        }
      }
    },
```

```
      "order": {
        "Destinations": {
          "destination1": {
            "Address": "https://order.azurewebsites.net/"
          }
        }
      },
      "product": {
        "Destinations": {
          "destination1": {
            "Address": "https://product.azurewebsites.net/"
          }
        }
      }
    }
  }
}
```

Notice in this configuration that we're using the wildcard *{**catch-all}* to handle all URLs that begin with the specified route. For example, */api/customer/foo* and */api/customer/bar* and */api/customer/very/nested/service* will all route to the customer microservice.

We list here the URLs of the microservices. We'll want to move all our microservices into a virtual network to ensure they're not accessible publicly, only through the YARP reverse proxy.

Because YARP is just an ASP.NET middleware running in a regular ASP.NET web app, we can use other ASP.NET middlewares too. In our Program.cs above we use https redirection. We could also add logging, authentication, error handling, health checks, caching, or any other ASP.NET request pipeline feature. This makes YARP very versatile.

YARP is a great reverse proxy that can scale as the microservice system scales. It has infinite customizability because it's just a NuGet package in our ASP.NET hosted application. We're taking ownership of a lot of the finer details though. By comparison, API Management allows us to outsource a lot of the details here to Azure.

Reverse Proxy Roundup

We looked at a few reverse proxy systems here. Which should you choose? The short answer is it depends. Let's review the pros and cons and best use-cases of each.

Name	Description	Pros and Cons	Best use-case
Kubernetes Ingress	Map DNS to a collection of k8s services	- Configuration can get complex - Easy to include TLS termination	Best when all your microservices are hosted in Kubernetes
Application Gateway	Layer 7 reverse proxy	- Can upgrade to WAF	Best for simple reverse proxy needs
API Management	Centralize and catalog an enterprise's APIs	- Centralize billing, throttling, authentication, security - Transform requests and responses	Best for enterprise API management across projects and teams
YARP	A NuGet library with simple configuration	- Must own hosting - Can add any ASP.NET middleware	Best when you want to really customize the experience

Summary

Packaging a microservice as a container offers an industry standard platform allowing us to deploy to many environments. In this chapter, we containerized an ASP.NET application, deployed it to ACR, and deployed it to many different container runtime environments. We used a reverse proxy to collect all the microservices behind a single subdomain, freeing us from complex CORS setup.

Containerizing a .NET application is easily done in one of two ways. A Dockerfile offers the most flexibility as we can specifically control all aspects of the Docker image creation. By comparison, the .NET SDK approach offers a hands-off build target that can execute even without Docker or Podman running.

Once the container is in place, there's a variety of mechanisms for hosting containers in Azure. AKS is upstream Kubernetes hosted in Azure. We get all the benefits of the open source Kubernetes ecosystem at the cost of some complex configuration. By comparison, pushing our image into ACA offers an opinionated abstraction built on top of Kubernetes. It is simpler in some respects, but look carefully, and you can see the Kubernetes bits showing through. Azure App Service is the simplest hosting mechanism, though it's not well suited if there's a lot of microservices involved.

With the microservices in place, we want to collect all the microservices behind a reverse proxy to give a single subdomain. This avoids complex CORS configuration, and eliminates environment-specific container images. If all the microservices are in Kubernetes, a k8s ingress is a natural choice. The ingress configuration is quite straightforward. Azure Application Gateway is a simple layer 7 reverse proxy. App Gateway outsources all the runtime details of a reverse proxy, but the configuration can get intense. API Management allows maximum control as we can configure advanced features such as billing and request/response rewriting. YARP is a more programmer-friendly reverse proxy as it's a NuGet package and an ASP.NET middleware, allowing us to use all other .NET middleware such as authentication, logging, and health checks. Reach for YARP if you want to own everything about the reverse proxy process.

ASP.NET fits naturally in container hosting on Linux. No longer are we tied to IIS and Windows servers. Whether we host with open source options like Kubernetes or Azure-specific services, ASP.NET is right at home in Docker containers.

CHAPTER 10

Healthy Microservices

In this chapter, we discuss ensuring maximum observability of microservices. OpenTelemetry has become the standard health monitoring tool, so we really lean in and look at the benefits of OpenTelemetry. .NET Aspire is a great way to easily set up OpenTelemetry and use it during local development and debugging. We can use custom logs, traces, and metrics to add additional visibility to microservices, allowing us to easily find the source of a future problem. In production, we can use Azure Application Insights to capture production logs, traces, and metrics through OpenTelemetry.

Is It Healthy?

When we look at a microservice, how do we know if it's running well? As you look at a service, if it's running correctly, you probably didn't notice. But if it's running poorly, you probably noticed a lot.

Let's begin by enumerating what could go wrong with a microservice:

- Not responding to web traffic.
- Processing data incorrectly.
- Using too much RAM.
- Running slowly.
- Threw an exception.
- The system crashed.
- Another process is behaving badly and choking the resources.
- Running system updates.
- The hardware failed.

How do we compensate for services that behave this way? The naive approach – often our first attempt – is to throw stuff at it. Is it running slowly? Let's buy a bigger processor. Is it taking too much RAM? Let's add more RAM to the machine. Is another process interfering? Let's move it to its own machine. Is the hardware flakey? Let's run multiple copies. This can often buy us time, but it's a really costly endeavor.

As we reach for high availability, we need both redundancy and well-functioning systems. Let's look deeper at how to handle the problem correctly.

Where Do We Look?

We need a methodical approach to system diagnostics. We could definitely throw money at the problem, but that isn't a solid approach. Rather, we need to learn how the system functions and act methodically to correct the system when it fails.

When looking at a system, we can enumerate questions we'd like to know about the system:

- How many requests is it processing?
- How much RAM is it using?
- What percentage of requests are failing?
- What caused the exception?

As we enumerate these questions, groups start to form. Francisco Beltrao,[1] a software engineer at Microsoft, nicely enumerates three main groups of insights as he introduces these concepts to .NET developers: we need logging, tracing, and metrics.

Logging – Logs show us about events at a point in time. For example, the system started, or an exception was thrown. These logs may hold additional details like a stack trace, the date and time of the event, the currently processing URL, and the authenticated user if logged in. What distinguishes these from the other groups is they're a point in time - there's no duration.

Tracing – A trace helps us put together the user's journey (the sequence of events). In addition to the details in a log, each trace ties to previous and successive events through a correlation id or a request id. We can follow a user's journey from the browser app to the API Gateway through the microservices to the data store with traces. Though

---

[1] https://devblogs.microsoft.com/dotnet/observability-asp-net-core-apps/

logs can tell us if the database timed out, traces can tell us if this led them to abandon their cart or if they passed a bad parameter. Traces could tell us their journey through the sales funnel.

Metrics – Metrics add a time component to the investigation. Logs mark a point in time, an event. By comparison, metrics don't need an initiation point; metrics are ongoing statistics about the system. How many requests per second are we processing? What percentage of requests are failing with an HTTP status that isn't 200? Is the CPU usage higher than normal?

As we're investigating a system, we need all three groups of insights. Let's log when an exception happened and when a new release is deployed. Let's trace requests going between systems to understand user usage patterns and give context and reproducibility to exceptions. And let's harvest system and application metrics to understand if the system is constrained or behaving badly.

OpenTelemetry

OpenTelemetry has emerged as an industry-standard mechanism for logging, tracing, and metrics. .NET builds support for OpenTelemetry into pre-existing .NET base class libraries. We can use OpenTelemetry to add tracing to our application.

OpenTelemetry began as an effort to unify OpenTrace and Google's OpenCensus. It has since grown to a CNCF[2]-backed project to include metrics, tracing, and logging. There are implementations for Spring, ASP.NET Core, Express, Rust, Java, Ruby, Python, and more. There's also support for other platforms and tools such as databases, hardware devices, and web servers. For example, we can add OpenTelemetry to Nginx to capture the server-side of static file hosting. OpenTelemetry provides options for logging, metrics, and tracing. In OpenTelemetry, all data is pushed to the provider.

As of this writing, OpenTelemetry's .NET implementation focuses primarily on tracing, and supports metrics as well. The OpenTelemetry logging standard is still emerging, so .NET support for pushing logs is just beginning. The .NET implementation adapts .NET concepts into OpenTelemetry concepts, providing incredible backward compatibility and system visibility for this new technology. The system still functions the same, but concepts are renamed. For example, in OpenTelemetry, a "span" identifies work being done, including start and end times, attributes or tags describing the activity,

---

[2] CNCF is the Cloud Native Computing Foundation. See also `https://www.cncf.io/`

and the parent activity that spawned it. In .NET, *Span<T>*[3] means something completely different. Therefore, the .NET OpenTelemetry implementation calls this an Activity.[4]

The beauty of a single standard for logs, traces, and metrics is that a lot of platforms support it. Even the environment variable names are becoming more standard. For example, here's a *Dockerfile* that adds OpenTelemetry into React and the Nginx server that hosts the static files:

```
FROM node:alpine as build

WORKDIR /src

COPY package.json package.json
RUN npm install

COPY . .
# build .env
# prefix OTEL attributes with `VITE_` to pass through `vite build`
ARG VITE_OTEL_EXPORTER_OTLP_ENDPOINT
ARG VITE_OTEL_EXPORTER_OTLP_HEADERS
ARG VITE_OTEL_RESOURCE_ATTRIBUTES
ARG VITE_OTEL_SERVICE_NAME
RUN echo "VITE_OTEL_EXPORTER_OTLP_ENDPOINT=$VITE_OTEL_EXPORTER_OTLP_ENDPOINT" > .env
RUN echo "VITE_OTEL_EXPORTER_OTLP_HEADERS=$VITE_OTEL_EXPORTER_OTLP_HEADERS" >> .env
RUN echo "VITE_OTEL_RESOURCE_ATTRIBUTES=$VITE_OTEL_RESOURCE_ATTRIBUTES" >> .env
RUN echo "VITE_OTEL_SERVICE_NAME=$VITE_OTEL_SERVICE_NAME" >> .env

RUN npm run build
# ASSUME: it produces a dist folder

FROM nginx:alpine-otel
```

---

[3] https://docs.microsoft.com/en-us/dotnet/api/system.span-1
[4] https://github.com/open-telemetry/opentelemetry-dotnet/blob/main/src/OpenTelemetry.Api/README.md#introduction-to-opentelemetry-net-tracing-api

```
RUN echo "load_module modules/ngx_otel_module.so;" | cat - /etc/nginx/
nginx.conf > /tmp/nginx.conf; mv /tmp/nginx.conf /etc/nginx/nginx.conf
COPY nginx.conf /etc/nginx/conf.d/default.conf

WORKDIR /usr/share/nginx/html
COPY --from=build /src/dist .

# nginx already has `CMD [...]`
```

And then *nginx.conf* starts with this:

```
otel_exporter {
  # From the server's perspective:
  # TODO: set url to a valid OTEL endpoint during the build
  endpoint aspire:18889;
}
otel_trace on;
otel_service_name "nginx-react";

server {
  listen       80;
  server_name  react-server;

  location / {
    root   /usr/share/nginx/html;
    try_files $uri $uri/ /index.html;
    otel_trace_context propagate;
    otel_span_name "$request_method $request_uri";
  }
}
```

This is wonderful! For a completely unrelated system, the exact same OpenTelemetry configuration works great.

OpenTelemetry is clearly becoming the standard for all systems. We can easily configure the OpenTelemetry collector details in each system, and pipe logs, traces, and metrics in a standard way into all the systems that need it. This is brilliant!

Aspire

.NET Aspire is a great way to get OpenTelemetry and other great defaults into a new or existing project. Aspire's dashboard injects OpenTelemetry settings as environment variables, and Aspire's ServiceDefaults project nicely configures logs, traces, and metrics for all projects that consume it. Though we could definitely add the OpenTelemetry libraries manually, it's so much easier to add Aspire to the project to do it for us.

To add Aspire to an existing project, in Visual Studio's solution explorer, right-click on a project, choose the Add menu, and choose .NET Aspire Orchestrator Support. This creates the AppHost project, the project that starts all microservices, and the ServiceDefaults project, the project that rigs up sensible defaults for many .NET web technologies.

To begin a new project with Aspire preinstalled, in Visual Studio, go to File ➤ New Project, and choose the .NET Aspire starter template. In this template is the AppHost project that starts the dashboard, the ServiceDefaults project with sensible web defaults, and both an API and UI project showing how Aspire's service discovery facilitates one microservice calling another.

Now that we have Aspire in place, let's look more closely at the OpenTelemetry details. In the ServiceDefaults project is this handy configuration:

```
private static TBuilder AddOpenTelemetryExporters<TBuilder>(this TBuilder builder) where TBuilder : IHostApplicationBuilder
{
  var useOtlpExporter = !string.IsNullOrWhiteSpace(builder.
  Configuration["OTEL_EXPORTER_OTLP_ENDPOINT"]);

  if (useOtlpExporter)
  {
    builder.Services.AddOpenTelemetry().UseOtlpExporter();
  }
  // …
```

This little function nicely notices the standard *OTEL_EXPORTER_OTLP_ENDPOINT* environment variable. If it exists, it sets up .NET's OpenTelemetry library. Inside the library, it looks for the standard environment variables and configures it to push logs, traces, and metrics, authenticating if necessary. If it's unset, OpenTelemetry nicely stays dormant, and the application doesn't consume extra cycles collecting traces or metrics only to be thrown away.

Adding more Instrumenters to .NET Aspire

As we're collecting traces with .NET's OpenTelemetry library, we can hook into a large collection of existing NuGet libraries that harvest a lot of detail. Here's a snippet of the ServiceDefaults project expanded with a lot more collectors:

```csharp
public static IHostApplicationBuilder ConfigureOpenTelemetry(this
IHostApplicationBuilder builder)
{
  // ... snip ...

  builder.Services.AddOpenTelemetry()
    .WithTracing(tracing =>
    {
      tracing.AddAspNetCoreInstrumentation()
        .AddGrpcClientInstrumentation()
        .AddHttpClientInstrumentation()
        // Added some more trace providers
        // (requires more NuGet packages)
        .AddEntityFrameworkCoreInstrumentation()
        .AddSqlClientInstrumentation()
        .AddNpgsql() // PostgreSQL
        .AddRedisInstrumentation();
    });
  // ... snip ...
```

With this configuration (and after installing the NuGet packages) we're now capturing internal events from ASP.NET, HttpClient, gRPC, Entity Framework, SqlClient, PostgreSQL's database driver, and Redis's database driver. Granted, we may not need all these if we're not using all these libraries. It's really handy to collect all the details from any of these libraries automatically though.

Given the Aspire OpenTelemetry trace setup, Figure 10-1 shows we get a great view of the request as it navigates between microservices.

CHAPTER 10 HEALTHY MICROSERVICES

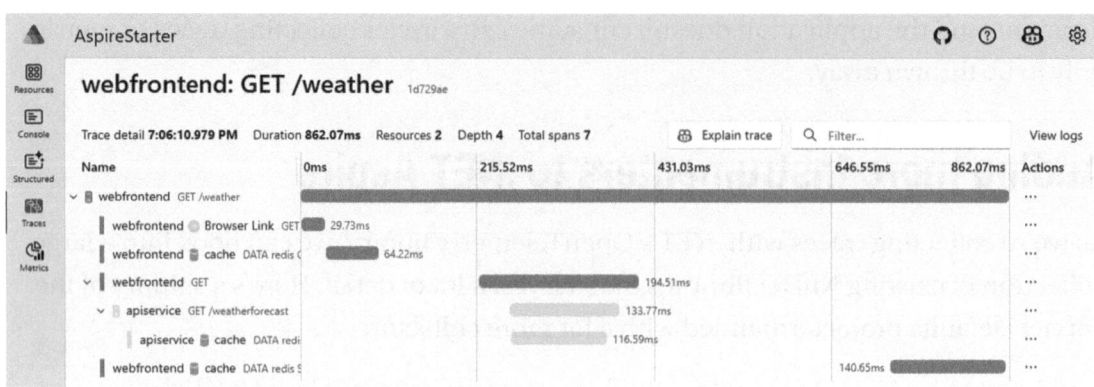

Figure 10-1. *.NET Aspire Traces*

Source: `https://learn.microsoft.com/en-us/dotnet/aspire/get-started/build-your-first-aspire-app`

In this section, we've focused on the OpenTelemetry aspects of Aspire. But it's hardly just an OpenTelemetry sink and visualization tool. It also nicely handles service discovery, starts and debugs projects, executables, and containers, and allows us to quickly visualize logs, traces, metrics, and microservice dependencies. Aspire also helps deploy the suite of microservices to Azure Container Apps (ACA), Kubernetes, and Docker Compose.

Custom Logs, Traces, and Metrics

With .NET Aspire in place, we're capturing OpenTelemetry logs, traces, and metrics. We can visualize these with the Aspire dashboard. Aspire launches the suite of microservices. How can we add our own logs, traces, and metrics? We'll see that we're using .NET classes that have been in place since .NET Framework. Yet now they pipe into OpenTelemetry.

Kathy, the Code Whiz developer, is tasked with adding specific details about the locations users ask for and the Google Routes API response code. Let's add some new logs. In the GoogleRouteService project from Chapter 5, open the `GoogleRouteService.cs` file. At the top of the class, change the class declaration to take in an `ILogger<T>`.

```
public class GoogleRouteServices(ILogger<GoogleRouteServices> logger)With
```
this logger injected in, we can log additional details about the call:
```
public async Task<DiscoveredRoutes> GetRouteInfo(Addresses addresses,
string apiUrl, string apiKey)
{
  logger.LogInformation($"GetMapDistanceAsync from {addresses.
  OriginAddress} to {addresses.DestinationAddress}");
```

With these few lines, Kathy is able to log details about this point in time. But this doesn't tell the full story. Let's add the custom trace and spans, or in .NET terms, the activity and tags.

Still in *GoogleRouteService.cs* file, at the top of the class, add a static *ActivitySource*:

```
public class GoogleRouteServices(ILogger<GoogleRouteServices> logger)
{
    public const string ACTIVITY_SOURCE_NAME = "DistanceMicroservice.
    GoogleRouteServices";
    private static readonly ActivitySource activitySource = new
    ActivitySource(ACTIVITY_SOURCE_NAME);
```

This ActivitySource is static because we want exactly one for the entire lifetime of the application. If we were to create a new ActivitySource for each instance, we could easily overwhelm OpenTelemetry with trace instrumenters. Though not required, the name as a string will help us wire this into OpenTelemetry.

In the constructor, we pass a unique name. By convention, we can use the full namespace and class name. Optionally we can also pass a version as the second parameter.

In the body of the *GetRouteInfo* method, add this around the API call to get the activity:

```
public async Task<GoogleDistanceData> GetMapDistanceAsync(string
originCity, string destinationCity)
{
  // ... code omitted for brevity ...
  using var activity = activitySource.StartActivity("GoogleRoutesApi");
  activity?.SetTag("googleRoutes.originAddress", addresses.OriginAddress);
```

```
activity?.SetTag("googleRoutes.destinationAddress", addresses.
DestinationAddress);

HttpResponseMessage response = await httpClient.PostAsJsonAsync(apiUrl,
routeRequest);

activity?.SetTag("googleRoutes.status", (int)response.StatusCode);
// ... code omitted for brevity ...
```

We want to put this at the beginning of the work we want to track. In this case, it makes sense to put it right before calling Google's Route API. We add using here, so it'll automatically end as the method finishes.

The activity might be null here. As noted in the documentation, if there's no exporter listening for trace events, .NET can optimize the execution by not returning an object.[5] For this reason, we'll use the null coalescing operator introduced in C# 6.[6]

We also added tags to include additional context to the content we're looking to track. These tags are free-form values. We can add tags for any interesting behaviors we'd like. In this case, we want to capture origin and destination cities, but we really don't want to log the API key in the trace details.

Let's add one more tag for the results:

```
discoveredRoutes.Message = $"Number of routes found: {discoveredRoutes.
Routes.Length}";
        activity?.SetTag("googleRoutes.routesFoundCount", discoveredRoutes.
        Routes.Length); // <-- add this line
```

If Kathy ran the microservice right now, she would note that the activity is null. Indeed, this is the desired behavior when no one is listening for the OpenTelemetry traces. Let's add the traces to the OpenTelemetry exports. In the *ServiceDefaults* project, in *Extensions.cs*, in the *ConfigureOpenTelemetry* method, we need to reference this *ActivitySource*. Sadly, we can't reference the string constant we created earlier because that would create a circular dependency. We could duplicate the string, but now we have a magic string defined in two places. Let's pass in a list of sources:

---

[5] https://docs.microsoft.com/en-us/dotnet/core/diagnostics/distributed-tracing-instrumentation-walkthroughs#activity
[6] https://docs.microsoft.com/en-us/dotnet/csharp/language-reference/operators/member-access-operators#null-conditional-operators--and-

CHAPTER 10 HEALTHY MICROSERVICES

```
public static TBuilder ConfigureOpenTelemetry<TBuilder>(this TBuilder
builder, string[] sources) where TBuilder : IHostApplicationBuilder
{
  // ... snip ...
  builder.Services.AddOpenTelemetry()
    // ... snip ...
    .WithTracing(tracing =>
    {
      tracing
        .AddSource(sources) // <- add this line
        .AddSource(builder.Environment.ApplicationName)
```

We modified the method definition to take in a list of sources, and exported the sources to OpenTelemetry. Next modify the *AddServiceDefaults* method at the top of the file to pass it in

```
public static TBuilder AddServiceDefaults<TBuilder>(this TBuilder builder,
string[]? sources = null) where TBuilder : IHostApplicationBuilder
{
  builder.ConfigureOpenTelemetry(meters ?? [], sources ?? []);
```

One more spot gets everything wired up. In the *DistanceMicroservice* project in *Program.cs*, let's modify the *AddServiceDefaults* call to pass in the ActivitySource:

```
builder.AddServiceDefaults(sources: [GoogleRouteServices.ACTIVITY_
SOURCE_NAME]);
```

That's it! Kathy has created a new Activity (span) and added custom tags to it.

Start the solution, open the Aspire dashboard, and switch to the traces tab. Run the microservice a few times, and notice the traces and additional details.

Let's upgrade again. Let's build a custom metric that counts success and fail calls to this service. We'll follow much of the same steps that we did for adding traces as we add metrics. Let's begin in *GoogleRouteService.cs* file. Just inside the class definition, add a new meter:

```
public class GoogleRouteServices(ILogger<GoogleRouteServices> logger)
{
  public const string DISTANCE_METER_NAME = "DistanceMicroservice.
  GoogleRouteServices";
  private static readonly Meter DistanceMeter = new(DISTANCE_METER_NAME);
  private static readonly Counter<long> DistanceSuccess = DistanceMeter.
  CreateCounter<long>("api-calls-success", description: "Successful
  distance measurements.");
  private static readonly Counter<long> DistanceFail = DistanceMeter.
  CreateCounter<long>("api-calls-fail", description: "Failed distance
  measurements.");
```

Then in the *GetRouteInfo* method, we increment the success or fail metric based on the response status code:

```
if (!response.IsSuccessStatusCode)
{
  DistanceFail.Add(1);
  discoveredRoutes.Message = $"Error: {(int)response.StatusCode} -
  {response.ReasonPhrase}";
}
DistanceSuccess.Add(1);
```

We're assuming here that the API call doesn't throw an exception. If we were worried about exceptions, we could wrap the API call in a try/catch, and increment the fail metric in the catch block.

If we fired up the microservice now, we'd notice the metric isn't getting logged. We've not told OpenTelemetry to export this metric. In the *ServiceDefaults* project, in *Extensions.cs*, in the *ConfigureOpenTelemetry* method, we'll add a list of meters:

```
public static TBuilder ConfigureOpenTelemetry<TBuilder>(this TBuilder
builder, string[] meters, string[] sources) where TBuilder :
IHostApplicationBuilder
{
  // ... snip ...
  builder.Services.AddOpenTelemetry()
    .WithMetrics(metrics =>
```

```
{
  metrics
    .AddMeter(meters) // <- add this line
    .AddAspNetCoreInstrumentation()
```

We're now passing in a list of meters and a list of trace sources. In the *AddServiceDefaults* method, we pass them through

```
public static TBuilder AddServiceDefaults<TBuilder>(this TBuilder builder,
string[]? meters = null, string[]? sources = null) where TBuilder :
IHostApplicationBuilder
{
  builder.ConfigureOpenTelemetry(meters ?? [], sources ?? []);
```

Then finally in the *DistanceMicroservice* project in *Program.cs*, we pass in the list of meters:

```
builder.AddServiceDefaults(meters: [GoogleRouteServices.DISTANCE_METER_
NAME], sources: [GoogleRouteServices.ACTIVITY_SOURCE_NAME]);
```

Now when we fire up Aspire and run the microservice, we can switch to Aspire dashboard's metrics tab and see our new metrics. Probably putting the metrics counters and tracing activity source in the microservice mixes concerns. Kathy adds a Jira task to refactor these pieces into their own static classes that won't cause cross-dependency concerns if this quick instrumentation bump adds value.

Logs are a great way to capture details about a point in time. Tracing can be an effective tool for discovering and auditing the relationships between components. Metrics allow us to count events within a timeframe. In the .NET implementation of OpenTelemetry, we use built-in .NET classes for logging, tracing, and metrics. The class names are slightly different from the official OpenTelemetry concepts, but hooking into the existing logging, tracing, and metrics system allows OpenTelemetry to instrument much older .NET projects than would be possible if logs, traces, and metrics were new OpenTelemetry constructs that sat on top. Aspire makes it easy to surface these details to the developer as one builds and troubleshoots the microservice. But how will Kathy debug the microservices in production? Let's look at Azure Application Insights.

CHAPTER 10   HEALTHY MICROSERVICES

Azure Application Insights

Azure Application Insights is the way to capture and visualize logs, traces, and metrics within Azure. Though we could definitely host our own Prometheus, Grafana, and Jaeger containers in Azure, using built-in tools gives us access to other systems that may not have OpenTelemetry sinks yet.

Kathy finds adding App Insights to OpenTelemetry is easy. In the *ServiceDefaults* project, in *Extensions.cs* is this commented out line:

```
//if (!string.IsNullOrEmpty(builder.Configuration["APPLICATIONINSIGHTS_CONNECTION_STRING"]))
//{
//    builder.Services.AddOpenTelemetry()
//        .UseAzureMonitor();
//}
```

To enable ASP.NET and OpenTelemetry to send data to App Insights, we need only uncomment these lines, redeploy, and set the environment variable to the connection string. Notice that we're not actually using the connection string; *UseAzureMonitor()* looks for this named environment variable automatically. Rather we're just checking that it's not blank.

Here's a full script that provisions the microservice in Azure App Service and provisions Azure App Insights:

```
RESOURCE_GROUP="rg-pro-microservices"
APP_NAME="wa-pro-microservices"
PLAN_NAME="sp-pro-microservices"
LOCATION="canadacentral"
CONTAINER_IMAGE="myregistry.azurecr.io/myapp:latest"
APPINSIGHTS_NAME="$APP_NAME-ai"
SERVICE_PLAN_SKU="F1" # Free tier for testing

az group create --name $RESOURCE_GROUP --location $LOCATION
az appservice plan create --name $PLAN_NAME --resource-group $RESOURCE_GROUP --is-linux --sku $SERVICE_PLAN_SKU
az webapp create --name $APP_NAME --resource-group $RESOURCE_GROUP --plan $PLAN_NAME --deployment-container-image-name $CONTAINER_IMAGE
```

```
az monitor app-insights component create --app "$APPINSIGHTS_NAME"
--location $LOCATION --resource-group $RESOURCE_GROUP
--application-type web
INSTRUMENTATION_KEY=$(az monitor app-insights component show --app
"$APPINSIGHTS_NAME" --resource-group $RESOURCE_GROUP --query
"instrumentationKey" --output tsv)
CONNECTION_STRING=$(az monitor app-insights component show --app
"$APPINSIGHTS_NAME" --resource-group $RESOURCE_GROUP --query
"connectionString" --output tsv)
az webapp config appsettings set --name $APP_NAME --resource-group
$RESOURCE_GROUP --settings APPINSIGHTS_INSTRUMENTATIONKEY=$INSTRUMENT
ATION_KEY APPLICATIONINSIGHTS_CONNECTION_STRING="$CONNECTION_STRING"
ApplicationInsightsAgent_EXTENSION_VERSION=~3
az webapp log config --name $APP_NAME --resource-group $RESOURCE_GROUP
--docker-container-logging filesystem

echo "App URL: https://$APP_NAME.azurewebsites.net"
# stream logs to the console:
az webapp log tail --name $APP_NAME --resource-group $RESOURCE_GROUP
```

This sample shows how we provision both the web app and the App Insights resources, and set the web app's settings to connect the two. If we were deploying to Kubernetes, after creating the App Insights resource, we could adjust the deployment to add a k8s secret with the App Insights connection string.

Aspire is great for local debugging, but it doesn't persist the logs, traces, and metrics. App Insights allows querying historical logs (within your configured retention period), allowing Kathy to visualize previous failures in much more detail.

Effective Monitoring

Understanding the health of a system of interrelated microservices is more than merely collecting all the system's logs, metrics, and traces. We also need to balance the frequency and detail of content with the usefulness of this data.

When gathering health data, it's easy to log too much, spam the logs, and make them useless. For example, a message with hard-coded values such as "here" or "executed this line" may be really helpful when writing the code but is really unhelpful when trying to diagnose a failure. If the content only includes hard-coded values like this, it's likely not a good message, and this code should be removed.

What is valuable data to save in logs, metrics, and traces? Save contextual data. Include the clues you'll need to understand how you got here, what options the user chose, and the operation results. Include extra detail in exceptional cases like stack traces and inner exceptions.

When writing logs, metrics, and traces, you may consider capturing the following:

- In the data tier, log SQL queries, nonsensitive query parameters, runtime duration, and any errors returned by the database.

- For REST queries, grab the URL, HTTP method, relevant headers, and the return HTTP status code and deserialized status message.

- For long-running tasks, log the start and end time and the number of items to process.

- In all logs, metrics, and traces, capture the currently authenticated user, the date and time of the event, the duration, the environment name, the current application name and version, and other system context. For example, the line number in the stack trace isn't that helpful without the product version number, release date, or Git hash to help find the correct version of the file.

- When capturing exceptions, grab the exception message, possibly the exception type, the stack trace (or at least the top file and line number), and loop through inner exceptions doing the same.

- For some special exceptions, grab additional details. For example, for an *AggregateException*, grab all the exceptions in the *InnerExceptions* list.[7] For *HttpRequestException*, harvest the *StatusCode*. For *DbUpdateException* coming from Entity Framework, grab details from the *Entities* list.

---

[7] https://docs.microsoft.com/en-us/dotnet/api/system.aggregateexception.innerexceptions#System_AggregateException_InnerExceptions

What data should we avoid saving? We shouldn't save anything that's hard-coded, redundant, or sensitive.

Avoid writing logs, metrics, and traces that include

- Don't capture messages like "Here," "Did the work," or other hard-coded messages that don't include context.

- Don't include sensitive data, including API keys or passwords, social security or credit card numbers, personally identifiable information, or other sensitive data. Logging this data may increase the scope of a system audit to include the security of the logging platform.

- Don't include the list of items searched. For example, if looking through a list of offices or countries, we only need the item we searched for and the fact it wasn't found. If we also log all the options, we'll get a lot of unhelpful matches when searching the logs for these office addresses or country names.

- Filter out noisy messages from underlying systems. For example, it can be helpful to grab the current URL passing through ASP.NET, but it isn't helpful to log each middleware function's input and output parameters. It's helpful to know what parameters we passed to the PDF generation library, but it isn't helpful to get all the state changes inside the library if we treat the library as a closed box.

As our health monitoring strategy matures, it can be helpful to publish deployment dates and versions, together with the Git hash of the software that produced this version. For example, if we notice that all system metrics are slower after the deployment, we can deduce there's a performance regression in this version. If we notice fewer failed requests, we know that we've correctly solved the issue. If we notice the volume of logs dramatically increases with a new version, we know there's likely a problem to address.

Finding the correct balance of message detail and helpfulness is a continuous process of refinement. We likely won't get it right the first time, but we can continue to refine our logging, metrics gathering, and tracing systems to ensure these systems are valuable debugging tools.

CHAPTER 10   HEALTHY MICROSERVICES

Debugging with Logs

How do we diagnose a system failure if we can't hook up a debugger? What if the cause of the failure has since disappeared? The messages we have captured from our system health monitors can be useful debugging tools if we've configured them correctly. Let's walk through a scenario where we can use logs to debug a failure.

Kathy, the Code Whiz developer, notices a problem with the system. In the Grafana[8] dashboard, she finds an increase in HTTP 500 errors indicating the maps microservice is failing in some cases. She's tasked with diagnosing and correcting the failure. With the test data she used to build the service on her local machine, the system works just fine. Now what?

Inside Grafana, Kathy creates a custom graph from the Prometheus data. She graphs the HTTP 500 errors over time and notices a correlation: the failures always seem to happen at 4 pm on Thursdays. Now what?

Do we add additional "it got here" messages and deploy a new version to production before next Thursday? This is hardly a robust and deterministic solution. Let's find a different solution instead.

Kathy pivots over to the log files and looks through the error messages from last Thursday. Unfortunately, 80% of the logs are nearly identical stack traces. These logs aren't very helpful. Kathy adds a new task in Jira to better handle these errors, possibly avoiding catching exceptions at each place and letting the central error logger catch them all, avoiding the redundant stack traces in the logs. Sadly, she concludes that the logs aren't helpful in their current state. The only piece that's helpful is OpenTelemetry recorded the inbound URL of the message that began this work. From the query string parameters, she now has the source and destination cities.

In the code, Kathy fires up the mapping microservice in Visual Studio, browses the Swagger test page, and plugs in both cities. "Still works on my machine." That wasn't it.

Kathy pivots over to Jaeger to look at tracing information. She zooms into last Thursday and identifies a trace that matches the inbound URL. From the nested trace tree, Kathy can see that Bob from accounting launched the request. He often catches up on the week's orders on Thursday afternoon. Could this be relevant?

---

[8] See https://grafana.com/docs/grafana/latest/getting-started/ to get started with Grafana

As Kathy traverses up and down the trace spans in Jaeger, the innermost span has a tag that clues her in. Adding the Google results as a custom tag to the OpenTelemetry setup is really paying off. In this case, the results returned from the Google Maps API are `OVER_QUERY_LIMIT`. Here's the cause.

It appears our business is doing so well that we've exceeded the API limits of Google Maps. That's a good problem to have. So how do we monitor this limited resource? We could add specific metrics to count usage of this limited resource that could flow into Prometheus and get graphed in Grafana. We could add caching to the maps-info microservice. After all, the distance between two addresses won't change, given the same road conditions and closures. Kathy creates a few more tasks in Jira to address these changing business requirements. In the meantime, Kathy suggests that Bob complete the orders each day until the developers can add these new changes.

The scenario we explored here used the system health metrics to diagnose a system failure. Each of the components is helpful in painting a picture of the system's health and in diagnosing its failures.

Metrics are really helpful for learning about current or impending failures. Over time, these measurements can help us understand what normal looks like and help us discover when the system is not functioning normally. Over time, we'll learn what metrics are helpful, and we can add or remove metrics to get the proper visibility into the system.

Traces are really helpful for learning about the impact of interrelated systems. We can follow a single user's journey through each of the microservices and dependencies in the system. We can understand how the authentication state can impact web requests and how parameter validation failures can lead to system instability in downstream systems.

Logs are really helpful in digging into the specifics of a failure. The stack traces, system state variables, and other contextual information give us enough detail to recreate the problem – even if we can only do so in our minds. We can return to the code, write a failing unit test, and prepare a proper correction with this information.

Using all these systems to help us "debug with logs" is a really helpful and powerful technique. When systems are designed to expose the correct level of detail, it can be easy and joyful to diagnose system failures. By comparison, if we fill the health monitors with lots of noise, they can be burdensome to use.

In each development sprint, it's often helpful to find the noisiest, unhelpful message in the logs or traces and remove this message. In each sprint, let's also find the noisiest error and solve the problem. After we've done this a half-dozen times, the logs will likely be much more valuable and the system will be much more stable.

Sometimes we need more details from the systems to diagnose a specific issue. We can turn up the log level for a time to capture additional detail. In some scenarios, it may be helpful to identify a specific namespace and turn up those logs to Debug. But be diligent in turning them back down when finished, or else the next time you're using the logs, they'll be overrun by irrelevant noise.

Summary

In this chapter, we looked at ensuring services are healthy. We learned about logging for capturing events, tracing for capturing the relation between events, and metrics for capturing system state over time. Each of these data sources can tell different parts of the story, allowing us to easily monitor the services and debug error failures. We saw how OpenTelemetry can direct logs, traces, and metrics to any OpenTelemetry sink, and how OpenTelemetry has become the standard way for harvesting these data. When developing and debugging locally, Aspire is a great dashboard for collecting logs, traces, and metrics. In production, Azure Application Insights also accepts OpenTelemetry data, allowing easy problem diagnostics. We can easily debug with logs, traces, and metrics when they contain valuable insights. We ensured the logs are useful by adding context and eliminating excess noise.

Index

A

ACA, *see* Azure Container Apps (ACA)
ACI, *see* Azure Container Instance (ACI)
ACR, *see* Azure Container Registry (ACR)
Active Server Pages (ASP), 64
Advanced Message Queuing Protocol
	(AMQP), 17, 18
Aggregate root, 49–51
Aggregates, 49–51
Ahead-of-time (AOT), 67
AKS, *see* Azure Kubernetes Service (AKS)
Alerting, 22, 25, 26, 126
AMQP, *see* Advanced Message Queuing
	Protocol (AMQP)
Analyzing data, 160
AOT, *see* Ahead-of-time (AOT)
API, *see* Application Programming
	Interface (API)
API Gateway pattern, 12, 13
APIM, *see* Azure API Management (APIM)
Application Gateway, 209, 211, 212,
	217, 218
Application Programming Interface (API),
	3, 88, 89, 95, 158, 207, 227
Architecture patterns, 29, 30
ASP, *see* Active Server Pages (ASP)
Aspire, 84, 85, 224–226
ASP.NET, 64, 175, 218
    hosting options, 86
    Minimal APIs, 76–79, 86
    MVC, 69–72, 86
    Razor Pages, 73, 74, 86
    Web API, 74–76, 86
"At least once" delivery guarantee, 116
Auto mechanic's toolchest, 29
AWS, 84, 129, 194, 206
Azure API Management (APIM), 168, 212,
	213, 217
Azure App Fabric, 206
Azure Application Insights, 231–233, 238
Azure App Service, 203–205, 218
Azure container, 189
Azure Container Apps (ACA), 202, 203,
	218, 226
Azure Container Instance (ACI), 206
Azure Container Registry (ACR), 22, 194,
	205, 217
Azure Data Factory, 154
Azure DevOps, 4, 22, 23, 27
Azure functions, 79–82, 86
Azure Kubernetes Service (AKS),
	197–201, 218

B

Backends for Frontends (BFF)
	pattern, 12–13
Base Class Libraries (BCL), 65, 221
BBoM, *see* Big Ball of Mud (BBoM)
BCL, *see* Base Class Libraries (BCL)
Benefits, microservices
    data autonomy, 7
    fault isolation, 5, 6
    scalability, 4, 5

INDEX

Benefits, microservices (*cont.*)
    service autonomy, 3, 4
    team autonomy, 3
Big Ball of Mud (BBoM), 61
Bounded context, 48, 49, 57, 59
Brokered system, 112–113
Broker-less system, 112
Business process communication
    callback, 16
    fire and forget, 15
    pub/sub, 16
    RPC, 15

C

Cascading failures, 107
CCC, *see* Cross-cutting concerns (CCC)
Centralized logging system, 24
Chaos Monkey, 168
Choreography, 139, 142, 143
CI/CD, *see* Continuous Integration/Continuous Deployment (CI/CD)
CLR, *see* Common Language Runtime (CLR)
Code Whiz, 46, 59–61, 161, 165, 226
Color coding, 52–54
Command message type, 111
Command Query Responsibility Segregation (CQRS), 145, 146, 155, 162
Common Language Runtime (CLR), 63, 65
Communication methods, 9, 14, 88, 107
Competing consumer, 113–115, 123–124
Component tests, 20, 172, 173
    mocking, 172
    stub, 173
Consistency, **A**vailability, and **P**artition (CAP) theorem, 137–138

Consistency guarantees, 137
Consumer-driven contract testing, 174, 178
    consumer project, 179–181
    ConsumerTests, 182–186
    ProviderTests, 186, 187
Consumption models
    competing consumers, 113, 114
    independent consumers, 114, 115
Containers, 9, 22, 84, 189, 197, 206, 232
Continuous Integration/Continuous Deployment (CI/CD), 4, 21, 22, 156
Contract testing, 173, 174, 178, 188
Coordinated Universal Time (UTC), 25
CORS, *see* Cross-Origin Request Header (CORS)
CQRS, *see* Command Query Responsibility Segregation (CQRS)
Create, Read, Update, Delete (CRUD) methods, 76, 79, 82, 146
Cross-cutting concerns (CCC), 23, 28
    alerting, 25, 26
    architecture testing, 26, 27
    logging, 24
    monitoring, 23, 24
Cross-Origin Request Header (CORS), 201, 206, 207, 209

D

Data analytics, 3, 9
Data autonomy, 7
Database
    choices, 131
    splitting, 159–163
    types, 129
Database administrators (DBAs), 130
Database systems, 129, 131, 154
Data, decentralizing, 133, 162

Data dependencies, 162
Data integrity management, 160
Data transactions, 159, 162
Data warehouse, 154, 155, 163
DBAs, *see* Database administrators (DBAs)
DDD, *see* Domain-driven design (DDD)
Debugging, 84, 194, 236–238
Decomposition, 60, 61
Delivery guarantees, 127
    at least once, 116
    at most once, 115
    once and only once, 116
Dependency injection (DI), 65, 69, 77, 171
Deploying microservices
    CI/CD automation tools, 27
    containers, 22
    pipelines, 22, 23
    versioning, 21
DI, *see* Dependency injection (DI)
Direct communication, 107
Dispute handling, 55
Dispute Management subdomain, 59
DistanceMicroservice, 91, 92, 104
Distributed systems, 8, 87, 137, 139
Distributed transaction, 116, 137, 140
DLR, *see* Dynamic Language Runtime (DLR)
Docker container, 9, 119, 189, 218
Dockerfile, 83, 190, 217
    Alpine Linux, 190
    build tools, 191
    COpY line, 192
    dockerfile file, 193, 194
    dockerignore file, 193, 194
    dotnet commands, 190
    FROM line, 191
    .gitignore file, 193, 194
    .NET CLI, 191
    pattern, 192
    updation, 192
Domain-driven design (DDD), 147
    aggregates and aggregate roots, 49–51
    bounded context, 48, 49
    developers, 62
    domain, 47
    subdomains, 47
    Ubiquitous language, 48
Domain events, 16, 53–56, 147
Domain experts, 51, 54, 56, 58, 60, 62
Domain models
    focus on behavior, 60
    Rate Engine subdomain, 59
Domains, 47, 51, 58–59, 206
Duplicate data, 116, 134–136
Durability guarantee, 137
Dynamic Language Runtime (DLR), 64

E

ECR, *see* Elastic Container Registry (ECR)
ECS, *see* Elastic Container Service (ECS)
EDMX, *see* Entity Data Model XML (EDMX)
Elastic Container Registry (ECR), 194
Elastic Container Service (ECS), 206
Emerging contexts, 56
End-to-end (E-to-E) tests, 19, 167, 177
    business logic, 175
    ConfigureServices, 177
    create test, 176
    DistanceApp.cs file, 175
    DistanceApp fixture, 177
    Entity Framework Data Context, 178
    Program.cs, 176
    WebApplicationFactory<Program>, 178
Enterprise Service Bus (ESB), 9, 36
Entity Data Model XML (EDMX), 67
Entity Framework Core (EF Core), 65–67

INDEX

ESB, *see* Enterprise Service Bus (ESB)
Event-driven architecture, 36, 43, 109
    pros/cons, 36, 37
    use case, 37
Event message type, 111
Event payload, 147, 149
Event sourcing, 147, 163
    data, 147
    definition, 147
    event payload, 147, 149
    inventory management system, 151, 152
    online system, 152
    orders activity, 150, 151
    payments, 149, 150
    shipping address, 147
Event storming
    color coding, 52–54
    description, 51
    legend, 53
    meeting, 54, 55, 58
    setup, 52
Eventual consistency, 43, 152, 153, 163
External Configuration Store pattern, 14
Extract, Transform, Load (ETL) tools, 154

F

Fault isolation, 4–6
Feature flags, 159, 163
FIFO, *see* First In, First Out (FIFO)
File Transfer Protocol (FTP) server, 89
First In, First Out (FIFO), 110

G

Google Remote Procedure Calls (gRPC), 18, 90
    communication, 98
    HTTP/2/Protocol Buffers, 98

    IDL definition file, 99
Google Route Service, 91–94
Google's Distance API
    app settings, 95
    DistanceMicroservice.http, 96
    Endpoints Explorer, 95
    launchSettings.json file, 96
    results, 96
    Swagger, 97, 98
Google's Routes API, 95
Grafana, 23, 25, 236, 237
gRPC, *see* Google Remote Procedure Calls (gRPC)

H

Healthy microservices
    Azure Application Insights, 232, 233
    considerations, 219
    logging, 220
    methodical approach, 220
    metrics, 221
    monitoring, 234, 235
    naive approach, 220
    OpenTelemetry, 221–223
    tracing, 220, 221
HTTP, *see* Hypertext Transport Protocol (HTTP)
HTTP verbs, 3, 18, 76, 89
Hybrid architecture, 11
Hypertext Transport Protocol (HTTP), 9, 17, 88, 173, 221, 234
Hyp-Log, 45, 58, 60, 61, 87, 129, 165

I

IDL, *see* Interface definition language (IDL)
Incorporating gRPC

NuGet packages, 102
Program.cs file, 102
project file, 102
Protos folder, 99
Usings.cs file, 100, 101
Independent consumers, 114–115, 126, 127
Inline microservice calls, 134
Integration tests, 22, 31, 171, 186
Interface definition language (IDL), 98
Internet of Things (IoT), 63, 68, 89
Interprocess communication (IPC), 14, 87, 88, 105
Inventory management system, 151, 152
Inversion of Control (IoC), 65, 79
Invoice and dispute management contexts, 58
Invoice management system, 61
InvoiceMicroservice project, 120–123
IoC, *see* Inversion of Control (IoC)
IoT, *see* Internet of Things (IoT)
IPC, *see* Interprocess communication (IPC)

J

Jaeger, 232, 236, 237
JIT, *see* Just-in-Time (JIT)
Just-in-Time (JIT), 63, 64

K

KEDA functions, 82–84, 86
Kubernetes (k8s), 197
    cluster, 200
    elements, 197
    Ingress, 200, 201, 218
    pods, 197
    YAML file, 197–199

L

Layered architecture, 34
    pros/cons, 34, 35
    use case, 35
Linux containers, 189, 196
Load aggregate, 56, 57
Log aggregation, 24
Logging information, 24, 168

M

Managed Extensibility Framework (MEF), 64
Map Info Controller
    Swagger, 97, 98
MassTransit library, 113
Materialized view, 155, 156, 163
Meetings
    domain models, 60
    emerging contexts, 56
    single context, 57
    split process, 55, 56
MEF, *see* Managed Extensibility Framework (MEF)
Message brokers, 18, 27, 110
MessageContracts class, 119
Messaging, 109, 126
    architecture, 109
    buffering, 110
    business process communication, 15, 16
    command, 111
    consumers, 126
    delivery, 115
    drawbacks, 125, 126
    duplicate messages, 115
    event, 111
    format, 17

Messaging (*cont.*)
    independent processing, 110
    loosely coupled, 109
    ordering, 117
    query, 111
    RabbitMQ running, 119
    vs. RPC style, 109
    scaling, 110
    transport, 17, 18
    types, 110, 126
Message routing, 126
    brokered system, 112
    broker-less system, 112
Micro-kernel architecture, 38, 39, 43
    pros/cons, 39
    use case, 39
Microservices, 41–43, 87
    architecture, 10, 11, 27, 28, 129, 130
    availability, 131, 133
    business, 130
    callers, 105
    challenges, 7, 8
    communication, 15, 27
    cost, 9
    database, 131
    domain functionality, 165
    duplicate data, 134–136
    hosting options, 206
    inline microservice calls, 133, 134
    invoice microservice, 118
    libraries, 6
    messaging, 109, 118
    packaging, 217
    patterns, 12, 27
        API Gateway pattern, 12, 13
        BFF, 13
        External Configuration Store pattern, 14
    pros/cons, 42
    React app, 207
    reverse proxy, 207
    rule, 130
    separate domain, 206
    sharing data, 133
    single source of truth, 131
    testing (*see* Testing)
    use case, 42
Mocking, 33, 172–173
Mocks, 20, 27, 174, 175
Model-View-Controller (MVC), 13, 64, 69, 75
Modern .NET, 66–68
Modular monolith, 33, 43
    pros/cons, 33
    use case, 33
Monitoring, 23, 24, 233–235
Monolith hell, 2, 8
Monolithic applications, 129, 130, 137
Monoliths, 1–3, 5, 31, 32, 43, 104, 156
MVC, *see* Model-View-Controller (MVC)

N

.NET Aspire, 224, 238
    ActivitySource, 227
    AddServiceDefaults method, 229, 231
    ConfigureOpenTelemetry method, 230
    DistanceMicroservice project, 229, 231
    GetRouteInfo method, 227, 230
    GoogleRouteService.cs file, 226, 227, 229
    OpenTelemetry, 224, 226
        logs, 226, 231
        metrics, 226, 231
        traces, 226, 231

OTEL_EXPORTER_OTLP_
    ENDPOINT, 224
ServiceDefaults project, 224, 228
tags, 228
traces, 225, 226
Visual Studio, 224
.NET Core, 65, 66
Netflix, 1, 168
.NET Framework, 63–65, 68, 166
.NET Microservices
    containerization
        Dockerfile (*see* Dockerfile)
        .NET SDK, 194, 195, 217
    deployment
        ACA, 202, 203
        Azure App Service, 203–205
        k8s (*see* Kubernetes (k8s))
        options, 196, 205, 206
Next Generation Windows Services
    (NGWS), 63
NGWS, *see* Next Generation Windows
    Services (NGWS)
No-SQL, 129
NuGet packages, 91, 102, 103, 169

O

Object relational mapper (ORM), 160
OLAP, *see* Online Analytical
    Processing (OLAP)
OLTP, *see* Online Transactional
    Processing (OLTP)
Online Analytical Processing (OLAP), 154
Online system, 152
Online Transactional Processing
    (OLTP), 154
Open Source Software (OSS), 168
OpenTelemetry, 84, 221–223, 231, 238

Orchestration, 139, 144
Order creation process, 143
Order Microservice, 114, 117, 134, 142
ORM, *see* Object relational mapper (ORM)
OSS, *see* Open Source Software (OSS)

P

Parallel activity, 139
PaymentMicroservice project, 122, 123
PayPal, 1, 8
Persistent-based Pub/Sub model, 16
Pipeline architecture, 37, 38, 43
Pipelines, 21–23, 27
Prometheus, 23, 24, 232, 236, 237
Protocol buffers, 17, 18, 90, 98
PubSub Demo, 124, 125
Publish/Subscribe (Pub/Sub), 16
Python, 3, 9, 221

Q

Query message type, 111

R

RabbitMQ, 25, 119, 120, 125
Rate Engine subdomain, 58, 59
Remote Procedure Call (RPC), 15, 108
Remote Procedure Call (RPC)-style
    communication, 87, 88, 105
Representational State Transfer (REST),
    18, 89, 90
REST, *see* Representational State
    Transfer (REST)
Reverse proxy, 207
    APIM, 212, 213, 217
    Application Gateway, 209, 211, 212, 217

Reverse proxy (*cont.*)
    Kubernetes ingress, 207, 209, 217
    YARP, 213, 215–217
Routing slip
    activities, 141
    error condition handling, 141
    pattern, 140, 142
RPC, *see* Remote Procedure Call (RPC)

S

Sagas
    choreography, 142, 143
    definition, 139
    with local transactions, 140
    orchestration, 144
    routing slip, 140–142
Scalability, 4, 5
Scaling microservices, 108
Scaling servers, 1
Search Engine Optimization (SEO), 68
SEO, *see* Search Engine Optimization (SEO)
Sequential business processes, 138
Service autonomy, 3, 4
Service-based architecture, 43
Service discovery, 12, 85, 104–105, 205
Service mesh, 169
Service-oriented architecture, 9, 40
    pros/cons, 40, 41
    use case, 41
Service testing, 26, 174
Sharing data, 133–134, 157
Silverlight, 65
Single context, 57
Software developers, 29, 51
Software patterns, 29, 31, 43
Software programmers, 10

SPLAT, 46, 50, 61
Split process, 55, 56
Splitting, database, 159–162
Splitting functionality, monolith
    feature flags, 159
    moving code, 157, 158
    strangler pattern, 159
SQL Server Integration Services (SSIS), 154
SSIS, *see* SQL Server Integration Services (SSIS)
Strangler pattern, 159, 163
Stubs, 20, 27, 173, 174
Subdomain, 47–48, 58, 59
SUT, *see* System Under Test (SUT)
Swagger, 79, 97, 98, 236
Synchronous communication, 88, 107, 108
System Under Test (SUT), 19, 20

T

TCP web sockets, 17
TDD, *see* Test-Driven Development (TDD)
Team autonomy, 3
Telemetry data, 131, 145, 146, 238
Test-Driven Development (TDD), 165, 188
Testing, 18
    architecture, 26, 27
    automation, 21
    code, 167
    competing consumers, 124
    components tests, 172, 173
    contract testing, 173, 174
    cost of errors, 165, 166, 188
    end-to-end, 19
    E-to-E testing, 175, 178
    gRPC endpoint, 103, 104
    integration tests, 171

.NET Framework, 166
performance, 167, 168
pyramid, 18, 19, 167, 169, 188
security, 169
service testing, 174
stub, 20
system failure, 168
unit, 20
unit tests, 170, 171
Test pyramid, 18, 19, 167, 169
Three-tier architecture, 10
Tightly coupled architecture, 9, 105
Transactional consistency
CAP theorem, 137
transactions, 138, 139
Transactions, 1, 116, 137–141, 143, 154
Transitive latency, 107
Transportation mechanisms, 17, 18
Transport mechanisms
considerations, 90
gRPC, 90
REST, 89, 90
Troubleshooting, 23, 24, 26, 126
Twitter, 1, 8

U

Ubiquitous Language (UL), 46, 48, 49
UI, *see* User Interface (UI)
UL, *see* Ubiquitous Language (UL)
Uniform Resource Identifiers (URI), 89, 187
Unit tests, 20, 170, 171
URI, *see* Uniform Resource Identifiers (URI)
User Interface (UI), 10, 34, 167

V

Versioning, 21–22, 108, 174
Visual Basic, 64

W, X

Webhooks, 26, 77
WCF, *see* Windows Communication Foundation (WCF)
WF, *see* Windows Workflow Foundation (WF)
Windows Communication Foundation (WCF), 64, 66, 68
Windows Presentation Foundation (WPF), 64, 67
Windows Workflow Foundation (WF), 64
Wire Tap pattern, 114, 115
WPF, *see* Windows Presentation Foundation (WPF)

Y, Z

YARP, *see* Yet Another Reverse Proxy (YARP)
Yet Another Reverse Proxy (YARP), 213, 215–218

GPSR Compliance

The European Union's (EU) General Product Safety Regulation (GPSR) is a set of rules that requires consumer products to be safe and our obligations to ensure this.

If you have any concerns about our products, you can contact us on ProductSafety@springernature.com

In case Publisher is established outside the EU, the EU authorized representative is:

Springer Nature Customer Service Center GmbH
Europaplatz 3
69115 Heidelberg, Germany

Batch number: 09329304

Printed by Printforce, the Netherlands